Ahsan Academy of Research
(Springs, South Africa)

Moral and Spiritual Transformation in Islam
(Selected Lectures and Writings)

Vol. 1

Muhammad Fazlur Rahman Ansari

Edited by
Abdul Kader Choughley

Tawasul International
Centre for Publishing, Research and Dialogue

© Ahsan Academy of Research

All rights reserved. No part of this publication may be reproduced, stored in a retrieval system, or transmitted in any form or by any means, electronic, mechanical, photocopying, recording or otherwise, without the prior permission of the copyright owner.

First Edition 2019
ISBN 978-0-620-81005-0

Edited by Abdul Kader Choughley

Ahsan Academy of Research
(Springs, South Africa)
info@ahsanacademy.co.za
www.ahsanacademy.co.za

SHELVCRAFTTM Shelving | Racking | Display | Shop Fiting Ph: 012 666 8933
Email: sales@shelvcraft.com Website: www.shelvcraft.com

Tawasul International
Centre for Publishing, Research and Dialogue, Rome, Italy

CONTENTS

Fazlur Rahman Ansari: Life And Thought 5
Acknowledgements 11
Biographical Sketch 13
Introduction 33

Part One: Islam: Meaning And Message 39
   1. Islam: The Way of Unity and Progress 41
   2. What is Islam? 53
   3. Philosophy of the Shahādah 69

Part Two: Moral Transformation in Islam 85
   4. Surah Al-Fātihah and the Concept of Khalifat-Allah 87
   5. The Principle of Unity 101
   6. The Qur'ānic View of Disunity 123

Part Three: Dynamics of the Sunnah 135
   7. The Inner Dimensions of the Sunnah 137
   8. Philosophy of Worship ('Ibādah) in Islam 147

Part Four: Islam and Knowledge 159
   9. The Holy Prophet's Contribution to Knowledge 161
   10. Islamic Theological Education 171
   11. Our Intellectual Emancipation and Islamic Reconstruction 187

Part Five: Islam and Modern Challenges 197
12. The Challenge of the Twentieth Century 199
13. The Age of Doubt. 211
14. Westernised Muslims 227

Part Six: Inner Dimensions of Islam 239
15. Tasawwuf: Spiritual Pursuit in Islam 241
16. Mysticism and Tasawwuf: An Overview 253
17. Discipline in Dhikr 257

Part Seven: Reflections 263
18. Three Key Concepts 265
Brotherhood 265
Dimensions of Tabligh 267
Status of Women in Islam 269

Fazlur Rahman Ansari: Life and Thought
(Chronologically Arranged)

1914 - Born on 14 August 1914 in Muzaffar Nagar (UP) to a noble family tracing their lineage to the distinguished Sahābah, Khālid Abu Ayyub Ansari.

1918 - Commenced hifz of Qur'ān.

1921 - Obtained certificate of hifz from Madrasah Islamiyah (Muzaffar Nagar).

- Family relocated to Meerut where he commenced the Dars-i-Nizāmi course.

1924 - Remained as student at Madrasah Islamiyah. Enrolled at Meerut College to pursue study of English.

1931 - Contributed articles for the following English newspapers *Muslim Standard of Ceylon, Royal Islam of Singapore.*

1932 - First meeting at College with Mawlana Abdul Aleem Siddiqui.

- Established relationship with Mawlana Siddiqui who entrusted him with the tabligh mission.

- Wrote his debut book *The Beacon Light* in refutation of Christian polemics against Islam.

1933 - Passed the Intermediate Science course at Meerut College.

- Completed Dars-i-Nizāmi course at Madrasah Islamiyah.

- Enrolled at Aligarh Muslim University for a BA Degree

	-	Wrote his second monograph *Christian World in Revolution*.
1935	-	Obtained prestigious award in recognition of his achievements in his combined BA/BSc degrees.
	-	Received a gold medal for establishing a new record in Philosophy (98%).
	-	Awarded Haqqi prize for best student in Arabic in BA exams.
	-	Wrote the following monographs: *Muhammad The Glory of the Ages Islam in Europe and America*.
1936	-	Enrolled for post-Dars-i-Nizāmi course under Professor Sayyid Sulayman Ashraf at AMU.
	-	Married the eldest daughter of Mawlana Siddiqui, Amat as-Subuh Sabiha.
1937	-	Apart from proficiency in English, Urdu and Arabic, started learning German.
	-	Turning point in his tabligh activities.
	-	Deputed by Mawlana Siddiqui to work in Singapore and Malaya to counter anti-Islamic propaganda.
	-	Was editor of *Genuine Islam* magazine.
	-	Co-ordinated old Malaya Muslim Missionary Society
	-	Organised Far Eastern Missionary Front.
	-	Wrote *Islam and Communism, Trends in Christianity* and *Humanity Reborn*
1938	-	His tabligh activities lasted eighteen months.
	-	Major contributions in defending Islamic law from media especially the *Straits Times* of Singapore.
1939	-	Selected as a fellow to pursue postgraduate

	-	studies in Germany.
	-	Outbreak of Second World War prevented his proposed study abroad.
	-	Pursued Bachelor of Theology at AMU 1941.
	-	Passed with distinctions in Islamic subjects.
1942	-	Completed his MA course in Philosophy with meritorious achievement -First Class First.
	-	Elected President of the Philosophical Society of AMU.
	-	Studied MA course independently in subjects which included Politics, Economics and Comparative Religion.
	-	Commenced with his PhD in philosophy under the supervision of Syed Zafar al-Hasan
	-	Became warden of Aftab hostel–a post which he held for three years.
1944	-	Appointed member of Education Planning Committee for two years mandated by Qua'id-e-Azam Muhammad Ali Jinnah.
1947	-	Could not submit his PhD dissertation after Syed Zafar al-Hasan migrated to Pakistan.
	-	Another copy destroyed during Partition of India.
	-	Studied Homeopathic course.
	-	Accompanied Mawlana Siddiqui along with his family to Karachi (Pakistan).
	-	Continued to work as private secretary to Mawlana Siddiqui.
	-	Editor of *Sindh Information* (Karachi).
1949	-	Mawlana Siddiqui initiated him into the spiritual orders at the hatim of the Ka'bah.

- Granted ijāzah (authority) in spiritual matters.
- Commencement of tabligh tours.
- Accompanied Mawlana Siddiqui as private secretary during the extensive two - year tabligh activities.

1952 - Joined Jam'iyat-al-Falāh, and was Editor of *Voice of Islam* for two years.

1954 - Lectured at Karachi University.
- Participated in World Interfaith convention.
- Demise of Mawlana Siddiqui in Madinah.

1955 - Elected as Chief Successor of Mawlana Siddiqui by the Halqah Aleemiyah-Qādiriyyah in Karachi.

1957 - Second World Tabligh Tour spanning several countries.

1958 - Establishment of the World Federation of Islamic Missions (WFIM).

1959 - Conducted short courses in English for foreign students in Karachi.
- Participated in the World Parliament of Religions.

1960 - Continued teaching at St. Patrick College, St. Joseph College and College of Home Education on various Islamic subjects.
- Embarked on Third World Tabligh Tour which lasted eight months

1961 - An influential Italian woman accepted Islam at his hands.

1962 - Conducted classes as Professor for 'ulama at the Academy for Islamic Studies (Quetta University).

1963	-	Declined appointment as lecturer in Department of *Tasawwuf* and Ethics (Quetta University).
1964	-	Established Aleemiyah Institute of Islamic Studies
	-	Founded the *Manzil* magazine in Urdu and Gujarati as well as *The Minaret* in English.
	-	Undertook Fourth World Tabligh Tour which lasted five months.
1965-8	-	Focused on the growth and development of the Aleemiyah Institute.
1969	-	Fifth World Tabligh Tour which lasted four months.
	-	Founder of the Islamic Research and Publication Bureau.
1970	-	First historic visit to South Africa.
	-	Memorable lecture at Stellenbosch University.
	-	Completed his doctorate at Karachi University 1972.
	-	Elected as expert on Board of Islamic Studies (Karachi University).
	-	Led a two - man delegation to Uganda.
	-	Second historic visit to South Africa.
1973	-	Toured Seychelles and Sri Lanka for tabligh purpose.
	-	Wrote his monumental *The Qur'ānic Foundations and Structure of Muslim Society*.
1974	-	Admitted to hospital for cardio- vascular disease.
	-	Demise after prolonged illness on 6 June.

Acknowledgements

Mahdie Kriel has made pioneering contributions in transcribing, compiling and editing lectures and articles of Mawlana Ansari. He deserves credit for his substantial interest and remarkable devotion to promoting the life and thought of Mawlana Ansari through his publications. In more than one way, Mahdie has provided collaborative support for my works on Mawlana Ansari. When I presented my ideas on this proposed work he granted me permission and his dua's. The title of the book was suggested by Mahdie, which encompasses the versatile contributions of the distinguished scholar of the twentieth century.

It has almost been twenty years since the first edition of *Islam to the Modern Mind* edited by Yasien Mohamed appeared in 1999. The study on the eminent scholar, Mawlana Ansari, was inspired by Anver Essa of Shelvcraft. His profound admiration for this prominent figure in Islamic resurgence culminated in the number of books which he published. Several editions with a print run of ten thousand copies were distributed at no cost to individuals, academics, universities and organisations in many parts of the world. This was a mammoth task which Anver and his family members meticulously carried out.

Another important work *Islamic Intellectual Revival of the Modern Mind* contains articles and lectures which have been compiled and edited by Mahdie Kriel. In fact these two books are the foundational sources of Mawlana Ansari's significant contribution to contemporary Islamic thought. Two other works commissioned by Anver, *Fazlur Rahman Ansari: Life and Thought* and *Islam: An Introduction* by Abdul Kader Choughley are representative of Ansari's immense fame. The groundswell of interest in all these works can be gauged from the international interest to his Islamic contributions.

South African Muslims had been honoured in the first half of the twentieth century by the presence of the spiritual luminary, Mawlana Abdul Aleem Siddiqui. His message of moral and spiritual armament was anchored on his tabligh vision. Mawlana Siddiqui's lectures in 1934 and 1952 were transcribed by Mahdie Kriel and edited by Yasien Mohamed. *The Roving Ambassador of Peace* was widely acclaimed for its lucidity and concise presentation of this great scholar's Islamic learning. Another study *Abdul Aleem Siddiqui and His Mission* by Abdul Kader Choughley focuses on the revered scholar's multidimensional approach to tabligh.

It will be no exaggeration to state that Anver's publishing efforts on Mawlana Ansari and Mawlana Siddiqui are unsurpassed. To date, seven books of exceptional scholarly merit have been published and are indispensable reference works on Islamic reformist thought.

Anver has consistently maintained a low-key profile; his unassuming personality and passionate commitment to Islamic studies are his outstanding traits. His ambitious plans to extend the scope of academic research are illustrative of his vision to promoting Islamic scholarship.

May Allah bless his noble initiatives.

Biographical Sketch

Mawlana Muhammad Fazlur Rahman Ansari: Early Influences

Muhammad Fazlur Rahman Ansari was born on 14th August 1914 in Muzaffar Nagar (UP) India. His father Mawlana Muhammad Khalil (d. 1943) was considered to be an accomplished scholar with strong sufi leanings. His mother Husn Arā Begum (d. 1955) was noted for her piety, generosity and instilling Islamic values among her children. Thus Mawlana Ansari was born in a religious environment where learning *('ilm)* was combined with moral upbringing *(tarbiyah)*. These traits found fuller expression in the later years of his intellectual and spiritual career.

Their family traced their lineage to the distinguished Sahābah, Abu Ayyub Ansari. Among his ancestors was the sufi-scholar, Shaykh Abdullah Ansari of Herat (Afghanistan) whose migration to India during the eleventh century was an epoch-making period for his descendants who assumed important positions in disseminating the message of Islam. Likewise another influential Ansari figure was Mawlana Karim Buksh who was reputed for his unwavering devotion to the *sunnah* and total absorption in *tasawwuf* practices. More importantly, his contributions towards the reform of Muslim society attested to the Chishti teaching of 'service to mankind.'

Mawlana Ansari had doting parents under whose pastoral care his education began. At the tender age of **four years, four months and four days**, this child prodigy commenced his *hifz al-Qur'ān* (memorisation). Among the *ashrāf* (Muslim nobility), the *basmala* or induction ceremony of the Qur'ān learning was a notable social event. It was almost like the rites of passage in fathoming the world of the Qur'ān held in veneration among Muslims. Mawlana Ansari's hifz ceremony was a remarkable achievement and a source of immeasurable pride for the family. The hifz tradition, a phenomenon steeped in centuries of

Islamic tradition across the Muslim world, also served as a benchmark for a family's religious status.

Mawlana Ansari's retentive memory was considered a Divine blessing. He commenced his hifz at an extremely early age. Based on family accounts he was able to present the memorised passages without any error. Furthermore his mother, Husn Arā was astonished at her son's remarkable ability to memorise the Qur'ān and recite passages at random without revision. He completed his hifz at a tender age of six years and six months. In 1921 he obtained the certificate of hifz al-Qur'ān from Madrasah Islamiyah, Muzaffar Nagar.

Mawlana Ansari's acknowledgement of his parents' contribution in shaping his intellectual career is expressed in the following words:

> The deepest debt of gratitude I owe, however, to my beloved parents of revered memory: Muhammad Khalil Ansari and Husn Arā Begum, who, through their noble character and fruitful teachings and loving concern for my well-being, built up the foundations of my personality and sponsored and guided my education at all stages, thereby enabling me to undertake this work (*The Qur'ānic Foundations*).

Madrasah Islamiyah Meerut offered the traditional Dars-i-Nizāmi course which Mawlana Ansari successfully completed in 1933. He initially enrolled as a part-time student in 1921 at the institution and always stood out as a student of exceptional ability and accomplishment. His versatility enabled him to pursue several courses (in many instances unrelated courses) concurrently and independently. It was his stoic spirit and indomitable determination that spurred him to levels of academic excellence.

Biographical Sketch

Mawlana Ansari's Intellectual and Spiritual Career: An Overview

The period 1932-3 was a turning point in Mawlana Ansari's intellectual and spiritual career for the following reasons:

- his first meeting with the roving ambassador of Peace, Mawlana Abdul Siddiqui
- his enrolment at the prestigious Aligarh Muslim university (AMU)

It was no fortuitous circumstances that he met Mawlana Siddiqui in 1932. A brilliant scholar at the Meerut College, Mawlana Ansari enjoyed considerable following among his peers. At the same time, Mawlana Siddiqui had returned from his tabligh tours and was warmly received at the Makhdum Sāhib mosque. Mawlana Ansari was introduced to him and a strong bond of love developed between the two and soon he became a regular visitor at Mawlana Siddiqui's home. The relationship reflected the kindred spirit both shared in regard to their respective Islamic and Western educational backgrounds. Mawlana Siddiqui was eminently
suited to hone Mawlana Ansari's academic skills to the tabligh mission for which he dedicated his life. Moreover in the company of Mawlana he developed a maturity of outlook and was inducted into the realms of *tasawwuf*. This unique combination of *ta'lim* (education), tabligh and *tasawwuf* in presenting a holistic presentation of Islam provided Mawlana Ansari with a renewed vigour to serve the cause of Islam. Under the mentorship of Mawlana Siddiqui, he unleashed his potential as a scholar of extraordinary merit. Mawlana Siddiqui entrusted him with the responsibility of replying to some of his correspondence and contributing articles to magazines, etc. His writings were done at the behest of Mawlana Siddiqui and which largely focused on Islamic missionary journalism and practical missionary work. There was no doubt that he had recognised Mawlana Ansari's capabilities in the field of tabligh.

The Beacon Light

In 1932 when he was only eighteen years he wrote *The Beacon Light*, a first class missionary book on Islam and much earlier he started writing for Colombo's (Sri Lanka) *Muslim Standard* and Singapore's *Real Islam*. Mawlana Siddiqui's pressing tabligh engagements did not give him sufficient time to respond to the spate of anti-Islamic literature published by Christian missionaries in Singapore. Polemical works denigrating Islamic teachings and the personality of the Holy Prophet (SAW) continued unabated and, no doubt, there was an orchestrated campaign to thwart tabligh activities among Muslims. Mawlana Siddiqui's role was two- pronged: to promote the universal values of Islam in Singapore and create a forum for interfaith discussion.

The Beacon Light, a seminal work of Mawlana Ansari, was a refutation of the missionary's tirade against Islam. It was Mawlana Ansari who volunteered to write a monograph in defense of Islamic teachings. In a short period of four hours the monograph was completed and in the words of an international law specialist was a flawless piece of work.

Mawlana Ansari's academic debut was followed by his initiation into *tasawwuf*. The world of Islamic spirituality opened up before him through his association with Mawlana Siddiqui. In many respects, Mawlana Ansari's intellectual horizon was broadened and the spiritual dimensions to his personality raised opportunities for his future tabligh mission. Thus his contributions must be examined in the light of Mawlana Siddiqui's pioneering role during this period Two strands of thought, intellectual and spiritual, were woven into the rich tapestry of Mawlana Ansari's multi- faceted career. Tabligh which blended with spirituality assumed greater importance for Mawlana Ansari in the distinguished company of Mawlana Siddiqui. Like his spiritual mentor, Mawlana Ansari's intellectual horizon broadened at the prestigious institution, Aligarh Muslim University (AMU) which was recognised as the cultural centre of Islam in terms of its exemplary academic ethos.

Mawlana Ansari at Aligarh Muslim University: 1933-47

Mawlana Ansari's prolonged stay at AMU (1933-47) may be divided into two phases. The first phase 1932-7 saw his meterioc rise as a student of exceptional ability. His undergraduate studies – BA, BSc and BTh attested to his versatile genius. An eighteen month hiatus (1937-8) inducted him into his first tabligh tour to Singapore. Thereafter, the second phase: 1939-47 brought him into prominence on two levels: his conceptualisation of Islamic Philosophy and Comparative Religion which he would develop in later years at the Aleemiyah Institute and his writing output based on a wide range of contemporary issues. These periods brought him closer to Mawlana Siddiqui both intellectually and spiritually. There was no doubt that Mawlana Siddiqui's *faidh* (spiritual blessings) opened up opportunities derived from this companionship. Moreover, Mawlana Ansari served as Mawlana Siddiqui's private secretary, a position which he held until the latter's death in 1954.

Mawlana Ansari joined the seat of Muslim learning and culture at AMU in 1933 and enrolled for the BA course. The subjects included in the curriculum were English Literature, Philosophy, Theology, Arabic and Urdu. He graduated in 1935 with a First Class First. It was a remarkable feat for Mawlana Ansari to pursue two degrees concurrently –BA and BSc for which he received the coveted Gold Medal. Another remarkable achievement enhanced his academic profile when he established a new record in Philosophy for obtaining **98% in Philosophy** in the BA examinations. In addition to the prestigious awards, he received the Haqqi Prize for meritorious achievement in Arabic. It must be noted that his undergraduate years were a preparatory period for his greater accomplishments in later years at the institution.

In the meantime, Mawlana Ansari had been pursuing a post Dars-i-Nizāmi course, Bachelor of Theology (BTh) under the eminent scholar, Professor Sayyid Sulayman Ashraf (d. 1939) who was appointed lecturer in 1902 and later served as chairman, Department of Muslim Theology.

Mawlana Ansari studied Qur'ānic tafsir and the vast corpus of hadith literature, *'Ilm al-Kalām* (scholastic theology) and *tasawwuf* under Sayyid Sulayman Ashraf. He paid glowing tribute to his teacher from whom he acquired knowledge of the Qur'ān and Islamic theological sciences.

Three important points emerge from Mawlana Ansari's association with Sayyid Sulayman Ashraf. Firstly, as a student he was able to master both classical and literary texts at an advanced level. Secondly, the degree he pursued was equivalent to a specialised study in Qur'ān and hadith.

This required a comprehensive and methodological study of the primary sources of Islam. His profound understanding of these sources are reflected in his writings with particular reference to his major work, *The Qur'ānic Foundations and Structure of Muslim Society*. Lastly, as a celebrated sufi, Sayyid Sulayman Ashraf complemented, by his personal example, the fusion of shari'ah and *tasawwuf*. Like Mawlana Siddiqui's mentorship in the path of *tasawwuf*, Sayyid Sulayman's teachings about the rich repertoire of classical sufi texts had a definite impact on Mawlana Ansari.

After Mawlana Ansari's graduation, Sayyid Sulayman Ashraf had an occasion to make the following remark:

> Hafiz Fazl-ur-Rahman Ansari is a young man with a personality radiant with virtue and exceptional intelligence. As regards his academic distinctions, he holds a place of pride among the alumni of the Muslim University. He has studied the Islamic theological sciences for the most part under me, and has accomplished the task with industry and ability. In *tasawwuf* and philosophy too, he possesses an extraordinary interest and has studied certain classics in both the subjects from me. Islamic missionary work is his goal in life and I pray that Allah Almighty may

bestow the choicest success on his labours in that field.

A similar sentiment was echoed by Professor Abdul Aziz Memon, Chairman: Department of Arabic concerning Mawlana Ansari's versatility. He commented:

I have not seen anyone who can equal him in gentleness of manners, excellence of character, love for knowledge, profoundness of concern for the important Islamic problems and courage for shouldering great tasks.
Moreover, in spite of his young age, he does not stand below any seasoned elder in experience and executive ability.
In short, I consider him capable of every good and great pursuit and fit to prove himself equal to any grand task that might be entrusted to him. *Hardly I have seen any student at this University who could excel or even equal him in his attainments which seldom combine in a single person.*

Like many intellectuals at AMU, Mawlana Ansari's admiration for Iqbal was on account of his contributions to Islamic philosophy. His poems were soul-stirring; his critique of Western civilisation was rigorous and the message for the Muslim *ummah* was optimistic. Moreover, Iqbal had studied in Cambridge and Germany and his writings were enriched by his stay in Europe. His iconic status for students in India could thus not be ignored in their personal quest to study abroad. Mawlana Ansari's inspiration from Iqbal in this regard was quite understandable. In a letter dated 1937, Mawlana Ansari sought advice from Iqbal about his intentions to pursue higher Islamic studies in Europe. Iqbal replied:

As far as Islamic studies are concerned, lecturers at the universities of France,

Germany, England and Italy conceal their specific agendas under the guise of academic research and objective studies. Under these circumstances and keeping your noble intentions in mind, I state without hesitation that your study in Germany will be futile. Instead, go to Cairo (Egypt) and master the Arabic language. Study the Islamic culture, political history, *tasawwuf*, *fiqh* and *tafsir* so that you may be able to reach the true spirit of Muhammad (SAW). Again, if you are endowed with exceptional intelligence (and potential) and you are passionately inclined to serve Islam, then you may set out your goals as you deem appropriate.

Iqbal's advice as mentioned in the letter contributed significantly to Mawlana Ansari's career.

The extensive reading by Mawlana Ansari at AMU covered a wide range of subjects. Therefore, it was hardly surprising that he read voraciously during his undergraduate studies. If his *Beacon Light* introduced him as a student of Comparative Religion, his other book *Muhammad The Glory of the Ages* expressed his mastery of the sīrah literature and trends in modern scholarship in the field of Islamic studies.

Viewed in this historical context, Mawlana Ansari's scholarly contribution to the life and teachings of the Holy Prophet (SAW) at a comparatively young age of twenty years must be appreciated. His mastery of the original sources in Arabic and critical assessment of Western scholarship enabled him to provide an unembellished account of the Holy Prophet's message to humanity.

Mawlana Ansari's profound study of the Holy Prophet's sīrah is clearly elaborated in *The Qur'ānic Foundations*. His coherent arguments in refuting the Christian-Jewish campaign of vilification and presenting a biographical sketch of the Holy Prophet (SAW) based on Western sources illustrate his devotion to the Holy Prophet (SAW). For more than forty years, Mawlana

Ansari's writings and lectures focused on an unconditional commitment to the Prophet's message derived from the Qur'ān and *sunnah*. References to the Holy Prophet are aimed at establishing a special rapport with his great personality and imbuing a believer with traits that are embodied in the beautiful conduct of the Holy Prophet.

Tabligh Mission in Singapore: 1937-8

It was during the latter part of 1937 that Mawlana Ansari was deputed on his first tabligh mission by Mawlana Siddiqui. The rise of evangelist activities in the Far East Asia especially in Malaya Peninsula necessitated the presence of a forceful scholar who could stem the tide of this growing problem among the Muslim masses in this region. In his *Welcome Address* in Singapore, he categorically stated that he came as the ambassador of the intellectual empire of Islam to reinvigorate and reconstruct Muslim intellectual life. In other words, Singapore and by extension the Malay Peninsula required a renaissance of faith in all aspects of their lives. His pertinent remark about Singapore's future Islamic role vis-à-vis the decline of Muslim countries in other parts of the world reflected his sense of optimism. Mawlana Ansari was ready to assist in raising up a great new edifice of Islamic civilisation among people "who entered the flow of Islam at a time when the Islamic world had lost its initial vitality and was on the way to succumb to the cultural onslaught of the anti-Western civilisation and could not therefore enjoy the opportunity of building up enduring and vigorous national Islamic traditions and culture."

Mawlana Ansari's tabligh period (1937-8) was productive in Singapore. He actively promoted the collective identity of the Muslims in the region and sought through his writings to resist campaigns that undermined shari'ah provisions in Malaya. In 1938 a Bill meant to establish the supremacy of Islamic Law in Malaya was introduced in the Federal Status Legislature Council. The entire press dominated by non-Muslims launched a scathing attack on the Federated Muslim States (F.M.S) Mohammedan Offences Bill. Among the press, the powerful *Straits Times of Singapore* led an editorial campaign captioned "Go to Mosque or Go to Prison" which provoked a series of correspondence and articles undermining the proposed Bill.

Mawlana Ansari wrote a forceful reply in the *Straits Times* to refute the arguments of all the opponents of the Bill. The editor who was instrumental in writing a scathing editorial was deeply impressed by Mawlana Ansari's rational exposition that he wrote another editorial, seemingly an apology. His tacit endorsement of Mawlana Ansari's academic credentials was couched in persuasive language: "that subtle and learned logician."

It must be noted that the period under review (1937-8) nurtured Mawlana Ansari's academic profile: a scholar with a profound understanding of the challenges facing Muslim communities; an *'ālim* who framed and developed educational programmes compatible to the aspirations of the Muslims, and a *muballigh* who complemented pragmatism and Islam's destiny with progressive orthodoxy. In retrospect, Mawlana Ansari symbolised Islam's unique role as a da'wah-based dīn capable of responding to modern day challenges.

Likewise, the lecture tours by Mawlana Ansari to South Africa in 1970 and 1972 were a watershed in the history of South African Muslims. His lectures left an indelible impression on South African Muslims by articulating an Islamic worldview for the new generation of modern educated Muslims.

Academic Honours

In 1939 Mawlana Ansari was selected as Fellow of the Alexander von Humbold Stiftung of Berlin and was to proceed to Germany to pursue his postgraduate studies. However, with the outbreak of the Second World War in 1939, travel facilities to Germany were equally hazardous and disruptive; thus he had to abandon his ambitious plans. He resumed his studies in Bachelor of Theology and graduated in 1941 with a First Class First.

Again, the period 1941-2 marked a millstone in his intellectual career and pointed out to his remarkable versatility. He took up the MA course in Philosophy and graduated in 1942. His major subjects included Metaphysics, Ethics, Psychology and Islamic Philosophy for which he was required to study the original sources in Arabic and Persian. The pioneering study in Muslim philosophy entitled *History of Muslim Philosophy* examines the growth and development of this discipline and its close association with the sciences, humanities and arts. Thus a comprehensive study of Philosophy in relation to other disciplines entailed a scientific and rigorous approach combined with an extensive examination of Western sources. At the AMU with its enviable record of producing the best minds in these disciplines, Mawlana Ansari could not have found a suitable place to pursue his long-cherished ambitions. As the President of the Philosophical Society of AMU, he made important contributions as well. His devotion to learning went beyond the formal curriculum programme. On his own he studied an additional MA course in subjects as diverse as Politics, Economics, Law, Comparative Religion and History of Civilisation and Culture. The world- renowned philosopher, Syed Zafar al-Hasan became his supervisor for his doctorate which he commenced in 1942. Mawlana Ansari's topic *Islamic Moral and Metaphysical Philosophy* was intended to make groundbreaking research in this field. For five years research work was conducted in an extensive manner.

Even before the completion of Mawlana Ansari's doctoral thesis, Syed Zafar al-Hasan had recorded his impressions in 1945:

> Hafiz Fazlur Rahman MA., BTh. (Alig) has now been known to me intimately for twelve years. He is recognised by his teachers and his fellow students as an exceptional student, head and shoulders above others, always securing a First

class, standing first and often enough scoring record marks. For some time he has now been working with me on a philosophico-religious theme for his doctorate, which I am sure is going to be a great dissertation.

Hafiz Fazlur Rahman is a very capable man and has had a vast experience of the world. Already he has published a number of books and pamphlets and articles on Islam and Islamic topics which have been greatly appreciated. He is one of the very few really promising young scholars I know of.

In habits and manners Hafiz Fazlur Rahman is a perfect gentleman – who combines in his person true Islamic culture and occidental (Western) learning and I am sure he will, wherever he goes, add lustre to his own self, his teachers and his great alma mater, the Aligarh University.

Mawlana Ansari's Doctoral Thesis: Challenges and Opportunities

By all accounts Mawlana Ansari's thesis was to be a pioneering contribution in Islamic philosophy. Moreover, his detailed studies of tafsir together with his immense grasp of classical texts provided him a scholarly edge to develop his understanding of *tafsir* and the Islamic moral and metaphysical philosophy.

Mawlana Ansari's assiduous study on his doctoral thesis was not without difficulties. The concepts of Islamic moral and metaphysical philosophy were a new terrain in this discipline and entailed wading through a vast corpus of literature in several languages. As there were no previous studies dealing with this topic, the prospect of formulating new approaches became equally daunting. In fact, five years of intensive study indirectly prepared him for his future role as the exponent of the Qur'ānic teachings derived from the multiple levels of philosophy.

When the thesis was completed and submitted to Syed Zafar al-Hasan for moderation, the latter had left Aligarh for Karachi preceding the establishment of Pakistan; and thus was unable to present it to the relevant persons in the Philosophy department. After Syed Zafar al-Hasan's death in 1949, efforts were made to trace the research manuscript but could not be found among his belongings. Prior to this, the only other copy of Mawlana Ansari's thesis was destroyed during his migration to Pakistan in November 1947. His entire library was looted and destroyed in Amritsar (Punjab) and shattered all hopes of retrieving the "fruits of years of laborious and painstaking research."

World Tabligh Tours: 1949-69

The epoch-making and historic tabligh journey during 1949-50 and which lasted for fifteen months was uniquely associated to Mawlana Siddiqui and Mawlana Ansari. In many respects, the tabligh journey was unprecedented even during the nineteenth and twentieth century. The countries selected had their respective socio-political pecularities and the Muslim communities were exposed to a number of challenges. In fact, the emerging Muslim communities exposed to the predominantly Western cultures had the formidable task of establishing a viable Islamic presence through institutional forms like the mosques and Islamic centres. The crisis of Muslim identity was inevitable if they failed to address concerns that were directly related to Islamic beliefs and teachings.

In sum, the five tabligh tours which spanned over twenty years were undertaken by Mawlana Ansari to forge solidarity among diverse Muslim communities in far-flung countries across the continents. He also established Islamic outreach programmes for the purpose of articulating the collective Islamic identity in countries he visited. He strongly maintained that the fusion of knowledge and moral training was the Islamic ideal for Muslim communities.

History of the Aleemiyah Institute

Mawlana Ansari held important positions at higher institutes of learning. For example, he was appointed lecturer at the University of Karachi to teach Comparative Religion, Islamic philosophy and other disciplines during the period 1960 – 64.

In 1964 Mawlana Ansari took five years leave without pay in order to establish the Aleemiyah Institute. His growing preoccupation with World Federation of Islamic Missions (WFIM) which required extensive travels abroad forced him to resign from the post. It was at the insistence of Professor Ishtiaq Hussain Qureshi, then Vice - Chancellor of the University, that he continued to be associated with the institution as Director of Research studies in the Department of Islamic Studies, a position which he held until his demise in 1974.

Mawlana Ansari also studied various branches of medicine during his student days at Aligarh. In 1966, in Karachi, he was registered as an authorised practitioner of homeopathy.

The multidimensional personality of Mawlana Ansari unfolded at three levels: his academic career, tabligh mission and *tasawwuf* responsibilities. These three areas were contributing factors to his fame as an 'ālim-scholar.

The nucleus of the Islamic Institute was formed when Mawlana Ansari had introduced short courses on Islamic studies in a modest flat at Sadar, Karachi to foreign students who wished to be enlightened through the medium of English on Islamic culture and civilisation. The courses continued until the Aleemiyah Institute took a formal shape at the Islamic Centre in July 1964. The first batch of students who hailed from Pakistan, East Africa, South Africa, West Indies and South America pursued the fully-fledged courses in Islamic theology and modern thought.

The Aleemiyah Institute owing to its unique educational programme and dynamic approach carved out a niche as a premier institution of learning and attracted considerable interest from many parts of the world. The list of the first batch of graduates is an indication of the diverse backgrounds of

Muslim students who later served the cause of Islam.

Besides the degrees conferred by the Aleemiyah Institute, the students were given all possible facilities to obtain modern degrees at undergraduate/postgraduate levels according to their preferred areas of specialisation from the University of Karachi. It must also be remembered that Mawlana Ansari's association with the University as lecturer and Director of Research facilitated the accreditation of degrees at his Institute.

Mawlana Ansari's life was filled with challenges. One such example was his doctorate in Philosophy thesis which he had completed in 1947. The fruits of his labour lost during the Partition years did not deter him from resuming his doctoral programme at University of Karachi. In 1970 he was awarded the PhD degree in Philosophy. His topic was *Islamic Moral Code and its Metaphysical Background*. His thesis was commented by an eminent scholar of Philosophy, Dr Manzoor Ahmad as follows:

> It is indeed a comprehensive account of the Moral Code provided by the Qur'ān, a like of which, to my knowledge has not been formulated with such an extensiveness by anyone in the history of Muslim literature.

Three years later (1973), Mawlana Ansari would incorporate his extensive years of study on the Islamic Moral Code in *The Qur'ānic Foundations and Structure of Muslim Society*.

Towards Journey's End

Mawlana Ansari was a diabetic patient. His strenuous world tabligh journeys, public lectures, writing and teaching took a heavy toll on his health. After the completion of *The Qur'ānic Foundations*, his health deteriorated rapidly. It must be remembered that Mawlana Ansari also started another project concurrently with this work which was to focus on the hadith literature in relation to the teachings of the Qur'ān. This work was a momentous undertaking and Mawlana Ansari could not make significant progress owing to the frailty of his physical condition. With his health unattended and to a large extent diabetes uncared for, irreversible damage was caused to his kidneys.

It was on Friday 3 May 1974 that he was admitted to the National Institute of cardio-vascular disease suffering from a mild heart attack and oedema of the lungs. On Thursday 30 May the doctors announced that his kidneys were non-functional and not responsive to the treatment. The concentration of urea in his blood shot up to extreme levels. He was therefore brought home where homeopathic treatment was administered. According to Dr Muhammad Ali Shah, his disciple *(murid)* and allopath physician, he had not come across any case in the annals of medical history, where the mental faculties were so active and vibrant despite the severity of ailments Mawlana Ansari suffered from. He mustered enough courage to give a concise talk to the medical staff on duty regarding Islamic teachings and the spiritual dimensions of Islam.

Mawlana Ansari's mental alertness and concern for the mission of Islam was attested by his family members and close associates. His daughter said in the last days she saw her father walking slowly up and down the room reciting the poignant verse of the last Emperor of the Mughal dynasty, Bahādur Shah Zafar:

(From the giver and taker of life)
I sought and obtained a life span of four days.
Two have gone in longing (or wishing)
And two in waiting.

As in verse, so in real life, he spent all his life devoted to one single end, one single goal - the mission of Islam.

This verse alluded to the last days of the Mughal Emperor who was sent to exile in Burma (Myanmar) after the War of Independence in India. An accomplished poet, he symbolised the last vestige of the glorious and often turbulent Mughal rule.

Mawlana Ansari's zeal for the Islam and his mission sustained the last days of his life: His devoted colleague and lecturer at the

Aleemiyah Institute, Mawlana Sayyid Abdul Hayy Bukhari said:

Mawlana Ansari's concern for the ummah and its future was ingrained in his mind and soul. He said: "After all this hard work and life-long research, I have been able to discover certain truths and diagnose the ailments of the Muslim ummah. How I wish that Allah grants me a few years more to work, so that I may put in my little contribution which is the best in me, for the furtherance of the cause of Islam and Muslims."

But Allah willed that he should rest after a life that was full of hardship, trials, tortures and self-sacrifice. Before he was hospitalised, he had given a particular task to some of the members of the teaching staff of the Aleemiyah Institute. When the writer of these lines visited him in the hospital, he lay in a state of swoon. After a short while, he opened his eyes, looked at the writer, there appeared a feeble smile on his lips, and he said. "How is the work progressing?" He was so weak that his voice sounded as if coming from quite afar. When he was told it was progressing in the normal way, he sighed and said: "Tell them that I shall see it when I come back home."

He did come back home, but not to stay, for soon he had to leave for his eternal abode of bliss.

His humility and devotion to his mission were rewarded with an abundance of knowledge, which often was beyond the realm of human comprehension. On his death bed he said to his wife, Amatas - Subuh Sabiha, his life companion:

I feel as though the world of knowledge has only now been unveiled to me and all my life I have been a child grasping tentatively for a ray of knowledge here and there.

Mustafa Fazil, Mawlana Ansari's only son who succeeded Muhammad Ja'far as khalifah of the Qādiriyyah order, provides the following account of his father's last moments:

> It was the early hours of Monday 6th June 1974, when Dr. Ansari was in intense pain and realising that the doctors could not do anything he then said "Ok, It is now time to leave." He asked me to open all the doors and windows of the room and to give him space. His powerful voice echoed with the melody of *Surah Rahmān*, expressing from the core of his heart his gratitude to his Lord. As he approached the end of the surah, his voice started to fade in slower rhythm. During all this time, he raised his right hand umpteen times as if shaking hands. The whole house appeared to be electrified. With his voice gone, one could see his tongue uttering 'Allah, Allah, Allah....' And then the movement stopped – the saintly soul had departed to meet the Owner, the Lord Almighty, the Beneficent, the Merciful.

A multitude of mourners attended Mawlana Ansari's *jan āzah* (funeral service). There at the eastern gate of the Islamic Centre, North Nazimabad, Karachi, lay the earthly remains of the noble soul that worked tirelessly and heroically for the cause of Islam.

In Pursuit of Excellence

Apart from public lectures, there were also *majālis* (religious sessions) held at the homes of Mawlānā Ansari's hosts:

- Mawlana Ansari was accommodating to people from different backgrounds and spoke according to their levels. 'Ulama, professionals and common people visited him and there was no formality *(takalluf)* in his interaction with

Biographical Sketch

them. He had that charming smile that endeared people to him. He spoke directly, frankly and honestly. Moreover, it was his spirituality *(ruhāniyat)* that drew people closer to him. Never had visitors seen an 'ālim combine academic excellence with spirituality.

- The *majālis* focused on the universal message of Islām and love for humanity, themes that were woven into his worldview - a poignant reference to sufis who embodied this universal message. Mawlana Ansari's traditional appearance *(hulyā)* concealed his status as an illustrious scholar with a mind and soul that characterised the era of Islam's glorious past. He was a true representative of intellectual trends that gave shape and character to Islamic scholarship.

- Humility was the hallmark of his character. As much as he shunned self-importance he emphasised personal and spiritual growth-the grades of *tazkiyah* that empower a Mu'min (believer) to unleash his potential to be able to achieve the goals of Divine pleasure *(ridā ilāhi)*. It was not uncommon to see throngs of visitors who would discuss their personal matters with him only to leave with a smile on their faces.

- Mawlana Ansari's conversations were based on the Qur'ān, *sunnah*, lives of the *salf al-sālih*. His exposition of *tasawwuf* was forceful and passionate, spirited and charming as well.

- There was no doubt that his 'ibādāt *(tahajjud salāh, dhikr...)* governed his everyday life. It was the early hours of the morning that revealed his profound spiritual communion with Allah. A restless soul his devotional practices *(awrād)* were conducted in seclusion. The hosts were not inconvenienced.

- Mawlana Ansari's meticulous observance of the *sunnah* was mirrored in his *tahajjud salāh*. No taxing lecture programmes or other commitments for the day could deter him from his devotional practices in the early hours of the morning. The rapport between an *'abd* (servant) and the Almighty Allah through *salāh* and *dhikr* are 'triggers for transformation' which sustain the human personality to achieve the spiritual ideal – Divine pleasure. Mawlānā Ansari personified this spiritual ideal.

- His politeness was proverbial. At the meeting held at the University of Natal (UKZN) he spoke for the allotted time and personally received the next speaker (Rev. Hurley) and led him to the podium. Time management was thus rigorously followed.

A pertinent reminder was given to the audience on the fleeting nature of life and the futility of creating dissension (*fitnah*) by the following comparison:

"This life here is like the stock of an ice-vendor. He buys the ice from the factory and invests a capital in order to obtain a profit. But he gets back only that much of money in accordance with the quantity of ice he is able to sell. That portion that turns into water is lost in the earth and unreclaimable. All that we do out of love for this world, is like the ice that turned into water and is lost in the earth."

References:

Yasien Mohamed, *Islam to the Modern Mind* (Paarl, 2006).
Mahdie Kriel, *Islamic Intellectual Revival of the Modern Mind* (Cape Town, 2011).
Umair Mahmood Siddiqui, *Dr. Fazlur Rahman Ansari: The Ghazali of His Age* (Karachi, 2016).
Abdul Kader Choughley, *Fazlur Rahman Ansari: Life and Thought* (Springs, 2012).

Introduction

The study aims to examine the contributions of Dr. Mawlana Muhammad Fazlur Rahman Ansari (1914-1974) to contemporary Islamic thought. A long and extensive career spanning over forty years Fazlur Rahman Ansari (hereafter Mawlana Ansari) is considered an important figurehead in Islamic revival and tabligh. The twentieth century covers important religio-political developments in the Muslim world and scholarly response particularly among 'ulama and intellectuals are contextualised within the framework of Islamic resurgence.

The 'ulama regarded as bastions of traditional Islam have not been immune to the challenges of technological advancement in this century. They too have been faced with the dilemmas of responding to its pervasive influence which has changed the religious landscape of Muslim societies. Their attitude to science and technology has been ambivalent as examined in the study; and the discourse of Islamisation of knowledge assumes greater importance in relation to Mawlana Ansari's contributions. The 'ulama's worldview is also shaped by the Islamic institutions they are associated with.

Mawlana Ansari's pioneering contributions to Islamic resurgence encapsulate his multifaceted profile: *'ālim*, scholar, sufi and *muballigh*. These descriptions are elaborated in the volume to demonstrate his holistic vision of Islam as a dīn (way of life). This term has assumed different meanings in the latter part of the twentieth century in the Muslim world. For example, a politicised reading of this term has given rise to the Islamist groups investing new meanings. In contrast to this position, dīn is associated with the divine system with strong social connotations. Against these divergent interpretations, Mawlana Ansari's presentation of Islam in light of contemporary thought must be understood. Likewise, in the field of tabligh, his contributions stand out clearly. Unlike the traditional definition of tabligh which is confined to individual effort or institutional expression, Mawlana Ansari expands this concept as a 'collectivistic or social duty' that functions in the domains of moral and spiritual life. The international tabligh tours undertaken by him have added new dimensions to this concept: a network of missions connected to disseminating the message of Islam.

Mawlana Ansari's scholarly profile creates a deep understanding of the *tawhid* (unity) discourse. Viewed from this angle, his credentials are reflective of a rich Islamic tradition possessing the potential of guiding humanity as *khalifat-Allah* (vicegerent of Allah). This theme resonates in his writings and public lectures. Similarly, his presentation of *tasawwuf* is anchored in the Qur'ān, *sunnah* and the *salf al-sālih* (the earliest representatives of Islam). There is no doubt that Mawlana Ansari's conception of *tasawwuf* has relevance for Muslims living in modern society as a life- enriching experience that leads to Allah-realisation.

According to Mawlana Ansari, *islāh* (reform) and *tazkiyah* (spiritual purification) are the ideals to which Muslims should internalise in their lives because these are the embodiments of a dynamic Muslim society. It is interesting to note that scholarly tradition with strong links of Islamic activism has contributed significantly to Mawlana Ansari's profile as a reformer of international repute. His versatility is best illustrated in his major writings which seek to elaborate the following themes:

- The primacy of the Qur'ān and *sunnah* as contributors to world civilisation
- *Islāh* and *tazkiyah* as anchors of Islamic revival
- Islamisation of knowledge
- Tabligh: a methodological approach
- Islam and the West: A critique
- Vision of an Islamic society: the Qur'ānic paradigm

Introduction

Major sources for the study

The major sources for the study are based on Mawlana Ansari's writings in English. Of importance is his *The Qur'ānic Foundations and Structure of Muslim Society*, a voluminous study on the Philosophy and Moral Code as given in the Qur'ān. The dynamic orthodoxy formulated by Mawlana Ansari is also elucidated in this important work. Monographs which cover an array of Islamic subjects have been used to examine Mawlana Ansari's contributions to contemporary Islamic thought. The compilation of lectures has also augmented a broader understanding of his multidimensional career.

Islam to the Modern Mind: Lectures in South Africa 1970 & 1972[1] is an indispensable guide to understanding Mawlana Ansari's "scientific and philosophical exposition of Islam and for his candid counsels to Muslims in South Africa." It has a contemporary relevance for Muslim across the world to respond constructively to the challenges of secular modernity.

As the title aptly suggests, the book also conveys Mawlana Ansari's formulation of dynamic orthodoxy which is an antithesis to conservatism and modernism. The lectures edited by Yasien Mohamed, transcribed and compiled by Mahdie Kriel have stimulated great interest to study the life and works of Mawlana Ansari.

The work has been reprinted in 2017 as a fifth edition with editorial improvement by Mahdie Kriel. Another noteworthy feature of the edition includes references to the *ahādith* cited by Mawlana Ansari based on the classification adopted in specialist hadith works. The present work, however, omits the critical evaluation of Kriel's edition.

Islamic Intellectual Revival of the Modern Mind[2] is a collection of articles and lectures compiled and transcribed by Mahdie Kriel. It is also a useful work and covers a wide range of important topics by Mawlana Ansari.

The *Minaret Monthly*, organ of the World Federation of Islamic

---

[1] Yasien Mohamed: *Islam to the Modern Mind*.
[2] Mahdie Kriel, Islamic Intellectual Revival of the Modern Mindi, 41.

Missions, has published *Special Issues* in memory of Muhammad Fazlur Rahman Ansari. Biographical sketches and tributes form the themes of these issues.

A recent work *Fazlur Rahman Ansari: Life and Thought* by Abdul Kader Choughley is a noteworthy study about Mawlana Ansari's contributions to Islamic resurgence. It may be stated that no detailed study had been undertaken following his demise in 1974. Random articles have appeared in several magazines written by ex-graduates of Aleemiyah Institute (Karachi). However, these are not substantive contributions. The biographical impressions lack coherence and do not cover a comprehensive account of his Islamic reformist thought.

Belonging to a series of compilation are Umair Mahmood Siddiqui's latest editorial works: *The Beacon Light* (2015) and *Dr Fazlur Rahman Ansari: The Ghazali of His Age* (2016). These volumes are a synopsis of Mawlana Ansari's biography and include articles and booklets published as early as 1950.

The present work is a modest attempt to provide thematic significance to selected writings and lectures of Mawlana Ansari. The motivation for this compilation is to draw readers' interest to the treasure trove of his multidimensional contributions to Islamic resurgence in the 20th century. His influence continues to shape the Islam in contemporary world discourse.

Salient Features of the volume

- Selected lectures and articles are based on themes.
- References are cited from Mawlana Ansari's writings for an overview of the subject matter or topic under discussion.
- Where necessary, brief comments or quotations are given in the footnotes to facilitate a proper understanding of the points raised in the text.
- As far as possible, the topics (or chapters) are interlinked for the purpose of fluency, coherence and readability.

- Phrases linking paragraphs are inserted and syntax reconstructed to make the text reader-friendly. Also a few articles have been adapted to avoid repetition of ideas.
- Mawlana Ansari's translation of the Qur'ānic verses has been retained. It is evident that his translation was intended to convey a specific meaning within the context of his lectures or writings. Therefore a literal translation of the Qur'ānic verses is included in the footnotes.

It is hoped that the present work will encourage future studies on Mawlana Ansari's contributions to Islamic philosophy and Qur'ānic studies.

PART ONE

ISLAM: MEANING AND MESSAGE

The general view of mankind concerning religion is that its function is confined to the problem of salvation in the next world. But present day humanity has become increasingly interested in achieving salvation in the present world. Hence, religion has fallen into disrepute as something incapable of solving human problems relating to the earthly life; - nay, even as a definite impediment to human progress. Here Islam has a unique role to play, because it is definitely, directly committed to the salvation of humanity in both the worlds: the present one as well as the next.

All in all, Islam stands in history as eternal guidance for yesterday, today and tomorrow. The present may be gloomy because of the wrongs committed by the Muslims themselves during the different epochs of their history, including the present. But the future belongs to Islam, and to Islam alone!

1

Islam: The Way of Unity and Progress

What is the character of the universe which we inhabit and how are we related to it? There are two fundamental questions which have controlled all religions and philosophies of the world. In this connection each religious and philosophical system has tried to answer them in its own way.

Closely connected with these questions is the problem of the nature of relationship between mind and matter and spiritual and physical aspects of life. Hence, a solution of this problem alone can form the basis of our worldview and our life programme.

There are three distinct answers offered to our enquiry in this connection, namely the pre-Islamic religions, the post- Islamic empirical thought of the West and by Islam.

The pre-Islamic religions were deeply impressed by the notion of an acute conflict between man's moral and physical existence, or, in other words, between 'the biological within' and 'the mathematical without'.[1] This dualistic idea led them ultimately to find a way for the affirmation of the spiritual self in man to reject the physical reality as either meaningless or dangerous.

Hinduism regarded the world of matter as *maya*, an illusion and prescribed a life of renunciation for the spiritual development of its devotees. Likewise, Buddhism considered the physical world an obstruction in the onward march of the soul and pointed to the annihilation of the individual self and the severance of its emotional links with the physical world as the way to achieve *nirvana*. Similarly, Christianity recognised the antagonism between the physical and spiritual aspects of life and conceived the world of matter, or to use a more Christian term, the world of the flesh as essentially the playground of Satan. Consequently,

---

[1] The conflicting nature of man's physical and moral identity is critically examined in Ansari, *The Beacon Light* (Karachi, 2015), 78-81.

refined and cheerful moralist of earlier days, but by a sombre giant whom a kind of pre-sentiment was drawing more and more out of the pale of humanity. We should say that, in the moments of conflict with the most legitimate cravings of the heart, Jesus had forgotten the pleasures of loving, of seeing and of feeling.[4]

The post-Islamic empirical thought of the West adopts a path which is radically different from the pre-Islamic idealism. It asserts that the world of matter alone is real and worthy of our attention and the realisation of human destiny lies in the conquest of nature with the ultimate aim of achieving the highest amount of physical pleasure. However, it ignores all transcendental values[5] and spiritual considerations simply because they do not fall within the scope of empirical sciences. There is only one criterion of ethics which it recognises, (and that is the criterion of) practical utility for the enhancement of the earthly or 'carnal' pleasures of man.

Now, the physical world being essentially a battlefield of conflicting appearances and exclusively materialistic interpretation of reality, even though it may be concealed behind the otherwise fascinating mask of scientific spirit is bound to unbalance human life.

This is what the West is experiencing today. Nations are running at the throats of each other and individuals are indulging in the pleasures of the flesh in a way which precludes all possibilities of life's spiritual expressions. Peace and piety both

---

[4] Ernest Renan wrote his *Speeches and Essays* to win over liberals and secularists to Christianity. He became widely known in the nineteenth century Europe as a source of inspiration for modern Christian theology.
[5] The term *transcendental* is employed to illustrate the Islamic concept of the hereafter (*ākhirah*) as a reality.

have been left far behind.

Then is the message of Islam which stands between the ancient world that stressed the exclusive validity of the spiritual aspects of life and the modern world which interprets all reality in terms of matter? Has it any solution to offer to reconcile this sharp antagonism? Has it any teaching to give in the light of which we may develop all our faculties evenly and work out our destiny without prejudice against both our natural surroundings and the physical conditions of our life? Or our idealistic yearnings which are certainly not an illusion but a positive reality that are ingrained in our very nature?

Islam does not consider the universe as composed of two self-existing and conflicting entities. It conceives all life as a unity, because it proceeds from the Divine Oneness, and reality.[6]

In addition to this principle of harmony, Islam emphasises the purposive nature of all existence, whether spiritual or physical. Thus says Almighty Allah in the Holy Qur'ān:

$$\text{وَمَا خَلَقْنَا السَّمَاوَاتِ وَالْأَرْضَ وَمَا بَيْنَهُمَا لَاعِبِينَ}$$
$$\text{مَا خَلَقْنَاهُمَا إِلَّا بِالْحَقِّ وَلَكِنَّ أَكْثَرَهُمْ لَا يَعْلَمُونَ}$$

We have not created the heavens and the earth and whatever is between them in sport.
We have not created them but for a serious end: but the greater part of them understand not.

(44:38-39)

---

[6] For an elaboration on *tawhid*, see Ansari, *The Qur'ānic Foundations and Structure of Muslim Society*, vol. i (Kuala Lumpur, 2012), 173-89.

Thus our earthly surroundings are not a meaningless projection of the play of blind forces – a mere empty shell with no content. No, the tiniest particle of sand, the smallest drop of water, the frailest rose leaf, is full of meaning and music and functions under a definite and well-planned Divine scheme.

This being the character of the universe, what is the nature of man? Should we conceive him as a being who is originally born low and cannot attain the pinnacle of purity and perfection except through the tragedy of renouncing worldly pleasures or of passing through a continuous ordeal of transmigration?[7] This is the way Hinduism, Buddhism and some other religions go. Or should we believe him to have been born in sin and therefore incapable of working out his destiny except through a mysterious Divine sacrifice? This is the doctrine of Christianity. To these questions Islam replies in the negative. It is emphatic in its assertion that man is born sinless and is the chosen of Allah, as we read in the Holy Qur'ān:

لَقَدْ خَلَقْنَا الْإِنسَانَ فِي أَحْسَنِ تَقْوِيمٍ

Of the goodliest fibre We created man.

(95:4)

وَهُوَ الَّذِي جَعَلَكُمْ خَلَائِفَ الْأَرْضِ

And it is He Who has made you His vicegerent of the earth.

(6:165)

Starting his life with a sinless birth, man is entitled or we might say, destined, as an evolutionary being, to scale the loftiest

---

[7] Ansari explain transmigration of souls in the following words: "There are cycles upon cycles of rebirth through which every human being must pass times without number in order to attain salvation." Ansari, *Which Religion*, 10-11.

Moral and Spiritual Transformation in Islam

heights of perfection and to surpass all Allah's creation, including the angels, in his uniqueness and purity. Thus we read in the Holy Qur'ān:

وَاللَّيْلِ وَمَا وَسَقَ ﴿١٧﴾ وَالْقَمَرِ إِذَا اتَّسَقَ ﴿١٨﴾ لَتَرْكَبُنَّ طَبَقًا عَن طَبَقٍ

> *It needs not that I swear by the sunset's redness and by the night and its gatherings,*
> *And by the moon when it is at her full, that from state to state shall you be surely carried onwards.*
> (84:17-19)[8]

What then should be our attitude towards our material environment? Should it consist in renouncing the world and repressing our physical desires? Islam says nothing of the kind. Instead of recognising a conflict between the moral and physical existence of man, it emphasises the co-existence of these two aspects as the natural basis of life.

It maintains that our earthly sojourn is a positive factor in the Divine scheme of creation and the necessary stage in the evolution of our soul-life. Consequently, it seeks the affirmation of the spiritual self in man, not in renouncing the world of matter, but in the active endeavour to master it with a view to discover the basis for a realistic regulation of life. According to the celebrated poet of the East, Muhammad Iqbal 'the life of the ideal' is to maintain it as an organic unity.[9] It is therefore impossible for Islam to despise our earthly existence and activities, and there it differs radically with other religions of the world.

This realistic attitude of Islam may not, however, be identified

---

[8] Nay, I swear by the twilight, and by the night what it enfolds, and by the moon when it reaches its fullness: You shall proceed onwards from stage to stage (84:17-19).

[9] In other words, the life of the ideal reflects oneness (*tawhid*) which covers all facets of 'human faith and action.' See Ansari, Iqbal's Idea of a Muslim in *The Beacon Light*, 343-50.

with that of the modern West. The latter ignores our spiritual existence altogether and regards our earthly career as an end-in-itself, and that in a way which amounts to material worship. Islam, on the other hand, conceives it, not as an end, but as a means to a higher spiritual end. And what is the higher end? It is submission to the Will of Allah and seeking His pleasure, as the Qur'ān says:

قُلْ إِنَّ صَلَاتِي وَنُسُكِي وَمَحْيَايَ وَمَمَاتِي لِلَّهِ رَبِّ الْعَالَمِينَ ﴿١٦٢﴾ لَا شَرِيكَ لَهُ

> Say: Verily, my worship and my sacrifice and my living and my dying are for Allah, Lord of the Worlds, Who has no partner.

(6:162)

Viewed in this light, all our worldly actions, including the most insignificant ones, are transformed into religious acts the moment we give them a spiritual orientation, namely, the moment we perform them with the consciousness that we are acting in the light of Allah's commands. In fact, Islam conceives the whole life of a Muslim as a life of continuous worship. Allah says in the Qur'ān:

وَمَا خَلَقْتُ الْجِنَّ وَالْإِنسَ إِلَّا لِيَعْبُدُونِ

> I have not created the jinn and humankind but that they shall worship Me.

(51:56)

Thus the notion of worship in Islam is also radically different from that of other religions. In Islam there is no such distinction as 'religious' and 'secular'.[10] Every act of a true Muslim is a religious act because he has to perform all his works in obedience and conformity to Divine injunctions and has to dedicate all his

---

[10] Ansari endorses the views of the poet Iqbal who aptly says that dividing knowledge into old and new betrays the narrowness of mind.

faculties, spiritual or physical, to the cause of Allah's eternal scheme. Devotion and submission to Allah in this sense constitute the very meaning of our life in Islam.

Here Islam gives us the highest and the purest ethical standards. This statement is reaffirmed by Sir Richard Gregory who says that the concept of religious ethic has led to the highest idealism in human conduct.[11]

The notion of worship in Islam being what it is, it was absolutely necessary that Islam should not confine itself to the explanation of the metaphysical relations between man and his Creator but should also define exactly the relations between the individual and the society. And this Islam has accomplished to its eternal glory by giving us an exhaustive guidance which does not leave even the most trivial actions of our life untouched.

From what has been said above, the essential nature of the Islamic view of life must have become amply clear. But it is only the principle of 'unity in life' that has been emphasised so far. There is another fundamental principle, namely, 'movement in life' or progress, which requires elucidation. It points out to the direct outcome of its realistic conception of nature and man.

The Holy Prophet Muhammad (SAW) stands alone in the religious annals of the world as the advocate of scientific enquiry. The pages of the Qur'ān abound with passages which invite our attention to an empirical study of the natural phenomena and emphasises the conquest of nature by man. In fact, the inductive method of enquiry, which is the basis of modern scientific and philosophical thought is one of the most valuable gifts of the Qur'ān to the world.[12] Here are just a few Qur'ānic verses in support of this statement:

---

[11] Gregory, Richard, *Religion in Science and Civilisation* (London, 1940), 65.
[12] Cf. *Islam to the Modern Mind*, 28-31.

$$\text{إِنَّ فِي خَلْقِ السَّمَاوَاتِ وَالْأَرْضِ وَاخْتِلَافِ اللَّيْلِ وَالنَّهَارِ وَالْفُلْكِ الَّتِي تَجْرِي فِي الْبَحْرِ بِمَا يَنفَعُ النَّاسَ وَمَا أَنزَلَ اللَّهُ مِنَ السَّمَاءِ مِن مَّاءٍ فَأَحْيَا بِهِ الْأَرْضَ بَعْدَ مَوْتِهَا وَبَثَّ فِيهَا مِن كُلِّ دَابَّةٍ وَتَصْرِيفِ الرِّيَاحِ وَالسَّحَابِ الْمُسَخَّرِ بَيْنَ السَّمَاءِ وَالْأَرْضِ لَآيَاتٍ لِّقَوْمٍ يَعْقِلُونَ}$$

Assuredly in the creation of the heavens and of the earth, and in the alternation of night and day, and in the ships which pass through the sea with what is useful to man, and the rain which Allah sends down from the heaven, giving life to earth after its death and scattering over in all kinds of cattle, and in the change of winds and in the clouds that are made to do service between the heavens and the earth are signs for those who understand.

(2:164)

$$\text{وَمِنْ آيَاتِهِ خَلْقُ السَّمَاوَاتِ وَالْأَرْضِ وَاخْتِلَافُ أَلْسِنَتِكُمْ وَأَلْوَانِكُمْ ۚ}$$

$$\text{إِنَّ فِي ذَٰلِكَ لَآيَاتٍ لِّلْعَالِمِينَ}$$

And among His signs are the creation of the heavens and of the earth, and your variety of languages and colour. Herein truly are signs for those who know.

(30:22)

$$\text{أَلَمْ تَرَوْا أَنَّ اللَّهَ سَخَّرَ لَكُم مَّا فِي السَّمَاوَاتِ وَمَا فِي الْأَرْضِ}$$

Do you not see that it is Allah Who has made

subservient to you whatever in in the heavens and on the earth...?
(31:20)

It is no wonder therefore that during the ages of Islam's glory, its followers became the pioneers of civilisation and the inaugurators of the modern scientific era. This might sound strange to those who are accustomed to hear and read that Islam obstructs the way to progress and is an enemy of scientific learning. The truth lies just the opposite way and it can be honestly said that but for Islam there would have been no modern scientific progress. No less a person than Robert Briffault, the noted historian of civilisation, has admitted this fact in his well-reputed work *The Making of Humanity:* He says:

> Neither Roger Bacon nor his latter namesake has any title to be credited with having introduced the experimental method. Roger Bacon was no more than one of the apostles of Muslim science and method to Christian Europe. Science is the momentous contribution of Arab civilisation to the modern world, (though) it was not science alone which brought Europe back to life. Other and manifold influences from the civilisation of Islam communicated its first glow to European life.
>
> The debt of our science to that of the Arabs does not consist in discovering revolutionary theories. Science owes a great deal more to Arab culture: It owes its existence. The ancient world was, as we saw, pre-scientific. The astronomy and mathematics of the Greeks were a foreign importation, never thoroughly acclimatised in Greek culture. The Greeks systemised, generalised and theorised. But the patient ways of investigation, the accumulation of positive knowledge, the minute methods of science,

detailed and prolonged observation and experimental inquiry were altogether alien to Greek temperament... What we call science arose in Europe as a result of a new spirit of inquiry, of new methods of investigation, of the method of experiment, observation, measurement of the development of mathematics in a form unknown to the Greeks. That spirit and those methods were introduced into the European world by the Arabs.[13]

A vital point of difference between the spirit of the modern West and the spirit of Islam may however be emphasised again. While the modern West has employed science mostly for the satisfaction of its unjust craving for ill-used power and ill-gotten pleasure and for the cruel purposes of human destruction, Islam seeks in the scientific enquiry a means to the service of humanity and spiritual elevation. How beautiful the Qur'ān has inculcated the latter idea in the following verse:

﴿١٩٠﴾ إِنَّ فِي خَلْقِ السَّمَاوَاتِ وَالْأَرْضِ وَاخْتِلَافِ اللَّيْلِ وَالنَّهَارِ لَآيَاتٍ لِّأُولِي الْأَلْبَابِ

الَّذِينَ يَذْكُرُونَ اللَّهَ قِيَامًا وَقُعُودًا وَعَلَىٰ جُنُوبِهِمْ وَيَتَفَكَّرُونَ فِي

خَلْقِ السَّمَاوَاتِ وَالْأَرْضِ رَبَّنَا مَا خَلَقْتَ هَٰذَا بَاطِلًا سُبْحَانَكَ فَقِنَا عَذَابَ النَّارِ

> Verily, in the creation of the heavens and the earth, and in the succession of night and day, are signs for people of understanding, who standing, sitting and reclining bear Allah in mind and reflect on the creation of the heavens and of the earth and say : 'Oh, our Lord! You have not created all this in vain: Glory be to Thee!! Save us from the Fire.
>
> (3:190-191)

---

[13] Robert Briffault, *The Making of Humanity* (London, 1919), 202.

Islam, it may be emphasised, is not merely a faith, a 'religion' or a creed. It is a way of life – a life to be lived. It does not only respond to man's religious yearnings, but to human life as a whole. It does not only give us an infallible metaphysics, but also a comprehensive and sublime code of individual and social ethics, a sound economic system, a just political ideology, and many other things besides. It is not a solitary star, but a whole solar system, encompassing the whole and illuminating the whole.[14]

It should therefore be evident that the foregoing is a very brief discussion of a few Islamic fundamental beliefs to the study and fuller understanding of Islam. It is meant to stimulate thought, to bring out the fundamental distinction of Islam from non-Islam and to show that the notion of religion in Islam is infinitely richer and more sound than any other (belief systems) to which humanity subscribes.

---

[14] The distinction between Mysticism and Islamic spiritual quest (*tasawwuf*) is cogently outlined in *The Qur'ānic Foundations*, vol. i, 166-72.

2

What is Islam?

My life is passed mostly in agony and anguish because I am one of the soldiers of Islam on the battlefield who always have to face problems. I have to face those mighty anti- Islamic forces arrayed against Islam all over the world. In addition, I have to face Muslim ignorance, apathy and internal bickering over trivial issues while the enemy is blasting our fortress.

The enemy is taking away our best asset and the very flower of our nation is being kidnapped - the Muslim youth! They are leaving the fold of Islam in utter frustration in all the countries of the world. The apparently pious preachers of Islam are inviting Muslims to waste their energies on fighting amongst themselves.

Most Muslims are considered to be practising Muslims but tend to regard Islam as a cult, and not as a comprehensive way of life. According to us, it is constituted of certain rituals and ceremonials, and hair-splitting about 'aqā'id[1] This is where it ends. We do not consider the moral value of life because we have divorced religion from morality. Observe how far our devotional piety is divorced from our morality.[2]

I am confident that whatever Islam teaches is not a matter of interpretation but is given clearly in the Holy Qur'ān and the authentic sayings of the Holy Prophet (SAW). Islam is the only religion which is historical. It is not like Christianity, Hinduism or Buddhism, where the so- called facts of these religions are enshrouded in mystery and one feels mystified if one tries to find out exactly what their teachings are.

---

[1] 'Aqā'id (sing.'aqidah): Islamic belief system or creed. The 'aqā'id have been systematically formulated in manuals like 'Aqidah al-Tahāwi which is taught in institutions of higher Islamic learning (dār al-'ulum).
[2] Ansari, The Qur'ānic Foundations, vol. i, 323-8. The theme of morality is comprehensively discussed as an expression of Divine Law.

Islam was born in the broad daylight of history and it goes to the credit of our forefathers, the Sahābah, the Tābi'in[3] and the early Muslims. They took the greatest care in preserving the historical character of Islam so that today no one can claim ignorance.

When we compare what we have been taught in the Holy Qur'ān and the authentic ahādith of the Holy Prophet (SAW) with our view of its teachings in the age, we will notice a great difference. Remember that the ideological cultures of life, whether they have been based on philosophy or sociology or religion, may be divided into three types which are ideational, sensational and idealistic.[4]

When you study the philosophies and religions which were there before Islam, you will find that whether it was Hinduism, Christianity, Zoroastrianism or Buddhism, all these religions had the 'other - worldly view' i.e. they stood for *ideational culture*. The concept of the culture was that only the life to come was valuable, but not life here on this earth. Their philosophy was that this world is evil, the human body with all its demands are evil and that the social life is evil. Consequently, according to them, the salvation of mankind consisted of renouncing everything which was material and physical, sacrificing it at the altar of what they considered to be spiritual development. Therefore, the saint in Christianity was a celibate: a person who considered it a sin to give comfort to his body. In Hinduism and Buddhism we find a similar situation.[5] This was the ideational culture and its foundation was *mysticism*. Everything that was mystifying and mysterious found its place there.

By contrast, we have modern Western Civilisation with its *sensate culture*. The foundations of modern Western Civilisation are:

---

[3] *Tābi'in*: the generation after the Sahābah. They are included in the *salaf al-sālih* (pious predecessors) tradition.
[4] Ansari's extensive study on the sociology of religion comes to the fore in his important writings. Cf. *The Beacon Light*.
[5] Interestingly the lives and doctrines of Buddha and Jesus coincide with each other as discussed in Ansari, *Islam and Christianity in the Modern World* (Karachi, 1965), 78-91.

- From the point of view of metaphysics - its worldview is materialistic.
- From the point of view of morals, it is hedonistic (*the pursuit of sensual pleasure only*) and utilitarian (*an action is good only if it is materially advantageous in this world*).
- From the point of view of psychology, it is based on sensationalism. Study Western art, drama, poetry, fiction and their life as such and you will find that the basis of their outlook is sensational.
- From the point of view of politics, this civilisation is based on the concept of expediency. Thus opportunity is not based and defined on principles.[6]

What is the message of Islam and what is the message that the Holy Prophet (SAW) brought? My conclusion is that every teaching that the Holy Prophet (SAW) brought was absolutely unique, up to this day! The Qur'ān says:

إِنَّ هَٰذَا لَفِي الصُّحُفِ الْأُولَىٰ ﴿١٨﴾ صُحُفِ إِبْرَاهِيمَ وَمُوسَىٰ

And this is in the books of the earliest revelations, the books of Ibrahim and Musa.

(87:18-19)

However, the *suhuf*[7] of Ibrahim and Musa are not in the world anymore. There is the principle of continuity of divine guidance on which the Qur'ān stands.[8] However, when one examines its teachings and ideals for mankind one discovers the uniqueness of its message. For example, the Holy Qur'ān defines religion as

---

[6] Ansari echoes this viewpoint in the following words: "If the philosophy of materialism is correct then man should exploit man because according to that philosophy there is no moral bond of unity between human beings." *Islam to Modern Mind*, 291.
[7] Scrolls of divine revelation given to the Prophets in this verse.
[8] Ansari, *The Beacon Light*, 57-59.

follows:

$$\text{وَلَهُ أَسْلَمَ مَن فِي السَّمَاوَاتِ وَالْأَرْضِ}$$

All that is in the heavens and the earth are Muslim.

(3:83)

All creation submits to Allah involuntarily but human beings submit to Allah by free choice.
The Qur'ān says:

$$\text{هُوَ الَّذِي خَلَقَكُمْ فَمِنكُمْ كَافِرٌ وَمِنكُم مُّؤْمِنٌ}$$

It is He who has created you; and of you some are unbelievers and some are believers.

(64:2)

This obligation has been placed upon the human being because Allah has made him the highest in creation and has made him His *khalifah*.[9] The human being has to perform certain functions in terms of being His *khalifah fil-ard* as the vicegerent on the earth.

What is religion? The definition according to the Holy Qur'ān is absolutely different from any that has been given by any other religion, pre-Islamic or post-Islamic. The Holy Qur'ān says:

$$\text{فَأَقِمْ وَجْهَكَ لِلدِّينِ حَنِيفًا ۚ فِطْرَتَ اللَّهِ الَّتِي فَطَرَ النَّاسَ عَلَيْهَا ۚ لَا تَبْدِيلَ لِخَلْقِ اللَّهِ ۚ ذَٰلِكَ الدِّينُ الْقَيِّمُ وَلَٰكِنَّ أَكْثَرَ النَّاسِ لَا يَعْلَمُونَ}$$

So set your face upright for the dīn, the way of life, with single-minded devotion and loyalty, according to

---

[9] On the function and obligations of *khalifah*, see Choughley, *Fazlur Rahman Ansari: Life and Thought* (Springs, 2012), 62-4.

the nature in which Allah has created man.
Allah's universal laws never change. This is the standard religion. But most human beings do not understand this.

(30:30)

Religious life is to lead one's life according to those natural laws. Based on the above verse, Allah created man according to his own nature, which is *tawhid*.

This concept was not given by Christianity or any other philosophy, but the Qur'ān. It also negates ritualism or ritual piety in so many Qur'ānic verses. Ritual piety was the cornerstone of all other faiths: burn so many candles, have an altar like this or music like that. On the contrary, the Holy Qur'ān made it clear that there are two types of piety, formal piety and practical (or real) piety.

The Qur'ān says:

$$\text{لَيْسَ الْبِرَّ أَن تُوَلُّوا وُجُوهَكُمْ قِبَلَ الْمَشْرِقِ وَالْمَغْرِبِ}$$

There is no (it is not) piety in the adoption of a direction to the east or the west.

(2:177)

$$\text{فَأَيْنَمَا تُوَلُّوا فَثَمَّ وَجْهُ اللَّهِ}$$

Wherever you turn, Allah is there. (2:115)

Allah is not confined to the direction of the *qiblah*. The *maslahah*[10] and the *hikmah* (wisdom) which are there for which the

---

[10] In *fiqh* (jurisprudence) terminology *maslahah* means benefit or interest. A wider definition includes public interest which is in harmony with the objectives of shari'ah. See Mohammad Hashim Kamali, *Principles of Islamic Jurisprudence* (Cambridge, 1991), 267-282.

qiblah has been fixed is something else but don't think it is piety as such. To adopt a direction ritualistically is not piety.
The verse continues:

$$\text{وَلَٰكِنَّ الْبِرَّ مَنْ آمَنَ بِاللَّهِ وَالْيَوْمِ الْآخِرِ وَالْمَلَائِكَةِ وَالْكِتَابِ وَالنَّبِيِّينَ وَآتَى الْمَالَ عَلَىٰ حُبِّهِ ذَوِي الْقُرْبَىٰ وَالْيَتَامَىٰ وَالْمَسَاكِينَ وَابْنَ السَّبِيلِ وَالسَّائِلِينَ وَفِي الرِّقَابِ وَأَقَامَ الصَّلَاةَ وَآتَى الزَّكَاةَ}$$

> But piety is to believe in Allah, and the Last Day and the angels and all the Prophet's. It also means giving away of wealth out of the love of Allah to close family relations and orphans and the needy and the wayfarer and for those who ask the emancipation of slaves and to establish prayer and give charity.
>
> (2: 177)

The angels who are functionaries of Allah, maintain the divine order in the entire universe. This negates the theory of Sir Isaac Newton (d. 1727) who believed that God created this world and left it to itself and does not interfere.[11] The Qur'ān negates this view for we are to believe in the angels or *malā'ikah* of Allah. Divine interference in everything in the world is hereby affirmed. The divine guidance came in the form of Scriptures which have been prescribed and which ultimately, are to be found in the form of one *kitāb* (book). Here the verse does not refer to *kutub* (pl. of *kitāb*) because all those divine books, which came before, have been changed through interpolation. They lost their original purity except for one divine book called the Qur'ān. The verse continues, '...and all the Prophets...' affirming here the continuity of divine guidance. This is simple as far as '*aqā'id* goes.

Here the Qur'ān does not mention all those over-indulgences which later Muslims developed in order to fight one another and

---

[11] For a detailed account on Newton's religious thought, see Robert Iliffe, *Newton's Religious Life and Work* published by the Newton Project.

to come to blows and to call one another *kāfir* (disbeliever).[12] This verse is simple, direct and full of life. Do you know that academic, theological discussions are not full of life, rather they are only full of quibbling. This is a direct statement given that suffices for a Muslim. If a person believes in that, you have no right to say he is not a Muslim. These are matters of belief without any discomfort to yourself.

Then the verse comes to the real pitch and here comes the belief of discomfort and sacrifice in real practical demonstration that you are a Muslim and a *Mu'min*, that you believe in Allah and that orientation of life which has been given and expounded by the Holy Prophet (SAW). There is a saying: "If you ask from me my life itself, I will give it to you, but if you ask me about money well, it is a questionable matter."

We should note that Almighty Allah is emphasising first of all the practical virtues here in this verse. He does not first mention the devotional virtues like *salāh* but to social virtues first. He is mentioning *huquq al-'ibād* of which Muslims have lost sight of today, completely. So, Allah says that when you have performed the *huquq al-'ibād*[13] rightly, only then can you confidently come to His presence and offer the *salāh*. Ghalib (d.1869)[14] has aptly remarked:

> Will you go to the Ka`bah with this face? With all the crimes impinged on your face? Or should you not purify yourself first and then go to the Ka`bah which is a holy place?

This is the philosophy of faith in the Holy Qur'ān. Firstly, testing of *imān* (faith) through sacrifice for others. All those who might need your help, help them first, then come to Allah

---

[12] Ansari censures Muslim groups who are judgemental and rigid in their interpretation of theological issues for which there exists difference of opinion.
[13] The second volume of *The Qur'ānic Foundations* examines the categories of duties from a Qur'ānic perspective.
[14] Mirza Ghalib was a prominent Urdu and Persian poet during the last days of the Mughal Empire.

Almighty and be a *musalli*.[15] And after helping deserving persons, you will still have to pay the *zakāh*. Somebody mentioned: "We pay so much taxes to the government how can *zakāh* still be due from us?" For that person's information, irrespective of the government taxes, and even after giving charity, a person has to pay *zakāh*. A Muslim is not born to be the top dog of this world only, but an angel of the heavenly bliss. If a Muslim believes that he is only in the category of animals, then he may keep his dog's bone in his mouth and take pleasure in being a millionaire or a multimillionaire. Such a person has no place with Allah. Nowhere in the Qur'ān does Allah Almighty say "Be wealthy" or that "Allah loves you to be wealthy." But the Qur'ān has condemned wealthiness and extravagance in so many places in the most terrible fashion. Let us take an example from our beloved Prophet (SAW).

Once, a person came to the Holy Prophet (SAW) and pleaded with him to pray for his progeny for the blessings of this world. The words that the Prophet (SAW) prayed are the key to the entire problem. He prayed:

O Allah, give to my progeny that which will suffice for their basic needs.

The Holy Prophet (SAW) prayed for his progeny, who were dear to him, for nothing more than their basic needs. The Holy Qur'ān says:

إِنَّمَا أَمْوَالُكُمْ وَأَوْلَادُكُمْ فِتْنَةٌ ۚ وَاللَّهُ عِندَهُ أَجْرٌ عَظِيمٌ

This fact cannot be denied that your wealth and progeny are a means of test and trial for you.
But in the presence of Allah is the highest reward.

(64:15)[16]

---

[15] One who performs *salāh*.
[16] Your riches and your children may be but a trial: Whereas Allah, with Him is the highest reward (64:15).

Your reward will not come to you from your wealth, large shares in your company nor from your progeny. You may take pride in your children but...[Wealth] *and the army of sons are adornments only of this worldly life.* (18:46)[17]

I am trying to bring to your attention the unique characteristics of Islam - maybe at another occasion I will tell you how the Muslims have distorted most of them. I refer to the last part of the - verse in (2:177): *[And] establish the salāh and pay the zakāh.*

According to the Qur'ān, the money which a Muslim has is not his. Allah proclaims:

إِنَّ اللَّهَ اشْتَرَىٰ مِنَ الْمُؤْمِنِينَ أَنْفُسَهُمْ وَأَمْوَالَهُم

Allah has purchased the life and wealth of every believer.

(9:111)

He is no more the owner. Man is only the trustee of all his possessions. As proclaimed by Allah, this money is not meant to be a curse for you, spend it! Then alone can it be a blessing for you. Hoard it and it will lead you to hell! The verse from the Holy Qur'ān clearly states:

وَيْلٌ لِّكُلِّ هُمَزَةٍ لُّمَزَةٍ ﴿١﴾ الَّذِي جَمَعَ مَالًا وَعَدَّدَهُ ﴿٢﴾ يَحْسَبُ أَنَّ مَالَهُ أَخْلَدَهُ ﴿٣﴾ كَلَّا ۖ لَيُنبَذَنَّ فِي الْحُطَمَةِ ﴿٤﴾ وَمَا أَدْرَاكَ مَا الْحُطَمَةُ ﴿٥﴾ نَارُ اللَّهِ الْمُوقَدَةُ ﴿٦﴾ الَّتِي تَطَّلِعُ عَلَى الْأَفْئِدَةِ

Woe unto him (the man of wrong character), who amasses wealth and counts it. He feels that his wealth

---

[17] Wealth and sons are allurements of the life of this world (18:46).

will immortalise him. Never! He will be thrown in al-hutamah. And what will explain to you what the hutamah is? It is the fire that is kindled and rises above the hearts in extended columns.

(104: 1-7)[18]

What does it mean "Rise above the hearts?" You must have had a notion about *Jahannam* (hell), that it will be a big place with fires or furnaces. However, here Allah says that the hell is above the heart. This is the hell of losing the opportunity of doing good and earning salvation. This is the hell of losing the opportunity of working for the welfare of the less-fortunate until they become frustrated like in the Soviet Union and China and other countries of the world, and rise in bloody revolt and take away everything from the wealthy.[19]

So the Holy Qur'ān laid it down that it is permissible for a Muslim to earn by legitimate means only and not by any means, fair or foul. There is no such things as "all is fair in love and war." Wealth can be earned only through legitimate means and the Holy Prophet (SAW) has proclaimed:

Whatever is legitimate (halāl) has been made clear and whatever has been made illegitimate (harām) has been made clear.

It has not been left to our interpretation. There are some people who try to raise the banner of their own piety and things that were not made *harām* (unlawful) by the Holy Prophet (SAW) they proclaim to be *halāl* (lawful). They have no right to do that and are committing a very great sin.

---

[18] Woe to every kind of scandal monger or backbiter, who amasses wealth and counts it. He thinks his wealth will abide for him...(104: 1-3).
[19] See Ansari, *Communist Challenge to Islam* (Karachi, 2018), 224. This book, first published in 1951, is a critical examination of Communism. Ansari makes a pertinent remark about its negative impact on mankind in the following words: "[It] is a ruthless and dogmatic dictatorship that destroys religious and moral values."

What is Islam?

So, a Muslim is permitted to earn by legitimate means only as defined and fixed by the Holy Prophet (SAW) and not by our wishful thinking. In this manner a person may earn millions – but, then he cannot spend it as he wishes. The Holy Qur'ān is clear on this:

$$\text{وَيَسْأَلُونَكَ مَاذَا يُنفِقُونَ قُلِ الْعَفْوَ}$$

O Prophet (SAW), these Muslims ask you what they should spend in the way of Allah for the service of mankind? Say: all that is saved after spending on your basic needs.

(2:219)

Spending here means not as Fir'awn and Qārun,[20] but as Muslims. This is as far as *huquq al-'ibād* is concerned. Then the Holy Qur'ān comes to *huquq al-nafs*, the personal quality. The verse continues:

$$\text{وَالْمُوفُونَ بِعَهْدِهِمْ إِذَا عَاهَدُوا}$$

If you make a promise, fulfill it at all cost.

(2:177)

Here the Qur'ān is again talking of social ethics. This is practical piety. Allow me to give you an example of this and compare our most "pious" Muslims in this regard?

There are numerous examples, but I will quote only one from the life of the Holy Prophet (SAW).

The Companion Sayyidina Hudhaifah[21] was amongst the last to leave Makkah for Madinah. He was stopped by the guards of the

---

[20] Fir'awn (Pharaoh) and Qārun are synonymous with cruelty and materialism respectively. There are numerous references in the Qur'ān relating to their disobedience to Allah. See Qur'ān: 2:49, 28:78-62.

[21] *Sayyidina* is a honorific title addressed to the *Sahābah* and luminaries of Islam. The *Sahābah* epitomised the Prophetic conduct and were prepared to sacrifice their lives for the promotion of Islam.

Quraysh and prevented from leaving Makkah. However, he was told that he could leave Makkah only if he promised not to join the Muslim army in the forthcoming war, the battle of Badr. Sayyidina Hudhaifah promised to do so. Upon his arrival at Madinah he related the whole incident to our beloved Prophet (SAW). After some time had passed, the battle of Badr was imminent and our beloved Prophet (SAW) could raise only three hundred and thirteen poorly-equipped soldiers. The Makkans came with a great force and when Sayyidina Hudaifah came to join the army, the Prophet (SAW)reminded him of his promise. Sayyidina Hudaifah protested and said: "But sir, a promise under duress is not a promise." Our Prophet (SAW) replied, "For other human beings yes, but not a Muslim. A Muslim never breaks a promise no matter what the circumstances. No Muslim should break the law of Allah." And Sayyidina Hudaifah could not go to the battlefield.

But our promises of today! There is a whole dictionary of excuses which has been coined and kept ready. This applies to even elderly people sitting in the market place, dealing in transactions and breaking their promises. What is this, a new type of Islam according to our personal feelings and wishes? The verse continues:

وَالصَّابِرِينَ فِي الْبَأْسَاءِ وَالضَّرَّاءِ وَحِينَ الْبَأْسِ

Those who stick to perseverance and patience when in hardship and loss

(2:177)[22]

A Muslim can only face all these difficulties calmly and serenely because his motto of life is:

---

[22] And to be firm and patient in pain (or suffering) and adversely and throughout all periods of panic (2:177).

وَبَشِّرِ الصَّابِرِينَ ﴿١٥٥﴾ الَّذِينَ إِذَا أَصَابَتْهُم مُّصِيبَةٌ قَالُوا إِنَّا لِلَّهِ وَإِنَّا إِلَيْهِ رَاجِعُونَ

> *And give glad tidings to the sābirin – to those who cultivate and practise sabr – who, when a calamity befalls them, they say: Everything belongs to Allah and to Him we must return.*
>
> (2:155 – 156)

Why should we care? We are not going to live here for- ever. We are going to return to Him. Let us take an example from a period in history when the Muslims had sunk to a very low level in certain aspects of their lives. Politically, they were beaten by their enemies and morally, the highest among them were like the highest of today: given to wine, women and luxuries. At that time was born one of the greatest reformers in Islamic history amongst the followers of the Holy Prophet (SAW). He was Sayyidina Ghawth al-Azam, Muhiyyiddin Sayyid Abdul Qādir Jilāni.[23] What was the example set by him regarding the Qur'ānic injunction of [those] *who stick to perseverance and patience in hardship and loss*?

It is related that he was a business magnate of the highest order, although not leading that life. He led a life of *faqr* and earning wealth for the sake of Islam. His business was so successful that he had a merchant navy of his own.

One day while he was sitting in his *khanqah* (sufi lodge) with his disciples, his general manager informed him that the flotilla which was carrying merchandise and going from Basra had perished at sea. If this flotilla perished, then the whole business perished too. Sayyidina Ghawth al-Azam looked at the general manager, bowed his head for a few moments, raised it and said: "Alhamdulillah" (All thanks and praise belongs to Allah). He then

---

[23] A pre-eminent scholar and saint, Shaykh Abdul Qādir Jilāni was an embodiment of the Qur'ānic teachings and Prophetic conduct. His writings, particularly *al-Fath al-Rabbāni* (The Sublime Revelation), a collection of sixty two discourses is widely read as a prescribed work for spiritual reformation.

continued his discourse with his disciples. After about an hour or so, the general manager returned and said that the previous information was incorrect, the flotilla was caught in a very big storm but managed to reach the shore safely. Again Ghawth al-Azam looked at the general manager, bowed his head for a few moments, lifted his head again and said: "Alhamdulillah".

One of his close students said to him: "Sir, I am unable to understand this, that when the bad news came that the flotilla perished you said, "Alhamdulillah". And when the good news came you also said, "Alhamdullilah." What is this strange phenomenon?

Shaykh Abdul Qādir Jilāni smiled and said: "You are mistaken in thinking that I said: "Alhamdulillah" on the drowning or saving of the flotilla. I introspected or examined my inner-self to see if the shocking news or good news had the slightest effect on my emotion, and I found that there was none. And it was then that I said: "Alhamdulillah".

"Innā lillāhi" is not said while weeping and wailing and moaning. This is not that "Innā lillāhi". This should be said with the spirit, understanding and consciousness that the inner and outer condition should be in conformity with the principle of "Innā lillāhi". We have been commanded to be like this. The motto of life in the Qur'ān has been laid down for believers as follows:

$$\text{لِّكَيْلَا تَأْسَوْا عَلَىٰ مَا فَاتَكُمْ وَلَا تَفْرَحُوا بِمَا آتَاكُمْ ۗ وَاللَّهُ لَا يُحِبُّ كُلَّ مُخْتَالٍ فَخُورٍ}$$

Any calamity that may come to you, whatever you lose in life, never allow frustration or despair to overtake you. And any blessing of Allah that might come to you which make you happy, do not become elated at that. Allah does not like those who are weathercocks.

What is Islam?

$(57:23)^{24}$

Otherwise you are not behaving as a Muslim. When a calamity befalls you, you become like drones and when happiness comes, you lose the balance of your mind. Such people Allah says cannot be His *'ibād*, they cannot be His servants. In another verse we are told:

وَمِنَ النَّاسِ مَن يَعْبُدُ اللَّهَ عَلَىٰ حَرْفٍ ۖ فَإِنْ أَصَابَهُ خَيْرٌ اطْمَأَنَّ بِهِ ۖ وَإِنْ أَصَابَتْهُ فِتْنَةٌ انقَلَبَ عَلَىٰ وَجْهِهِ خَسِرَ الدُّنْيَا وَالْآخِرَةَ ۚ ذَٰلِكَ هُوَ الْخُسْرَانُ الْمُبِينُ

> There are those who believe, or render their devotion, loyalty or faith on flimsy foundation. When good comes to such a person, he becomes elated, and when a test comes from Allah, he performs a somersault.[25]

(22:11)

He laments with indignation to Allah! I have been hurt! I have been praying here at the masjid five times a day!

Allah says *about such worshippers or such Muslims that they are losers in the life as well as the Hereafter (22:11)*.

And this is a definite and evident loss in both the worlds.

So what are the characteristics of a Muslim here?

Then the Qur'ān, continues with the verse:

أُولَٰئِكَ الَّذِينَ صَدَقُوا

> They alone are truthful.

---

[24] In order that you may not despair over matters that pass you by, nor exalt over favours bestowed on you. For Allah loves not any vainglorious boaster (57:23).

[25] There are among men, some who serve Allah, as if it were on the verge: If good befalls them, they are well content with it, but if a trial comes to them, they turn on their faces: they lose both this world and the Hereafter. That indeed is a manifest loss (22:11).

(2:177)[26]

In their proclamation they are truthful to Allah and His Prophet (SAW) of Islam. It is not the person who performs the *salāh* five times ritualistically as a gymnastic exercise without spirit and understanding. Not is it he who remains hungry and thirsty from morning to evening in the month of Ramadān and violating every law that was given by the Holy Prophet (SAW) in connection with fasting. He eats so much at *suhur* (pre-dawn) that he belches the whole day and eats so much at *iftār* (breaking of fast) that he belches the whole night.

> *Those who possess the sterling qualities of character, they are true Muslims. They are possessors of taqwā.*
>
> (2:177)

My dear brothers and sisters in Islam. I have expounded on the message of Islam and its ideals but it is for us to take up this message and put into practice, Insha-Allah.

---

[26] Such people are Allah – fearing (2:177).

3

Philosophy of The Shahādah

مُحَمَّدٌ رَسُولُ اللَّهِ ۚ وَالَّذِينَ مَعَهُ أَشِدَّاءُ عَلَى الْكُفَّارِ رُحَمَاءُ بَيْنَهُمْ

Muhammad is the Messenger of Allah, and those who are with him are strong against Unbelievers but mercy personified to one another.
(48:29)

The universal message of Islam which was delivered more than fourteen hundred years ago was a multidimensional message. It consists of guiding principles for a successful life one earth and in the life hereafter.

The guidance which the Holy Prophet (SAW) brought is not confined to any one particular aspect of human life, but is the most comprehensive guidance. It refers to the spiritual and moral aspects. At the same time, it refers to the economic, political and all other facets of human life pertaining to the individual as well as the community.

The key to the individual and community happiness, peace and prosperity can be found in the teachings of the Holy Prophet (SAW). He laid down a basic foundation which consists of two principles, which are encapsulated in the *kalimah al-shahādah* (Islamic declaration of faith):

> *I testify that there is not god except Allah and I testify that Muhammad is His Messenger.*

The philosophy (and wisdom) enshrined in the *kalimah al-shahādah* is vast and deep. It bifurcates itself into the different branches of human life and applies itself in order to produce a unified guidance in the field of thought, as well as action.

The most important point I wish to make here is that a person is not a Muslim merely by pursuing a certain set of rituals or by proclaiming formally his belief in certain verities. Actually he is the pilgrim of eternity who tries to experience the Eternal Being i.e. Allah, and to transform his personality on that basis.

The kalimah has become a practice. When a child is born and grows up, the parents teach him to speak their language without learning the grammar. The same, my dear friends, has happened to the kalimah.

I am not saying that the formal declaration of the kalimah is something worthless. What I mean is that is that it is not the goal. In every journey there is a starting point, a means or vehicle and there is a goal. The starting point is merely the recital with goodwill and clear conscience of the kalimah. The vehicle with which this journey as 'pilgrim of eternity' is undertaken, is the model or example of the Holy Prophet (SAW) as we have been told:

$$\text{لَقَدْ كَانَ لَكُمْ فِي رَسُولِ اللَّهِ أُسْوَةٌ حَسَنَةٌ}$$

In the life of the Holy Prophet (SAW) of Allah you have an excellent example...

(33:21)

The Muslim, Hindu, Christian, Jew and atheist are all governed by an immutable law. They were sent down here to the earth to perform a certain function under the Law of the Almighty Allah. All have to move regardless of whether they perform the function correctly or not, guided or misguided, on the right or wrong path. They cannot just stay behind, for the Holy Qur'ān says:

$$\text{إِنَّا لِلَّهِ وَإِنَّا إِلَيْهِ رَاجِعُونَ ﴿١٥٦﴾}$$

Everything belongs to Allah and our return is to Him.
(2:156)

By free choice or under compulsion, every human being is heading towards that day and that occasion when he or she will stand before his or her Creator to render account. This world is for Allah because it has been created by Him and is owned by Him alone, without any partner, *wahdahu- lā-sharika-lahu*.[1] Thus, because He owns this world, He owns all human beings, and He also owns their destiny. This entire caravan of humankind is heading towards Him. It cannot stop. Whether Hindu or Muslim, Christian or atheist – everybody is heading towards Him.

The fact is that we are conscious of evaluating ourselves and of other human beings on the basis of two principles that exist simultaneously all the time, that is, the principle of good and evil.

We condemn evil, for by our very nature we are so constituted that whatever is shown to us to be good, we approve of and praise. Allah says in the Holy Qur'ān:

وَمِن كُلِّ شَيْءٍ خَلَقْنَا زَوْجَيْنِ

The life of this world and the life of human beings is built upon two opposite principles.
(51:49)[2]

The day comes and then follows the night. This is the contrast.

---

[1] The Arabic phrase reaffirms *tawhid* (monotheism) and represents the foundation of faith. See Ansari, *Through Science and Philosophy to Religion* (Karachi, 1965).
[2] And of everything We have created pairs ...(51:49).

$$ يُقَلِّبُ اللَّهُ اللَّيْلَ وَالنَّهَارَ ۚ إِنَّ فِي ذَٰلِكَ لَعِبْرَةً لِّأُولِي الْأَبْصَارِ ﴿٤٤﴾ $$

Allah alternates the night and the day. In this is a lesson for those who want to grasp the reality of things.

(24:44)

The lesson is not for those who want to walk like dumb- driven cattle or like the blind, but for those who try to understand the nature of life and what is the destiny of life is which can be rationally accepted by human beings to be their proper destiny. For them is a lesson in this dual principle of contrast.

The day is bright and the night is dark. The day brings energy and vitality to proceed further, and to take up another day's work. When the sun sets, the energies decline and it is human nature to seek some place where he can take refuge during the night. Most creatures, cattle, birds and even plants are also conscious of the fact that daytime is the working time and night time is the time for rest. Allah clearly states in the Holy Qur'ān:

$$ وَجَعَلْنَا اللَّيْلَ لِبَاسًا ﴿١٠﴾ وَجَعَلْنَا النَّهَارَ مَعَاشًا ﴿١١﴾ $$

And We made the night its cloak and the day a means of subsistence.

(78:10-11)

Consequently, the child becomes conscious of these two principles of light and darkness, happiness and sorrow, health and sickness, life and death, affluence and poverty. The human being has to lead his life as a slave of those two conflicting principles. In his state of affluence if he meets friendship, love and affection from others in his business or other enterprises, then he is happy. This he calls good. When he meets the contrary, he is unhappy and calls it evil. Good and evil perpetuate and run all through life so that it is impossible for a human being to come across only that which is considered by him to be good. He also has to taste evil. It is also impossible for a human being to always have evil and never to taste the good. It is Allah's good world. Evil cannot overpower good in a manner to cause it to vanish completely. I am coming to a very important point here. This is not mere philosophy.

Most of our miseries, if not all, are based upon a wrong understanding of ourselves and our surroundings. It is easy for a person to capture the good aspects of life so far as it pleases him, but it is very difficult for him to bestow good on others because the human being by nature is selfish. Human selfishness stems from insecurity in this life. If he had that security, he would never have liked to be selfish at all. But he has to be selfish basically, because he is always confronted with the image of impending catastrophe or evil if he is not on guard all the time. Thus we find that most human beings including the Muslims, who should behave better, are unable to understand their mission as human being in terms of good and evil which exist here. If a person meets evil from another person, his immediate reaction is to fly into rage under the impact of his animal self. The animal self is the seat of desires. His reaction: "I have been insulted, therefore, whatever is at my disposal, I am going to hit back."[3] And here starts all the miseries in the individual, family or communal life.

The Holy Prophet (SAW) said something different from what we normally feel under the impact of our animal self. He said: "Anger eats away *imān* as fire eats away the straw or wood."

This is a clear principle laid down by him. But I have seen in my travels around the world that some 'very good Muslims' can't keep their anger under control and don't feel that they are betraying their declaration of the *shahādah*.

This problem of the principle of good and evil has been there since the very beginning of human life on this earth. Consequently, every wise man or Prophet (SAW) who came,

---

[3] Ansari explains the spirit of goodwill as demonstrated by the Holy Prophet (SAW). It is not a 'moral theoretical principle' but an exemplary trait of a practising Muslim. See *Islam to the Modern Mind*, 292.

whether to India, Africa or Europe, never advocated evil against evil. You will find the teachers of mankind becoming very idealistic, sometimes to a degree where they become irrational. The Sermon on the Mount (of Prophet Isā) is a good example. The Christians call him the Prince of Peace, but I doubt whether Jesus actually preached it, because if you take this principle literally, we discover it is something irrational.[4]

In this Sermon they are taught: "If anyone slaps you on the right cheek, present to him the left cheek also. If anyone takes away your coat, give him the overcoat also." This is the teaching of the Sermon. However noble it might appear, and however idealistic and sublime it appears, it is something that is against human nature.

It is possible for a human being, if he rises higher in the moral scale, to forgive another person. If a person slaps him on the cheek, he may forgive him, but it is against human nature to present his left cheek also. The only thing possible is to forgive an insult, damage or harm that has been done.

Forgiveness is always the direction wise men moved in trying to bring peace by removing from human beings all those miseries and agonies that have come to them as a consequence of conflict. It is very natural that every human being should come across conflict, for every human being is a bottled personality. They are mutually exclusive. No two human beings are alike and consequently there must be a clash between them. Here comes the moral principle of how a Muslim should behave. It is from this point of view that I recited this verse:

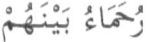

It is the characteristic of Muslims that they are 'mercy personified' to one another.

(48:29)

---

[4] Ansari's critique of Christian doctrine is succinctly expressed in his *Islam and Christianity in the Modern World*.

If they don't behave like that, they are not Muslims, whatever else they may do. The Holy Qur'ān describes the qualities of a Muslim to distinguish clearly whether he is behaving accordingly or not. The Qur'ān has not left it to our own wishful thinking or our own inner reactions or our own peculiar manner of thinking. May I add that the teaching which the Qur'ān has given us is an extremely rational one. It has taken into consideration the different levels of the moral tone of human beings and does not treat them the same like the Sermon on the Mount: "If anyone slaps you on the right cheek." Here, *you* refers to all human beings.

The Qur'ān, however, is conscious of differences between human beings in connection with their moral and spiritual development, the limitations of their inner temperament which is mostly physical. Thus the first principle laid down by the Qur'ān is:

﴿وَجَزَاءُ سَيِّئَةٍ سَيِّئَةٌ مِّثْلُهَا ۖ فَمَنْ عَفَا وَأَصْلَحَ فَأَجْرُهُ عَلَى اللَّهِ ۚ إِنَّهُ لَا يُحِبُّ الظَّالِمِينَ ٤٠﴾

> *The recompense of evil is an evil in the light measure. But whoever forgives for the sake of reform, for the sake of making the other party behave better and does not punish the guilty party, the reward is with Allah. Allah does not like those who transgress the bounds of justice.*[5]

(42:40)

If anybody slaps you once, you may slap him back. That is permitted. Here the Qur'ān is speaking of the law of equity in the court of Justice, not our personal human dealings. This law of equity[6] deals with that level where the parties concerned do not

---

[5] The recompense for an injury is an injury to it in degree: but if person forgives and makes reconciliation His reward is due from Allah. For Allah loves not those who do wrong (42:40).

[6] The recompense for an injury is an injury to it in degree: but if person forgives and makes reconciliation His reward is due from Allah. For Allah loves not those

settle the matter between themselves but take the matter to court. Then after giving consolation to the aggrieved party, Allah says that He sanctions recompense in equal measure. Here the Holy Qur'ān has given the solution of conflict at two levels. The first being the level of equity, i.e. revenge in equal measure, and the second being the level of forgiveness which is more meritorious in the eyes of Allah.

Then the Holy Qur'ān goes beyond that. It lays down the Law for those who might aspire to a higher status as human beings.

وَلَا تَسْتَوِي الْحَسَنَةُ وَلَا السَّيِّئَةُ ادْفَعْ بِالَّتِي هِيَ أَحْسَنُ

فَإِذَا الَّذِي بَيْنَكَ وَبَيْنَهُ عَدَاوَةٌ كَأَنَّهُ وَلِيٌّ حَمِيمٌ ﴿٣٤﴾

> Good and evil are not things of the same category. Always meet the challenge of evil what that which is good. When between two of you there is enmity, there is the possibility that under the pressure of your higher moral behaviour, he (the other) may be ashamed of his conduct and may become your friend.
>
> (41:34)[7]

Light and darkness are not of the same category. You cannot fight darkness with darkness. Therefore the command is to 'challenge evil with good.' If one is confronted with darkness, try to procure any source of light, even if it is a matchstick. Abusing darkness is not helping you. The only source of help to you is whatever source of light you might procure and use. Although the gloom of that darkness is so immense, the small light that you procured will at least dispel the darkness in your

---

who do wrong (42:40).
[7] Nor can goodness and evil be equal. Repel (evil) with what is better: then will he between whom and you was hatred become as it were your friend and intimate...(41:34).

immediate surroundings.

The Qur'ān advises that when a Muslim meets with evil, or is abused, he should not return with abuse, for then he is fighting darkness with darkness. When anyone does any evil to you, try to do something good, which in the end may lead to friendship.

This is what Allah is saying. But Allah also warns us here that meeting the challenge of evil with good cannot be adopted by every person; but

وَمَا يُلَقَّاهَا إِلَّا الَّذِينَ صَبَرُوا وَمَا يُلَقَّاهَا إِلَّا ذُو حَظٍّ عَظِيمٍ ﴿٣٥﴾

It can only be adopted by those who cultivate the quality of sabr (patience) and it can be practised only by those who cultivate magnanimity.

(41:35)

The person who cultivates the quality of *sabr* (patience), of serenity and calmness, perseverance, patience and magnanimity, he alone can walk this road. May I remind you that there is not a single teaching in the Holy Qur'ān that has not been practised by Muslims. It is not just a Sermon on the Mount about which nobody can prove that Jesus himself actually practised it. Whatever Islam has taught, has been practised by those people who have set a noble example of the Islamic teachings. Let us take an example from the life of Imām Abu Hanifa (d.767).[8]

He was a versatile scholar and an intellectual giant, head and shoulders above the other 'ulama. The other 'ulama became jealous of him and employed a person to abuse the Imām on his way home from the court building. This man had to provide a continuous mental torture to the Imām. Naturally, being a person of high stature, the Imām would not produce a counter-abuse. This abuse went on for a number of years. However, one

---

[8] For a recent study on Abu Hanifa's life and contributions, see Mohammad Akram Nadwi, *Abu Hanifah: His Life, Legal Method and Legacy* (Leicestershire, 2010).

day, when the Imām returned from one of his council meetings, his abuser was not there. Upon enquiry, it was discovered that the abuser had been arrested in a gambling den and was in jail. Imām Abu Hanifa immediately went to the police station and enquired from the police officer about a very good friend of his that was being held there. The officer was shocked that a friend of this great Imām could be in jail, and his shock was even greater when he heard the person's name. The officer said: "We have been waiting all along to arrest this abuser of yours and you call him your very good friend?" The Imām confirmed that the man was his friend and the abuser was released on the Imām's plea.

As the man came out of jail, the Imām got hold of his hand and said: "I am very sorry that you could not provide me with extra virtues and I hope that you will commence your job immediately." The man was so ashamed and fell at the feet of Imām Abu Hanifa and repented.

The police officer asked Imām Abu Hanifa to explain how the abuser could be his friend, and he replied: "The Holy Prophet (SAW) taught the Divine Law, that if a person injures or abuses you, then you get virtues to that extent from the account of that person, and if there is none, then from the general account. Thus the highest thing to earn is virtue. Therefore, who can be a greater friend than the one who gives you virtues as a daily gift which is the highest blessing from Allah?"

My dear brothers and sisters, don't take this as just another story. Try to think about this conflict between good and evil and what Allah has taught us and what His beloved Prophet (SAW) considered to be the behaviour of a Muslim.

People nowadays talk about: "He who stands making salām[9] in honour of the Prophet (SAW) is a polytheist (*mushrik*). He who does something in such a manner becomes a disbeliever."

---

[9] The controversy of *salām* in honour of the Holy Prophet (SAW) is most visible in the Indian subcontinent. Sectarian conflicts in the form of polemical debates characterise the intra-sectarian divide. See Barbara Metcalf, *Islam in South Asia in Practice* (Ranikhet, 2012).

Nobody talks about the morals of a Muslim while this is the

وَعِبَادُ الرَّحْمَنِ الَّذِينَ يَمْشُونَ عَلَى الْأَرْضِ هَوْنًا وَإِذَا خَاطَبَهُمُ الْجَاهِلُونَ قَالُوا سَلَامًا ﴿٦٣﴾

very foundation of Islam. Nobody tells Muslims what their behaviour should be like and what characteristics they should possess. The characteristics of the Muslim as mentioned in the Holy Qur'ān are numerous. Let me give you some examples:

> *The servants of the Merciful Lord are only those who walk on the earth in humility. And when they are confronted with mischief, these true Muslims say: 'Our mission is only peace.'*
>
> (25:63)

Those who walk on the earth in a light step are those who are grateful to Allah and to man, and have goodwill towards all. It is also those who behave like the refreshing morning breeze causing the buds to smile into flowers, bringing fragrance, vigour, happiness and peace to human beings. That is the role of the Muslim. By contrast, in every community you will find people whom the Qur'ān describes as *Jāhil* - ignorant people. It is the work of ignorant people alone to start mischief.

When true believers are confronted with the *Jāhils*, they are not going to entangle themselves with them. If you abuse me, I am not going to abuse you. If you talk aloud, I won't shout back. My mission as a Muslim is peace – salām! Don't engage in wrangles and quarrels. Of course, other qualities have also been mentioned.

وَإِذَا مَرُّوا بِاللَّغْوِ مَرُّوا كِرَامًا ﴿٧٢﴾

> *Muslims are those, (that) when they are confronted with anything that is vain or worthless, they bypass that event with dignity and grace.*
>
> (25:72)

I have mentioned only one basic aspect that has been made

obligatory by Allah in connection with Islamic life. I feel sad when I go from one community to the other and find that some people who are considered to be religious in their external outlook are the most mischievous on the face of the earth. Islam becomes a tool for mischief until the community is destroyed and divided into various parties and groups and matters go to the extent of litigation and court cases.

I have yet to meet many a Muslim who thinks in terms of the improvement of their personal character, and thereby the improvement of the moral behaviour of the community as a whole, in order that joy peace and happiness may come to every Muslim home and heart.

My dear brothers and sisters, it is high time that we take stock of the situation. The Holy Prophet (SAW) has laid down clearly that high morality is the measure of *imān*. He said:

> *The better the moral behaviour of a person, the greater is the imān.*

May I remind you in passing that the Holy Prophet (SAW) is Islam personified and he alone must be imitated.

Although the Holy Prophet (SAW) lived under the severest persecution he never abused anyone, nor did his hand harm anyone. Remember, the Holy Prophet (SAW) was the one who led the armies against the infidels of Makkah in the battles of Badr, Uhud, Hunayn and in those days the commander-in-chief was always the target and in the forefront because it was a personal war. Unlike today where the commander-in-chief sits a thousand miles away from the battlefield. Therefore, the main target of the infidels was the Holy Prophet (SAW) for they knew that if they could kill him the Islamic movement would die. All their swords, arrows and spears were directed towards him. This is the miracle of the Holy Prophet (SAW) which Muslims should remember.

Although the main attack was on his person, he only defended himself. His sword never harmed or even scratched his enemy. This was the manner he defended himself. This is the

Holy Prophet (SAW) about whom it was recorded that nobody was ever hurt by his tongue or his hand. In the worst moments of distress or persecution, the smile never left his face and the sweetness of his tongue never changed. This is the example he set for us![10]

We have an honest love for Islam, but my dear brothers and sisters, please learn to practise what Islam stands for. It does not stand for mere ritual. It is there primarily to transform us from human beings of a small stature into human beings of a high moral character. A poet said: "It is easier to kill a lion, but it is very difficult to control your ego." It develops into a raging storm immediately you raise your hand or tongue. If somebody abuses you once, the abuse is immediately increased against him. This is the *nafs al-ammārah*, and anybody who cannot tame this is a Muslim only in name. He is not a genuine Muslim because he is not pursuing the mission that was given to him as a Muslim.

My dear brothers and sisters, the Islamic way of life is grounded, oriented and founded in the highest spiritual idealism. To live for Allah alone who is All Holy, All Good and All Perfect and to live in imitation of the Holy Prophet (SAW), greater than whom no one was created in the entire creation. Remember, you have to carry the name of the greatest in Almighty Allah's creation as *khalifat-Allah*. The responsibility is very great. We will have to guard against behaving wrongly for we will not only damage our own dignity but also insult the name of that august personality of the Holy Prophet (SAW). This is a crime which I don't think Allah is going to forgive easily. He may forgive all crimes, but He says that the slightest insult to His beloved Prophet (SAW) and He will take away all your virtues. So beware of this aspect and be very cautious of your moral behaviour.

Please understand once and for all that Islam is not merely ritualistic gymnastics or an exercise in sectarian differences of opinion. This is not Islam. Islam means intense love for the Holy

---

[10] The ethics as enshrined in the Qur'ān were upheld by the Holy Prophet (SAW) in the battles he participated. Ansari, *The Qur'ānic Foundations*, vol ii.

Prophet (SAW)[11] and this intense love should manifest itself in changing your life. The Sahābah loved him and what was the consequence? They were changed from ordinary barbaric human beings into supermen for whom the angels would come and bow. This is what the love of the Holy Prophet (SAW) gave them.

We also love him, but we should also understand what the demands are of this love and how love should be manifested. Of course, it should be manifested in remembering him because a person always remembers his beloved. The greater the love, the greater the remembrance. One cannot love someone and not remember that person. Some people say that the Holy Prophet (SAW) brought the message and died, and what do we have with him now?

This is not Islam, nor *imān*. Remember, you do not know Almighty Allah but you believe in Him because the Holy Prophet (SAW) said that we must believe in Allah Who possesses special qualities (*sifāt*). We did not see Allah, but he saw Allah. Thus if you love the Holy Prophet (SAW) you also love Almighty Allah at the same time.

We heard the Holy Qur'ān from the lips of the Prophet (SAW) and because we love him and regard him as pure and holy and truthful, we agree with him. Thus, we know Islam only through the Holy Prophet (SAW). He is the basic personality in Islam and of *imān*. The better your *imān* in him, the better your Islam and your *imān* in Allah. You cannot approach Allah by bypassing the Holy Prophet (SAW) and you cannot understand the Qur'ān by bypassing the Holy Prophet (SAW). He is the only teacher. He is the source all blessings in this life and the hereafter. All the *awliyā-Allah* (friends of Allah) are his lieutenants, so cling to him in a manner that you may feel worthy of him and he may not feel sorry about you.

Do you know that the deeds of the entire *ummah* are presented to the Holy Prophet (SAW) every week? He has a tremendous

---

[11] Ibid., 63-70. In the section *Duties to the Holy Prophet*, The Qur'ānic verses emphasise unconditional loyalty to the Holy Prophet (SAW).

affection for his *ummah*. Therefore, when our deeds go before him and they are not good, what a terrible agony should it not cause him? Take care of this! Try to mould your life according to his *sunnah*, for that is the way to salvation.

As Iqbal says:

> Take yourself to the feet of the Holy Prophet (SAW) for he alone is all religion – the whole religion! If you cannot become a true lover of him and then all your prayers and deeds taken together make of you an *Abu Lahab*[12] and not a Muslim.

---

[12] Abu Lahab, was the implacable enemy of early Islam. His name personifies disgrace and contempt. See *Surah al-Lahab* 111:1-3.

PART 2

MORAL TRANSFORMATION IN ISLAM

- You cannot be godly if you are selfish.
- If you love Allah, love the human beings. The Holy Prophet (SAW) has proclaimed: *"All creation is Allah's family; he who honours Allah's family honours Allah, and he who insults Allah's family insults Allah."*
- Deal with every human being firstly as a human being, not as a Muslim, Christian or Jew, etc. Everyone of you is a human being first and foremost. This is what Islam has emphasised. There are inviolable rights for every human being and if you cannot stand by those rights, you are insulting your own humanity.
- Appreciate good wherever it is to be found, even in your enemy. Hate evil but not the evildoer. This is the Islamic principle of goodwill. Goodwill for all and ill- will towards none. Goodwill for all, irrespective of whether they are Muslim or Christian, etc.

4

Surah Al-Fātihah and the Concept of Khalifat-allah

Surah Fātihah contains several verses and is recited in each *salāh*. The Qur'ān opens with this surah. It is the quintessence of the Qur'ān. If one understands this surah, one understands much of the Qur'ān.

Almighty Allah says in the Holy Qur'ān:

$$قُلْ إِن كُنتُمْ تُحِبُّونَ اللَّهَ فَاتَّبِعُونِي يُحْبِبْكُمُ اللَّهُ$$

Say, if you love Allah then follow me, and Allah will make you His beloved.

(3:31)

The verse speaks of love by a Muslim for Allah and it speaks of love by Allah for a Muslim. What does it mean? It means that if we believe in the one true God, Allah, we can form contact with Him. We don't believe in something from which we cannot obtain blessing or reward. Neither do we believe in something that is just a distant force or power which has no concern for us. Or if it has a concern, it is only that of a ruler for its subjects - No!

Allah is the Ruler, the Creator, the Fashioner, the Guide. He controls everything in the universe. So Great, Majestic and Infinite and very different from us, yet He loves us. He loves us because He created us. For example, if an artist makes a piece of art with full devotion and love he would not allow any damage to be done to his piece of art. Likewise, if we make or possess something, we cultivate a love for it because we put our energy, heart and soul into it. Therefore, there is love for that thing or object expressed consciously or subconsciously.

How can we at all imagine that when Allah created us and fashioned us in the best mould as He says in the Holy Qur'ān:

$$لَقَدْ خَلَقْنَا الْإِنسَانَ فِي أَحْسَنِ تَقْوِيمٍ ﴿٤﴾$$

Verily, we have created man in the best form, with the best constitution.

(95:4)

but have no love and concern for us? When Allah has made the human being as such, He should love that which He created, and undoubtedly He does love it. Allah's relationship with human beings personifies mercy and love. In the opening surah (chapter) of the Qur'ān, in the very first verse, Allah introduces Himself with the attributes of love: *al-Rahmān, al-Rahim*. The first verse says:

$$بِسْمِ اللَّهِ الرَّحْمَٰنِ الرَّحِيمِ$$

..... *the Most Beneficent, the Most Merciful.*

In the second verse He says:

$$الْحَمْدُ لِلَّهِ رَبِّ الْعَالَمِينَ ﴿٢﴾$$

Praise is due to Allah alone, Sustainer of all the worlds.

Here again we have the attribute of love for the word *Rabb* means cherisher, sustainer, maintainer, protector, evolver and guide to the goal. These are the functions of the *Rabb*.

Then He repeats in the third verse that He is:

$$الرَّحْمَٰنِ الرَّحِيمِ ﴿٣﴾$$

The Beneficent, the Merciful.

In the fourth verse He says:

$$\text{مَالِكِ يَوْمِ الدِّينِ ﴿٤﴾}$$

Master of the Day of Judgement.

He is going to take account of our actions.

Then He invites us to receive His blessings and He comforts us: "Don't think of Me like some of the human beings that became great with whom contact becomes impossible. Despite the fact that I am infinitely great and that I am your Lord and your God, I love that you come to Me." And the inviter invites everyday from every masjid: "Come to *salāh*, Come to success!"[1]

The *mu'adhdhin* invites on behalf of Allah that we approach Him and request everything that is good. Thus, we are taught in the fifth verse of the surah:

We worship You alone and We seek Your help.

We affirm here our loyalty to Allah that we are not rebellious. We believe in Him and affirm it with this verse. Then we request Allah's help. The Holy Prophet (SAW) taught us that a Muslim should pray to Allah for the most ordinary things in life. But here, Allah is teaching us to ask the highest desire from Him while the lowest is left to our discretion. That highest desire is:

$$\text{اهْدِنَا الصِّرَاطَ الْمُسْتَقِيمَ ﴿٦﴾}$$

Guide us to the Straight Path

---

[1] Reference to the call of prayer (*adhān*).

Guide us to the path of glory, success, wisdom and beauty. Remember *ihdinā* (guide us) does not only mean pointing out the way but also to guide us on the Path to enable us to reach the goal. The goal has been mentioned in the surah. In verse seven we are told:

$$صِرَاطَ الَّذِينَ أَنْعَمْتَ عَلَيْهِمْ$$

The path of those on whom You have bestowed Your blessings.

Who are the blessed people? In the Qur'ān we are told:

$$وَمَن يُطِعِ اللَّهَ وَالرَّسُولَ فَأُولَٰئِكَ مَعَ الَّذِينَ أَنْعَمَ اللَّهُ عَلَيْهِم$$

Whoever obeys Allah and his Beloved Prophet (SAW) becomes the companion of one of those on whom Allah's blessings have come.²

(4:69)

They are the *Anbiyā* - Prophet's and below this rank is the *Siddiqin* – those who were the personification of truth in thought, word and deed. They were not message-bearers, but personified the divine truth in their personalities to the extent that no shortcomings could be found. The third category is the *Shuhadā* - those who sacrificed themselves for the sake of truth out of love for Allah. The fourth category is the *Sālihin*- those who led healthy lives in accordance with the divine code of life.³

Islam did not come to have followers who are Muslims only in name, rituals-based or holding certain *'aqā'd* (principles of

---

² And who obey Allah and the Messenger are in the company of those on whom is the Grace of Allah – of the Prophets, the sincere, the martyrs and the righteous: How beautiful is their company (4:69).
³ A segment of the verse is included in a *du'ā* (supplication) linked to Surah Fātihah.

belief) which they may not practise upon. Islam came to transform human beings in order for them to become worthy of companionship of any of those four categories.

A man is known by the company he keeps. Therefore, in order to be in the company of one of the four categories one has to be a true servant of Allah Almighty. Some people interpret this verse to mean that a person can also become a *nabi*. They are misguided and want to mislead people. *Nubuwwat* (Prophethood) has ended and the Holy Prophet (SAW) is the last and final Divine Messenger from Allah.[4] A person cannot become a Prophet (SAW) as a result of his *mujāhadāt* (spiritual labours) as prophethood is a gift from Allah.

But the companionship means: if a piece of iron stays in the company of a magnet, it becomes magnetised. It acquires new properties. Similarly, if a gardener stays in the company of fragrant flowers, he himself inhales fragrance by being in touch with the flowers. In sum, we have been asked by Almighty Allah to pray.

Did Islam come only to place upon us an obligation of praying without understanding, or performing some rituals and finding no change within ourselves after we have prayed? Did Islam come to impose upon us the hardship of fasting during the month of Ramadān just because (Allah forbid) He takes pleasure in putting us to hardship? He said clearly in the Holy Qur'ān:

وَجَاهِدُوا فِي اللَّهِ حَقَّ جِهَادِهِ ۚ هُوَ اجْتَبَاكُمْ وَمَا جَعَلَ عَلَيْكُمْ فِي الدِّينِ مِنْ حَرَجٍ ۚ مِلَّةَ أَبِيكُمْ إِبْرَاهِيمَ ۚ هُوَ سَمَّاكُمُ الْمُسْلِمِينَ مِن قَبْلُ وَفِي هَٰذَا لِيَكُونَ الرَّسُولُ شَهِيدًا عَلَيْكُمْ وَتَكُونُوا شُهَدَاءَ عَلَى النَّاسِ

---

[4] Deviant movements like Qadianism and Bahaism have made audacious claims to Prophethood. See Abdul Kader Choughley, *Abdul Aleem Siddiqui and His Mission* (Springs, 2013), 186-9.

In the code of guidance that Allah has sent, He did not intend hardship as the goal. It is the creed of your forefather Abraham. It is He who has named you Muslims so that the Messenger might bear witness to the truth before you, and that you might bear witness to it before all mankind.[5]

(22:78)

Allah sent Islam so that its followers can become bearers of witness to His existence and to the existence of that spiritual order that is there in the world.

The words *shahid, shuhud, mash-hud* and *mushāhadah* are all derived from the same root (*sh-h-d*). A person cannot be a *shahid* (witness) unless he has observed a certain thing. Who then will be recognised as a witness by mankind of the truth of Islam except he who can claim to have seen the working of His attributes though he has not seen the personality of Allah! Such a person is a *shahid* of what Allah Almighty does. Unless a person has reached this stage he has not fulfilled a condition for which Islam came.

Our function is not merely to pray and fast only as a mere ritual. Of course, we have to do it in order to become witnesses, to have personal and direct experience of Allah Almighty. That is why we have become the *ummah* of the Holy Prophet (SAW).

Let us take an example of history: There was a great saint, Sayyidina Junayd (d. 910 CE) of Baghdad. One day he was walking past the mosque when he heard the *adhān* (call to prayer) and when the mu'adhdhin said: *Ash-hadu-an-lā ilāha illal-lah*, the saint grabbed the *mu'adhdhin* by the collar and said: "You are a liar." The *mu'adhdhin* trembled for he knew that Sayyidina Junayd was an `ālim and a saintly person. The saint inquired

---

[5] And strive in this cause as you ought to strive (with sincerity and under discipline). He has chosen you, and has imposed no difficulties on you in religion, it is the religion of your forefather Abraham. It is He who has named you Muslims, both before and in this (Revelation) that the Messenger may be a witness (*shahid*) from you, and you be witness for mankind.. (22:78).

Surah Al-Fātihah and the Concept of Khalifat-allah

whether he has seen Allah? How can you say *Ash-hadu* (I bear witness) which is based on *mushāhadah* - personal observation. And if you have not observed Allah, what right have you to say: *Ash-hadu*. The saint approached him while being a state of spiritual ecstasy.⁶ A wise man who saw the happening told the *mu'adhdhin* to reply: "I am announcing this on authority of him who has seen Allah, *Muhammad Rasulullah*. Therefore I am not a liar." Recall the verse from the Holy Qur'ān:

قُلْ إِن كُنتُمْ تُحِبُّونَ اللَّهَ فَاتَّبِعُونِي يُحْبِبْكُمُ اللَّهُ

If you love Allah, imitate me, follow me and Allah will make you His beloved.

(3:31)

All these categories are the categories of the Beloved: *anbiyā, siddiqin, shuhadā* and *sālihin*.

What changes come in the human being when he or she becomes one of those whom Allah loves? In a *hadith al- Qudsi* we are told by Allah:

> When my servant loves me and proceeds towards me with intensity of love by leading a righteous, godly and pious life and beyond what I have prescribed as obligatory, then he arrives at the stage where I come to love him. When I make him my beloved, I become his ears with which he hears (hearing), his eyes with which he sees (sight), his hands with which he grabs. I become his feet with which he walks and his tongue with which he speaks.

---

⁶ In Sufi terminology, spiritual ecstasy (*sukr*) is an absence from self-awareness brought about through a powerful spiritual influence such as *dhikr* (remembrance of Allah). See Amatullah Armstrong, *Sufi Qamus: The Mystical Language of Islam* (Kuala Lumpur, 1995), 221.

And Bayhaqi (hadith collection) added:

I become his mind with which he thinks.

Allah is Unique and Infinite and Indivisible. He does not incarnate into any being. However, we know that if Allah becomes anybody's "eyes" we can understand that from such sight nothing would remain hidden. As for Allah becomes the "ears"- no sound would remain hidden from such a person and when Allah becomes your "feet"- there would be no place in the universe where those "feet" cannot go. If that "tongue" says that such and such a thing is going to happen, it is bound to happen. This is the goal of Islam, which has been set out for us. Don't think there is any vestige of *shirk* because the human remains human and God remains God. Nothing is detracted from the personality of Allah. Here is an illustration. The convex lens has neither light nor heat and is a dead, dark object. Focus the convex lens before the sun, and a small sun will appear on the palm of your hand and burn your hand. This small sun that is created is the image of the real sun, dazzlingly bright in its form and function, but in its nature is not. It is only an image that has been built up on the surface of your hand. This small sun has light and heat but is not self-existent. It remains at the will of the real sun. As long as the real sun remains and feeds the convex lens, the created sun will remain. If the convex lens is removed, the created sun will disappear.

This convex lens is like our spiritual heart. Through the love of Allah, the convex lens's focus and projection is increased through the *dhikr* (remembrance) of *lā-ilāha illal- lah*. It gradually acquires radiation from Allah and absorbs it. As it has been said by the Holy Prophet (SAW).

The heart of the believer is the Throne of Allah.[7]

---

[7] The metaphorical significance of the eyes, ears etc. must be understood in context of this hadith. In this category of hadith, the speech is attributed to Allah, wherein the Holy Prophet (SAW) simply acts as a carrier of the divine

It (heart) is the throne of Allah and should be actively made the throne of Allah. This is goal of Islam. When these qualities are gradually absorbed through the process Allah has taught to:

Establish the salāh to remember Him (20:14) and *Remember Me, I will remember you (2:102)*

Love is mutual, reciprocal, interdependent and it is out of Allah's intense love for us that He said to the Holy Prophet (SAW) to teach us: *Tell my servants -if they walk one step towards Me, I will move ten step towards them.*
This is real love and He does love us. Of course, most of us are unworthy of His love. We don't know how to love Him and we don't want to love Him. That is our greatest loss, for we cannot do any harm to Him nor take anything from His glory nor add anything to His glory. He is *Al- Samad.*[8] He is Absolute and Independent of everything.

That is why the path that has been prescribed by the Holy Prophet (SAW) is:

Imbue yourself with the divine attributes and divine qualities.

This is not *shirk* but real *tawhid* and requires proper understanding. This is the function of *khalifat-Allah* just like the convex lens is the *khalifah* of the sun. When man becomes *khalifat-Allah* he realises his potential status. In botany, every seed contains the plant that grows out of it, potentially. Similarly, every human being is *khalifat-Allah* potentially. He or she has to develop himself or herself in accordance with the code of Islamic guidance to become *khalifat-Allah.*

---

message.
[8] Refer to *surah al-Ikhlās:* 114 for its comprehensive meaning.

Islam is a treasure house of the blessings of Allah . We can benefit from this inexhaustible treasure house only if we follow the model of our beloved Prophet (SAW), love him intensely and to become like him in his nature – actually. A Muslim in the real sense of the word is to become Muhammad Rasullulah in nature. What else then? Allah says in the Holy Qur'ān:

لَقَدْ كَانَ لَكُمْ فِي رَسُولِ اللَّهِ أُسْوَةٌ حَسَنَةٌ

Verily, the best model is the Holy Prophet (SAW).[9]

(33:21)

A model is that which is imitated, with the spirit to become like that model. When a model is given to the factory for mass production to be reproduced and if that is not adhered to, then the factory has not done its job. The Holy Prophet (SAW) is the model and the Muslim should try his or her best to change according to that model. What were the qualities that Allah placed in that model? He could order the sun to stop; the moon to split into two or he could order space to give way in order to reach his Lord. Our beloved Prophet (SAW) was he most perfect *khalifat-Allah* and was the embodiment of what the Qur'ān says:

Allah has made subservient to you whatever is in the

---

[9] The *Sahābah's* intense love for the Holy Prophet (SAW) was translated into action. The *pen-portraits* of the Holy Prophet (SAW) in the hadith literature bring into bold relief his excellent conduct. See Ansari, *Muhammad, The Glory of Ages* (Karachi, 2017). Ansari reinforces the message of the Qur'ānic verse in the following words: "[The] repositories of spiritual knowledge merges seamlessly into the stages of *fanā* (annihiliation) through the love of the Holy Prophet (SAW). Thus the *uswah al-hasanah* (excellent conduct) is the highest ideal for Muslims." Choughley, *Fazlur Rahman Ansari,* 260.

heavens and the earth.

(45:13)

He was the personification of this mastery and therefore *khalifat-Allah* "par excellence" and the perfect model for anybody who wants to become *khalifat-Allah*.

But, we Muslims have become like a small worm that crawls in underground channels and we think we are doing good by leading this life of ignorance and heedlessness. Remember, the duty is not Allah or the Holy Prophet (SAW) but towards ourselves.

This is what Islam has come to teach and what our forefathers believed and practised. When we hear about our forefathers like Sayyid Abdul Qādir Jilāni, then we are amazed.

It is reported that the ruler of Baghdad came to Sayyid Abdul Qādir and brought with him two bags of gold sovereigns. He placed the bags before *Sayyidina*, who asked the ruler what the contents were. The ruler replied that it was a humble gift from a temporal king to the spiritual king. *Sayyidina* replied: "If you believe that I am a spiritual king, then you should pay homage in a spiritual manner and not in this material way." The king, however, insisted that Shaykh Abdul Qādir should accept his gift and he knew that this king was ignorant of the reality. *Sayyidina* took the two bags, one in each hand and pressed them, and behold – blood was flowing from those bags. The king trembled and *Sayyidina* said to him: "How unmindful of Allah and the Day of Judgement you are that you suck the blood out of your subjects and you bring that blood to one whom you think is the servant of Him!" The king trembled and fainted. When he came to his senses, he said: "I will function under your command!" This is *khalifat-Allah*.[10]

Sayyidina Mu'inuddin Chishti was commanded by the Holy

---

[10] Ansari belonged to the *Qādiri* spiritual order (*tariqah*). His devotion to Shaykh Abdul Qādir Jilāni is evident from his numerous reference in his writings to this illustrious saint (*wali*). See Ansari, *The Qur'ānic Foundations*, vol. i.

Prophet (SAW) to propagate Islam in India, the land of the Hindus.[11] The Hindu ruler searched for his greatest Hindu yogi in order to have a spiritual duel with Sayyidina Mu`inuddin upon his arrival in Ajmer. This yogi (Garam- pal) then challenged *Sayyidina* and said: "I can fly in the air, let us see who can fly the furthest." The yogi then flew in the air and *Sayyidina* commanded his wooden sandal to fly after him, hit him on the head and to bring him down. It actually happened!

We may think that these are stories of the past. If these facts of history are fiction then all history is fiction. Let me tell you about Mawlana Abdul Aleem Siddiqui. I was with him on our world tour during 1950 and we visited the capital of the Philippines, Qutabatu. A function was to be held on an open square scheduled to begin after Maghrib. After Dhuhr prayer, dark clouds appeared and by Asr, conditions worsened with signs of a big storm. After Asr, I mentioned to my teacher about the dark clouds and the rolling thunder and the impending storm, and he replied: "My dear son, why are you worried? We have come here to deliver the message of Allah. The rain is sent by Allah the earth belongs to Allah and the human beings are creatures of Allah. If He wants me to deliver the message it will be done."

After Maghrib we went to the open plain, where a huge crowd was waiting. The governor was the chairman and the chief justice (a Roman Catholic) was also there. His Eminence, Mawlana, jut began to deliver his talk when huge drops of rain started to fall. The huge crowd started to get up in order to flee to their homes, when Mawlana 'Abdul Aleem Siddiqui said: "My dear friends, don't be worried, the rain is going to stop right now." And the rain stopped. He reassured them that "[It] will not rain for as long as this function is on. However, after the function is over you will have ten minutes to get to your homes, and then a very big storm will come."

Not one drop of rain fell after the announcement and Mawlana Siddiqui delivered one of his finest lectures in an utmost carefree

---

[11] On his life and thought, see Khaliq Ahmad Nizami, *Tārikh-i-Mashā'ikh- i-Chisht* (Delhi, 1958).

manner and spoke for about one and half hours. The rumbling and thunder was there all the time. Then the chairman gave the vote of thanks. When the function was over, the people rushed to the platform in order to shake hands with Mawlana Siddiqui, who reminded them: "My dear friends, you were running away from here earlier and don't you see what is happening in the sky? Please, for Allah's sake, you have ten minutes to get to your homes and I am going to my hotel."

Exactly ten minutes later the storm came and the following morning, the water in the roads was about two metres high. Thousands of those who were Catholics, became Muslim. This happened in 1950! This is *khalifat-Allah* and this is Islam!

The goal of Islam is not to grope in the dark. The function of Islam is clearly expressed in the Qur'ān:

اللّهُ وَلِيُّ الَّذِينَ آمَنُوا يُخْرِجُهُم مِّنَ الظُّلُمَاتِ إِلَى النُّورِ

Allah is the friend of those who believe in Him genuinely, and He takes them out of the darkness into the light.

(2:257)

The work of man as *khalifat-Allah*, is to build roads, buildings and bridges. Thus the work is not possible without interference, that is, to change the function and shape of a thing which is called *tasarruf*. This interference is possible on the lower level of physical science and at the higher level, that is, spirituality. Those who acquire characteristics of *khalifat-Allah*, as spiritual or moral beings and servants of Allah, become mirrors through which His attributes are reflected. They can do greater wonders than the physical scientist.

`Allāmah Iqbal said: "If a person is a *mu'min* in the real sense of the word, he is no more the image but the reflector of His attributes." In the battle of Badr, when the *kuffār* (disbelievers) were more powerful, the Holy Prophet (SAW) picked up dust and threw it at them. The battle was fought with this and as the Qur'ān says:

$$وَمَا رَمَيْتَ إِذْ رَمَيْتَ وَلَٰكِنَّ اللَّهَ رَمَىٰ$$

> Although that dust was thrown at the army by the hand of the Holy Prophet (SAW), actually it was thrown by Me.

(8:17)[12]

because the Prophet (SAW) was Allah's *khalifah*.

My friends, whatever has been said, try and test it. Don't waste your lives and time in vain pursuit, and postpone till tomorrow. Resolve right now to attain that glory which Islam came to confer!

---

[12] When you threw (a handful of dust) it was not your act, but Allah's (8:17).

5
The Principle of Unity

The concept of Unity[1] is the foundation of the Muslim community and the very essence of Islam. As we all know, the most important principle that has been given to us in Islam is the principle of *tawhid* – unity. This does not mean that we should only believe in Allah as the one true God. It means many more things.

Tawhid is the basis of the philosophy of life in Islam. It means that Allah is One (*ahad*)), therefore all mankind is one family. Two groups are possible in this one family but both are concentric, that is, rallying around the same centre of humanity itself. About these two groups, the Qur'ān says:

$$\text{فَمَن شَاءَ فَلْيُؤْمِن وَمَن شَاءَ فَلْيَكْفُرْ}$$

Whoever wants to be a believer, let him be one, and whoever wants to be a disbeliever, let him be.

(18:29)

Those who accept the divine truth from Allah Almighty, this group has been formed for a definite mission as laid down in the Qur'ān:

---

[1] For an elaboration on this theme, see Ansari, *Islam: An Introduction* (Springs, 2013).

$$\text{كُنتُمْ خَيْرَ أُمَّةٍ أُخْرِجَتْ لِلنَّاسِ تَأْمُرُونَ بِالْمَعْرُوفِ وَتَنْهَوْنَ عَنِ الْمُنكَرِ وَتُؤْمِنُونَ بِاللَّهِ}$$

You are the best ideological group raised by God for the service of mankind in order that you may be a witness to the divine truth for all mankind. That you may invite and guide mankind to the path of truth, and believe in Allah. Command only that which is good and eradicate with all the forces at your command, all that is evil and believe in Allah.[2]

(3: 110)

Your function is to invite to everything that is good and to eradicate all evil. You have to do this strictly under the principle of unity: under One True God.

From this, you obtain your inspiration, your strength your sanction for being the teachers of goodness and piety for the entire mankind.

We have been called an *ummah*, a community who shares the same ideal. As soon as the ideal changes, the *ummah* does not remain one any longer. It can be considered as different communities or ideological groups.

As the Holy Qur'ān says:

$$\text{وَإِنَّ هَٰذِهِ أُمَّتُكُمْ أُمَّةً وَاحِدَةً}$$

This ummah that Allah established through His Beloved Prophet (SAW) is one ummah.[3]

(23:52)

It is indivisible and cannot be divided on the basis of race,

---

[2] You are the best of People, evolved for mankind. Enjoining what is right, forbidding what is wrong, and believing in Allah... [3:10].
[3] And undoubtedly this *ummah* of yours is a single *ummah* (23:52).

The Principle of Unity

language or on various groups of the north, south, east or west. This *ummatan wahidatan* (one community) was one concept on which this community started on its journey in history.

A command has been given by Allah who is the Lord and King of this universe and one who cannot be disobeyed under any pretext. Allah commands:

$$\text{وَاعْتَصِمُوا بِحَبْلِ اللَّهِ جَمِيعًا وَلَا تَفَرَّقُوا}$$

Stand fast by that principle of unity and solidarity that has been given to you and do not divide yourself into different groups.

(3:103)

This division has been taking place in history and also among Muslims on two grounds:

- Political – where there has been a clash between vested interests and personalities.[4]
- Theological bickering, quarrelling over petty things.

Regarding the clash of egos and personalities, we have been warned in the Holy Qur'an:

$$\text{وَلَا تَنَازَعُوا فَتَفْشَلُوا وَتَذْهَبَ رِيحُكُمْ}$$

Do not quarrel on the basis of your personalities; this division will weaken you and your prestige will vanish.[5]

(8:46)

---

[4] The political conflicts based on self - interest has a long history in Islam. Overshadowed by political opportunities Muslims have undermined Islamic solidarity as forcefully expressed in the Qur'ān.

[5] And fall not into disputes lest you lose heart and your power depart (8:46). The focus on personal disputes sets the tone for Muslim disunity.

You will enjoy no honour in the eyes of other communities. They will insult you because you no longer remain a challenge. The challenge can be met only by a group which is linked in a spirit of absolute unity. This hand has five fingers and each finger is weak in itself, but if I combine it into a fist, then it has hitting power and strength.

The clash of vested interests is something terrible. It is human nature to project one's ego. "I am better than so and so," but Allah says about this human nature:

اعْلَمُوا أَنَّمَا الْحَيَاةُ الدُّنْيَا لَعِبٌ وَلَهْوٌ وَزِينَةٌ وَتَفَاخُرٌ بَيْنَكُمْ

Know you all, that the life of this world is but play and amusement, pomp and mutual boasting...

(57:20)

The *nafs-ammārah*[6] (base self) is embedded in the human personality and takes different forms. Here we have been told that if Muslims want to be sincere and loyal to the One and True God and to the Holy Prophet (SAW) who is the leader of this *ummah* for all times, then they cannot bring about anything which pertains to their personal interest. The Holy Qur'ān is very clear on this point:

قُلْ إِنْ كَانَ آبَاؤُكُمْ وَأَبْنَاؤُكُمْ وَإِخْوَانُكُمْ وَأَزْوَاجُكُمْ وَعَشِيرَتُكُمْ
وَأَمْوَالٌ اقْتَرَفْتُمُوهَا وَتِجَارَةٌ تَخْشَوْنَ كَسَادَهَا وَمَسَاكِنُ تَرْضَوْنَهَا
أَحَبَّ إِلَيْكُمْ مِنَ اللَّهِ وَرَسُولِهِ وَجِهَادٍ فِي سَبِيلِهِ فَتَرَبَّصُوا
حَتَّى يَأْتِيَ اللَّهُ بِأَمْرِهِ ۗ وَاللَّهُ لَا يَهْدِي الْقَوْمَ الْفَاسِقِينَ ﴿٢٤﴾

Proclaim! If your parents and offspring, your

---

[6] The projection of egos stifles spiritual growth and hollows out positive traits that are dyed in the Holy Prophet (SAW)'s excellent conduct. Cf. The human soul is certainly prone to evil. (12:53).

brothers, your wives and kindred; the wealth that you have gained, the commerce in which you fear a decline; or the dwellings in which you delight are dearer to you than Allah and His Beloved Prophet (SAW) and the striving in His Cause, then wait until punishment descends upon you On the day when some faces will be brightened and others will be blackened...

(9:24)

But what have we done? History shows that Islam came to a people no more divided than the Arabs. They were divided by tribalism[7] which ensured hostility and fighting the extent to which has probably not been recorded about any other community in history.

They could fight and shed blood because of simple differences that could last for over a century. The Arabs were a condemned people because they had no idea of the One True God and no notion of the concept of unity. The greatest achievement of Islam was to weld these warring tribes into one brotherhood!

إِنَّمَا الْمُؤْمِنُونَ إِخْوَةٌ

The believers are but a single brotherhood.

(49:10)

Any person who becomes a believer, *ipso facto* becomes a member of the brotherhood and has to deal with a fellow Muslim as a brother. The Holy Prophet (SAW) has said:

The feeling of a Muslim for his brother is like one part of the body that has a feeling for the other part: if one part hurts the whole body pains.

---

[7] Ansari provides a graphic account on the intertribal wars that decimated chunks of Arab population in about *Muhammad The Glory of Ages* (Karachi, 2017).

The Qur'ān says that this community that has been raised with this mission is not based on race, language, territory or colour. It is a community based on an ideal towards which they strive to achieve under one banner.

The Holy Qur'an states clearly:

Allah loves that Muslims should combine into a wall of steel and then strive for the cause of Islam.

(61:4)

If individuals want to fight in the way of Allah as individuals, it has little merit in the eyes of Allah. The Companions of the Holy Prophet (SAW) heard the message, thought about it, assimilated it and absorbed it into their personalities and forgot about their egos. They heeded the warning in the Holy Qur'ān regarding Iblis, who fell from that high status, saying:

أَنَا خَيْرٌ مِّنْهُ خَلَقْتَنِي مِن نَّارٍ وَخَلَقْتَهُ مِن طِينٍ ﴿١٢﴾

I am better than him (Adam) because You created me of the fire and Adam of clay.

(7:12)

So Iblis was told:

And the curse shall be on you until the day of Judgement.

(15:35)

How can a person who believes in Allah - He who does not share His Majesty and Greatness and Sovereignty with anyone else, who is Unique and Absolute - yet believe himself to be great? If a person says with his lips his *shahādah*, and he worships at the same time his *hawā al-nafs* (base self), he is a *mushrik* according to the Qur'ān:

Have you not seen him who worships his ego?[8]

(25:43)

He asserts his ego in terms of his wealth and power, yet he is affirming that there is the One True Allah. A Muslim cannot be that! Grandeur and Greatness is only for Allah– for no one else, for we are dependent on Him.

O you who believe, you are all beggars at the door of God (you are mere shadows on the firmament of space and time, who are staying here at the Will of God

---

[8] Do you see such a one who has for his god his own passion (or impulses)? (25:43). Again, Ansari uses the term *mushrik* for people with bloated egos. Their mindset suggests that their material trappings lead to happiness. This, of course, is the prompting of their egos.

and His pleasure) only. Allah is not dependent on anyone and worthy of all praise.

(35:15)

إِن يَشَأْ يُذْهِبْكُمْ وَيَأْتِ بِخَلْقٍ جَدِيدٍ ﴿١٦﴾ وَمَا ذَٰلِكَ عَلَى اللَّهِ بِعَزِيزٍ ﴿١٧﴾

If Allah wants, He can wipe you from the face of the earth for He can create a new creation. Nor is that (at all) difficult for Allah.

(35:17)

What are you, O human beings? Here, Islam has gone to the extreme limit of self-effacement, teaching how to crush the ego. It is the human ego, which is responsible for all quarrels, which appears to be irresolvable. Theological bickering breaks the bond of brotherhood, for we are told in the Holy Qur'ān:

Allah is the truth. (22:6)

All divine Messengers who came from the time of Sayyidina Adam up to the time of our Prophet (SAW) came with truth:

Allah has sent his Messenger with guidance and with din (religion) of truth.

(48:28)

And about the world, we are told:

$$\text{وَمَا خَلَقْنَا السَّمَاوَاتِ وَالْأَرْضَ وَمَا بَيْنَهُمَا إِلَّا بِالْحَقِّ}$$

I have not created the heavenly bodies and the earth and all between them except in truth.

(15:85)

Consequently, what is the ideal of Islam for human life and the individual? What is the highest virtue that one has to achieve? Virtue of truth combined with sincerity and integrity, is what we have to achieve. Truth cannot be in a human being without moral integrity and thus we will find that the greatest statement in the Qur'ān about tawhid is pithily expressed in the surah *al-Ikhlās* (112). This surah has been named as such because the basis of a Muslim's `aqidah (belief) in Allah is truth and integrity. It is not just something vague or something about which we render lip service only. We may say the *shahādah* with our lips only, but remember the hypocrites of Madinah have been condemned in the Holy Qur'ān. They used to proclaim that they believed in Allah and the Last Day and in the Holy Prophet (SAW) as a Messenger of Allah, but Allah says:

$$\text{وَمِنَ النَّاسِ مَن يَقُولُ آمَنَّا بِاللَّهِ وَبِالْيَوْمِ الْآخِرِ وَمَا هُم بِمُؤْمِنِينَ ۝}$$

Among the human beings are those who proclaim that they believe in Allah and the Last Day, but Allah bears witness that they are not believers.

(2:8)

At another place, we are told:

إِذَا جَاءَكَ الْمُنَافِقُونَ قَالُوا نَشْهَدُ إِنَّكَ لَرَسُولُ اللَّهِ ۗ وَاللَّهُ يَعْلَمُ إِنَّكَ لَرَسُولُهُ وَاللَّهُ يَشْهَدُ إِنَّ الْمُنَافِقِينَ لَكَاذِبُونَ ﴿١﴾

O Prophet (SAW), these hypocrites come to you to proclaim that they believe in you as a Messenger, but Allah bears witness that they are indeed liars.

(63:1)

The hypocrites say with their lips, but their hearts do not agree with it. It is mere lip service. Belief in Islam is not belief unless it has to be clearly and positively proclaimed with one's tongue and considered as truth by the heart.

My brothers and sisters, Islam has provided clear guidance in this connection. There is no scope of misunderstanding or misinterpretation concerning unity among Muslims. Therefore, the punishment for the community in violating this principle is severe. If there was any possibility of different interpretations about the principle of unity, then the punishment would have been lighter – but here the punishment is very severe. May I say with all the sorrow and grief and great sense of shame that the Muslim community has been chastised very severely by Allah because we have violated the Divine law. We behave like hypocrites and proclaim one thing and act in another way, though we know what the truth is. We know that the manner in which we are acting is not what we have been prescribed by Islam. Our 'ulama have divided the category of *munāfiq* (hypocrite) into two: *munāfiq fil-'aqīdah* (hypocrite in belief) and *munāfiq fil-'amal* (hypocrite in action).

There are those who say that they are Muslims, however, violate the Law (*sharī'ah*) in their deeds (*a'māl*). Consequently, the history of the Muslims in this world has to be read in this light. Do you know that the community that the Holy Prophet (SAW) built up can be considered to be a community of supermen? They were so different from other human beings. They possessed a tremendous power of *imān billah* (belief in Allah), that the greatest of obstacles and the mightiest of armies could not withstand their impact.⁹ The whole world trembled before them although they were just a handful.

This progress continued during the time of Sayyidina `Umar and the khilafat of Sayyidina `Uthmān. Issues came up on the basis of which the ummah gave the appearance of division and Sayyidina `Uthmān became the first martyr with the dagger of a so-called Muslim. Sayyidina `Ali was killed, Sayyidina Hasan was poisoned, Sayyidina Husayn and his family were killed. They were killed by those who called themselves Muslims. Gibbon, the historian, wrote in *The Decline and Fall of the Roman Empire* that if `Umar had to live for another ten years, the entire world would have been Muslim!

To be sure, the ego came. Belief in Allah continued to fade into an image and mere idea. It was no longer that vibrant, living and dynamic *imān* or faith in Allah (SW). The living nature of that *imān* paralysed gradually, and that was the "rope" of Allah or *habl-Allah*. The better the *imān*, the better or greater will be the unity, and the better will be the character. Naturally, when there are people who call themselves Muslims and they stage all these atrocities against Muslim leaders and good Muslims, what can be said about their *imān*¹⁰.

The result was that Muslims lost the prize right at the moment when they were going to have it all. Those who were responsible did not understand at the time what was going to befall this *ummah*. Of course, this *ummah* had been built up in a strong manner by a master hand – the Holy Prophet (SAW). The *ummah* had that vitality that in spite of all the obstacles and handicaps, it could continue in power for centuries. But the

---

[9] The early battles of Islam fought by the *Sahābah* were unmissable signs of *imān* (faith) and *yaqin* (conviction). Their success is mentioned in several verses of the Qur'ān.

[10] The phenomenon of deviant Muslim sects committing atrocities against Muslims in the name of Islam has reached alarming proportions in the present century. Doctrinal differences have become a pretext for shedding innocent Muslim blood which is severely condemned in the following verse: If a man kills a believer intentionally, his recompense is in hell to abide there (forever): and the wrath and curse of Allah are upon him and a dreadful punishment is prepared for him, (4:93).

breakdown was inevitable.

Please Muslims, take a lesson from it. How much damage through disunity, have we caused ourselves? Read the history of Muslim struggle for unity. When Muslims had established themselves in Spain with all the glory, the great 'Abd al-Rahmān went into France to face the combined armies of Charlemagne. The Muslim army gained the upper hand and they were victorious. It was at the battle of Portiers, a few miles from Paris, which was a decisive victory for Muslims in Europe. What happened? The Muslim army consisted of two groups: Arabs and Berbers. The devil instigated into their minds as to who was going to get the better share. Fighting with one another started during the night. This information reached the ears of Charlemagne, who was retreating with his army and he returned to attack the Muslims as they were fighting amongst themselves. The enemy attacked with the utmost violence and the victorious Muslim army had to flee to the plains of France. Not only did they have to flee the plains of France but ultimately also the plains of Spain.[11]

This is the bitter pill of disunity. It caused the glorious Muslim Empire and Muslim civilisation of Spain to be blotted out of existence. These Muslims who had gone to Spain with a very small army under Tariq bin Ziyaad had conquered the whole of Spain. After they established their kingdom, the different governors of different provinces were afflicted by this poison of disunity.

Their egos ruled. Each governor wanted to become the chief ruler of Spain and sided with the armies of Isabella and Ferdinand on the temptation of getting the throne of another governor who was a Muslim. This is the history of Muslim Spain. Finally, Muslims lost Spain. They were killed in large numbers

---

[11] The account of Muslim defeat is documented in T.B. Irving, *Falcon of Spain* (Lahore, 1991). Muslim unity is in disarray: civil wars have unleased destruction in Muslim countries that Muslims themselves have become displaced refugees.

and all trace of their glorious civilisation was blotted out.[12]
The same happened in India where Muslims ruled for about eight hundred years (977-1857). When the British, who were just a handful, came to India, Muslims worked as their agents against the Islamic Empire. There was Mir Ja`far in Bengal and Mir Sādiq in South India[13] who played this role. It was only disunity between Muslims that brought their downfall as rulers of India.

Recently, I read a South African newspaper in Johannesburg. A story appeared on the front page of a man called Chaid Benton who died recently. This man was a so-called "hero". He came from England, travelled around Africa and ultimately became the "kingmaker" in Morocco. This man aided the leaders of rebellion in Morocco. When al-Hāfidh[14] raised the banner of rebellion against Sultan `Abd al-`Aziz, Benton aided the rebel leader and was responsible for the change of government. For him it was a game to replace one Muslim sultan after another. Ultimately, Morocco became so weak that the French came in and declared it a "protectorate."

What do you think about the *imān* of those Muslims who were behaving like stooges at the hands of those non-Muslims? They were ruining their faith and damaging their name, their community and their country! What do you think of their *imān*?

If Islam means a mere formal ritualism, accepted only as a cult and not the transforming alchemy, or as a comprehensive code of life and imān in Allah, then it is just a philosophical idea and

---

[12] A similar view is echoed in the following words: "They (Muslims) have not even left a distinct name, behind them though for nearly eight centuries they were a distinct people, the home of their adoption and of their occupation for ages refuses to acknowledge them, except as invaders and usurpers. A few broken monuments are all that remain to bear witness to their power and dominion..." Cited in Akbar Ahmed, *Living Islam* (London, 1993), 77.

[13] They were complicit with British colonialists to overthrow Muslim states in India. The defeat of Tipu Sultan in 1799 at the hands of the British was largely due to the conspiracy of Mir Sādiq, an agent working clandestinely against Muslim rule. See Ilyas Nadwi, *Tipu Sultan* (New Delhi, 2004), 253-7.

[14] Abd al-Hāfidh (d. 1937) signed the treaty of Fez, in 1912, giving the French a protectorate over Morocco. The French rule lasted over forty years.

not a religious truth. Then all these happenings are possible.

My dear friends, pardon me if you feel insulted, but I am one of you. This world Muslim community, according to the statistics of the U.N.O comprises seven hundred million souls.[15] These seven hundred million Muslims are to be found all over the world. We are seven hundred million! *Allahu-Akbar!* But we are not worth seven cents in the world. We are seven hundred million straws that one match-stick can turn into ashes. We are not seven hundred million Muslims when other human beings can control us so easily.

In today's newspaper, an article appeared about Jordan. Mind you, the ruler of Jordan, King Hussein, calls himself a *sayyid*, a descendant of the Holy Prophet (SAW). The Israeli cabinet decided that if they find that King Hussein's throne is in danger, then Israel would help him to ensure that he would remain as ruler. *Allahu-Akbar!* What a friendship! These two are known to be the worst enemies. The American senate and the president are all the time worrying how to save King Hussein whose country has been devastated from the bombs supplied by the USA. That same community which has been uprooted from its home by America? What love and affection can America have for this man and the Kingdom of Jordan? The establishment of Jordan has in now way eased the plight of the Palestinian refugees in the country. In 1967, Israel took control of Jerusalem and West Bank during the Six-Day War.

I am not a politician neither do I wish to talk politics. I am talking about one thing only – the degradation of Muslims by eroding the principle of unity. It has fallen into the abyss. Today's news was that the so-called guerrillas and the army of King Hussein clashed again. Both are supposed to be Muslims. Innocent men, women and children in Amman lying buried in the debris in more than half of that big city. At whose hands?

Not the Israeli or the Americans! It is the Muslims who have done this to themselves. *Allahu-Akbar!* The Holy Qur'ān proclaims:

---

[15] Renamed *United Nations*. Muslim population in the world exceeds 1.8 billion (2017) and is considered the fastest- growing religion as well.

The Principle of Unity

وَمَن يَقْتُلْ مُؤْمِنًا مُّتَعَمِّدًا فَجَزَاؤُهُ جَهَنَّمُ خَالِدًا فِيهَا وَغَضِبَ اللَّهُ عَلَيْهِ وَلَعَنَهُ وَأَعَدَّ لَهُ عَذَابًا عَظِيمًا ﴿٩٣﴾

He who deliberately kills his Muslim brother, his punishment is eternal hellfire and Allah's special wrath descends upon him! And Allah curses him, and Allah has prepared for such a person a special punishment.

(4:93)

The Holy Prophet (SAW) has proclaimed:

To abuse a fellow Muslim is fisq and to kill him is kufr[16]

The person who kills a fellow Muslim ipso facto goes out of the fold of Islam. He is a kafir (disbeliever). My dear friends, I am a foreigner, I am not here to give blame. I know that I cannot act as an arbitrator. I have seen much of this world as I have been around the world seven times. I have seen problems that emerged in the Muslim community and tried to straighten them – but to no avail. Who am I? Leaders of different groups honour me by requesting me to arbitrate on disputing matters. I spend all my time, but to no avail. What do they expect me to achieve? Remember, *hidāyah* (guidance) is in Allah's hands.

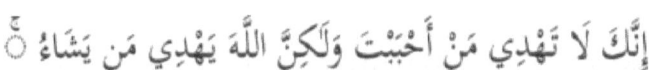

---

[16] The word *fisq* is used in the text. It refers to acts which are in open violation of the *shari'ah*.

It is true you will not be able to guide every one whom you love; but Allah guides those whom He wills.

(28:56)

After a few days I have to leave, and the contending parties know this. If the real *imān* and the understanding is not there between the contending parties, I cannot bring about transformation overnight. Not even in a century! What am I? My sincerity may be accepted by Allah and He may help in this matter but He said clearly in the Holy Qur'ān and laid down a fundamental principle:

> *I am not going to change your condition unless you have that attitude that you want to change your condition.*[17]

(13:11)

If that sincere attitude is there on both sides, whatever may be the differences, then Allah's blessings is bound to come. May I remind you that great men like Sayyidina Imām AbuHanifa, Imām Shāf'i, Imām Ahmad Ibn Hanbal,[18] Imām al-Ghazāli, before whom I consider myself not even worthy of a particle of dust off their feet, could not do anything. They made their contributions as they could as individuals and as great godly scholars. But, to change those conditions that existed and to extricate the community from the abyss into which it was going, could hardly be done by those very great men. Compared to me, they are probably 100 times greater. What am I going to do, my dear friends? I can only stand here and speak

---

[17] Allah will never change the condition of a people until they change what is in themselves (13:11).

[18] On the contributions of the four Imāms in the evolution of fiqh, see Muhammad Abu Zahra, *The Four Imams: Their Lives, Works and their Schools of Thought* (London, 2001). Ansari's admiration for the Imāms may be gleaned from Islam to the Modern Mind and Islamic Intellectual Revival and the Modern Mind.

Remind the followers of Islam what the principles of Islam are which will help them.

(51:55)

This life on earth to which we attach so much importance, according to the Holy Qur'ān, is merely a game.

Know you all that the life of this world is but play and amusement, pomp and mutual boasting and multiplying (rivalry) among yourselves.

(57:20)

It is just a series of fleeting shadows – dreams – and nothing beyond that. We are sleeping here and will wake up when we die, for in our sleep we are seeing a continuous dream. This is *hayāt al-dunyā*, (life of this world), and this is what our great Imāms have taught. The term of life that we possess about which none of us know when it is going to end:

Nor does anyone know in what land he is to die.

(31:34)

But this is a precious opportunity according to what the Holy Prophet (SAW) taught us:

Work for the life hereafter as if you are going to die tomorrow.

This life here is like the stock of an ice-vendor. He buys the ice from the factory and invests a capital in order to obtain a profit. But he gets back only that much of money in accordance with the quantity of ice he is able to sell. That portion that turns into water is lost in the earth and unreclaimable. All that we do out of love for this world, is like the ice that turned into water and is lost in the earth.

$$\text{مَا عِندَكُمْ يَنفَدُ ۖ وَمَا عِندَ اللَّهِ بَاقٍ}$$

What is with you must vanish: what is with Allah will endure.

(16:96)

$$\text{الْمَالُ وَالْبَنُونَ زِينَةُ الْحَيَاةِ الدُّنْيَا ۖ وَالْبَاقِيَاتُ الصَّالِحَاتُ خَيْرٌ عِندَ رَبِّكَ ثَوَابًا وَخَيْرٌ أَمَلًا ﴿٤٦﴾}$$

Wealth and sons are allurements of this world but the things that endure, are good deeds; but best in the sight of Your Lord are rewards and the best hope.

(18:46)

My friends, in this short life we do not control anything but depend absolutely on the Mercy of Allah.

$$\text{أَلَمْ يَأْنِ لِلَّذِينَ آمَنُوا أَن تَخْشَعَ قُلُوبُهُمْ لِذِكْرِ اللَّهِ}$$

Has not the time come for the believers that their hearts may melt in the remembrance of Allah.

(57:16)

Has the time not come that our hardened hearts may melt in fear of that accountability that stands before us? The nemesis and consequences of our evil actions that are to recoil like serpents and tighten around our necks. The problem of the importance of unity among Muslims should not have arisen. It is an insult to the Muslims. The problem of disunity on any account should not remain; it is the greatest insult for the Muslims. He who fears standing before his Lord on the Day of Judgement for rendering account, and he who abstains from ego worship, for him is Heaven or the Garden of Bliss. By contrast,

فَأَمَّا مَن طَغَىٰ ﴿٣٧﴾ وَآثَرَ الْحَيَاةَ الدُّنْيَا ﴿٣٨﴾ فَإِنَّ الْجَحِيمَ هِيَ الْمَأْوَىٰ ﴿٣٩﴾

He who plunges himself into the storm of his own ego, forgetting his Lord, forgetting his unavoidable destiny and loves the life of this world, his abode will be hell.[19]

(79: 37-39)

My brothers and sisters, for God's sake, Allah has been extremely kind to us. He sent His greatest blessing on this earth when He raised His beloved Prophet (SAW). He says in the Holy Qur'ān:

لَقَدْ مَنَّ اللَّهُ عَلَى الْمُؤْمِنِينَ إِذْ بَعَثَ فِيهِمْ رَسُولًا مِّنْ أَنفُسِهِمْ

---

[19] The Abode will be Hell-Fire.

Allah did confer a great favour on the believers when He sent a Messenger from amongst themselves after they had been in manifest error.

(3:164)

This blessing that has come to us - shall we then not benefit from it? How unfortunate it will be if we do not. The first step to benefit from this blessing is to eradicate this ego. Remember the warning from the Holy Prophet (SAW) that Iblis is not the enemy of Allah, but the enemy of man. The only enemy of Allah is the human carnal self: the ego. It has the audacity to stand before Allah – in this world where it is blind – but in the life to come it will tremble! It is the ego, the enemy of Allah. So take care of it, control it and become godly.

O believers, become godly. (3:79)

That is the way to light, truth and greatness. The acceptance of the devil as one's master does not pay. The devil will go with clean hands on the Day of Judgement and will deny any involvement in acts of evil. Iblis will say that he merely encouraged the motive to commit the sin, but did not sin himself and therefore he should be allowed to go scot-free. *Allahu-Akbar!*

يَوْمَ يَفِرُّ الْمَرْءُ مِنْ أَخِيهِ ﴿٣٤﴾ وَأُمِّهِ وَأَبِيهِ ﴿٣٥﴾ وَصَاحِبَتِهِ وَبَنِيهِ ﴿٣٦﴾

That day when man shall flee from his own brother, his mother, his father, his wife and children.

(80: 34-36)

And the leaders, let them not feel inflated and elated, whoever they may be, because if they misguided anyone, then that person is going to stand before Almighty Allah and say in his plea to Allah:

O Lord we were ignorant people, we were not leaders, we were merely masses, we obeyed our leaders, they misguided us. O Lord, today when You are going to punish us for our evil deeds, give these leaders double chastisement and curse them!

(33:67-68)

6

The Qur'ānic View of Disunity

As we all know, Islam is the religion of unity, but many of us do not know what the implications are when we make this statement. All we know is to be a good Muslim, to believe in Allah as the One True God and that we should not commit any type of *shirk*. Actually it is not the case. The principle of unity is the principle that permeates throughout the philosophy of life and the code of life in Islam.

Allah is One, therefore the entire universe is One because it has One Creator. Because the universe is one, it has been created by One Intelligent and All-Wise Being for a certain purpose. Therefore, this universe is a moral order and because Allah is One, all mankind is one family.

Truth is one and cannot be two-sided. Consequently, emotive faith (faith based on emotion or religion) and cognitive faith (faith based on knowledge or reason) are both united in a single or organic whole[1] in Islam. Hence, there is no conflict between faith and reason or faith and knowledge. Furthermore, Allah is One, therefore the entire humanity is one and the two sexes, male and female, are also basically the same. They are one, but are differentiated by their biological functions and are equally honourable as human beings. So this concept of unity goes on.

The point I wish to make is that the principle of unity permeates the entire fabric of Islam as a code of life. It is not merely saying that Allah is One, while Muslims remain in a disunited and disintegrated form. That is not Islam. As far as the principle of unity is concerned, the commandments, which have been given in the Holy Qur'ān are very clear and explicit. To violate a command is *harām*(unlawful) and to stick to *harām* leads to *kufr*. Thus, we have been commanded in

---

[1] Faith and reason are the twin concept of *tawhid*. The organic unity *(wahdat)* is forcefully expressed in *The Beacon Light*, 142-4. In a similar vein, there is no conflict between belief (*'aqidah*) and action (*'amal*).

the Holy Qur'ān:

$$وَاعْتَصِمُوا بِحَبْلِ اللَّهِ جَمِيعًا وَلَا تَفَرَّقُوا$$

Hold fast to the bond of unity which Allah has created in the ummah and never divide yourself (into sects or groups on any grounds whatsoever).²

(3:103)

This command is laid own in connection with Muslim unity. In connection with religious groups which have been forming throughout Islamic history, especially in the latter days we are told in the Holy Qur'ān. *Mushriks* have been qualified further:

$$مِنَ الَّذِينَ فَرَّقُوا دِينَهُمْ وَكَانُوا شِيَعًا ۖ كُلُّ حِزْبٍ بِمَا لَدَيْهِمْ فَرِحُونَ ﴿٣٢﴾$$

From among those who divide themselves on petty religious issues and divide themselves into mutually hostile religious groups and each and every group regards itself alone as on the right path and the other group as absolutely contemptible (and kāfir).

(30:32)

Allah Almighty says in the Holy Qur'ān in this verse that this action of division of the Muslim community into warring and hostile groups is an action equivalent to *shirk.* About *shirk,* Allah says in the Holy Qur'ān:

$$إِنَّ اللَّهَ لَا يَغْفِرُ أَن يُشْرَكَ بِهِ$$

---

² And hold fast, all together, by the Rope which Allah and be not divided among yourselves (3:10-3).

> *The only thing that Allah will not pardon on the Day of Judgement is shirk.*
>
> (4:48)

He may pardon all other sins but not *shirk*. Can there be any doubt in the light of these verses that this community and the Muslims of the world at large are not committing *shirk*? This community which has been divided into mutually hostile religious groups? In the Holy Qur'ān we are told, after this blessing of Islam has come to you.

﴿وَلَا تَكُونُوا كَالَّذِينَ تَفَرَّقُوا وَاخْتَلَفُوا مِن بَعْدِ مَا جَاءَهُمُ الْبَيِّنَاتُ ۚ وَأُولَٰئِكَ لَهُمْ عَذَابٌ عَظِيمٌ ١٠٥﴾

> *Do not become like those of the previous ummahs who divide themselves on the basis of petty religious issues and turned themselves into sects, for them is a grave chastisement.*[3]
>
> (3:105)

The principle of unity as spoken of in the *hadith* is very clear:

> *The Muslim community is an organic whole, a unity, indivisible, and the help of Allah comes only when they are in this state. Whoever gets out of this state and whoever gets out of this unity and creates disunity among them, will be thrown right away into the fire of hell.*

This principle of unity is an established fact of Islam and of the Islamic way of life, and we shall have to consider the value system in the light of social norms of Islam wherein this unity has been established. There are three fundamental norms of the Islamic way of life or social order: unity, justice and selfless service to the others.[4]

---

[3] Be not like those who are divided amongst themselves and fall in disputations after receiving clear signs. For them is a dreadful punishment. (3:105).
[4] Justice and self-sacrifice are values to be upheld and practised by Muslims. Their role models are the *salaf* (earlier representatives of Islam) who

Unity cannot be maintained unless the principles of justice are maintained, such as selfless service to others, love and goodwill. Therefore Islam has laid stress on the principle of justice. If one reads the available records of the history of mankind one will find that the Qur'ān is the first book in the known history of mankind where the concept of absolute justice has been given. For example in the Holy Qur'ān we are told:

$$\text{يَا أَيُّهَا الَّذِينَ آمَنُوا كُونُوا قَوَّامِينَ بِالْقِسْطِ شُهَدَاءَ لِلَّهِ}$$

O believers, stand by justice in everything and every dimension of life. Stand by and be for justice and not for the sake of any expediency (personal benefit) or any other motive, but purely for the sake of Allah.[5]

(4:135)

When we do anything for the sake of Allah, the ego is completely annihilated. All the sentiments will be placed before you on the Day of Judgement, as Allah says:

$$\text{وَلَوْ عَلَىٰ أَنفُسِكُمْ أَوِ الْوَالِدَيْنِ وَالْأَقْرَبِينَ}$$

.... Even though being just may damage you or go against you or against your parents or against your kith (relations).

(4:135)

---

internalised these qualities and left lasting imprints in Islamic history.

[5] O ye who believe! Stand out firmly for justice, as witnesses to Allah... (4:135). Yusuf Ali comments on the above verse: "Justice is Allah's attribute, and to stand firm for justice is to be a witness to Allah, even if it is detrimental to our own interests (as we conceive them) or the interests of those who are near and dear to us."
Yusuf Ali, *The Holy Qur'ān English Translation of the Meanings and Commentary* (Madinah, 1410, AH), 259.

Otherwise, by simply offering prayers, which are noble deeds, without doing justice will not lead to *taqwā* (Allah- consciousness). The Holy Qur'ān has gone further in connection with justice, for example justice towards one's enemies.

﴿٨﴾ اعْدِلُوا هُوَ أَقْرَبُ لِلتَّقْوَىٰ ۚ وَاتَّقُوا اللَّهَ ۚ إِنَّ اللَّهَ خَبِيرٌ بِمَا تَعْمَلُونَ

> O believers should it happen that there are a group or groups that are hostile to you or towards your religion and you are dealing with them, you should always deal justly with them in spite of all the injustice from their side ...

(5:8)

Your duty and obligation is to be just in your dealings with them. This is the principle of justice that supports unity. Why does disunity come into a community? If you analyse this problem you will find that disunity comes through the *clash of egos*. When these individual egos are projected, justice cannot be satisfied. The very name "Islam" means "the annihilation of the ego" or "submergence of the ego" into the Divine pleasure and Absolute Ego of God. It starts from this point and then gives the principle of justice in clear terms.

Greed is the other cause of disunity. The desire to acquire all the good of this world for oneself. Competition follows between all desiring individuals which leads to hostility and conflict and finally, disunity. They may be Muslims, but their personal interests are at a variance and therefore there can be no unity between them. In the light of this, Islam has laid down the other principle of selflessness and sacrifice for others. Here, may I add, that if you study Islamic guidance in its natural order of revelation as received by the Prophet (SAW) you will find that the priorities, such as selflessness, were left out by us. In the first year of the call, the message was:

$$\text{وَمَا أَدْرَاكَ مَا الْعَقَبَةُ ﴿١٢﴾ فَكُّ رَقَبَةٍ ﴿١٣﴾ أَوْ إِطْعَامٌ فِي يَوْمٍ ذِي مَسْغَبَةٍ ﴿١٤﴾}$$

$$\text{يَتِيمًا ذَا مَقْرَبَةٍ ﴿١٥﴾ أَوْ مِسْكِينًا ذَا مَتْرَبَةٍ ﴿١٦﴾}$$

$$\text{ثُمَّ كَانَ مِنَ الَّذِينَ آمَنُوا وَتَوَاصَوْا بِالصَّبْرِ وَتَوَاصَوْا بِالْمَرْحَمَةِ ﴿١٧﴾}$$

> *What do you understand about the most difficult and most rewarding virtue? It is the abolishment of slavery or feeding in times of distress and famine, an orphan who is known or near to you or the indigent who is down in the dust. And those who preach and teach and exemplify magnanimity and steadfastness, perseverance and human dignity, and those who practise and preach compassion towards one another.*

(90:12-17)

The word '*aqabah* means walking on the steep path. Then we are told that the most important virtue is: *abolishment of slavery* from the world. Abolishment of social injustice which existed in the form of slavery was given to the *ummah* as the highest virtue to work for. The most basic need of human beings is food, more basic than shelter. So here the most basic need is being emphasised as that of the highest virtue. And *imān* has been mentioned only after this. Look at the focus of Islam. It can take the form of opening a charitable institution, hospital or visiting a person who is sick or helping a person who is economically distressed. Also the word *marhamah* is a basic and all-comprehensive principle. This was the message of Islam in the first year of the Call and how was this message practised?

Regarding the virtues of these acts, we are told according the Holy Qur'ān:

$$\text{لَيْسَ الْبِرَّ أَن تُوَلُّوا وُجُوهَكُمْ قِبَلَ الْمَشْرِقِ وَالْمَغْرِبِ وَلَكِنَّ الْبِرَّ مَنْ آمَنَ بِاللَّهِ وَالْيَوْمِ الْآخِرِ وَالْمَلَائِكَةِ وَالْكِتَابِ وَالنَّبِيِّينَ}$$

> *Piety does not lie in the mere adoption of direction for performing a ritual ...*

(2:177)

but consists of a healthy set of beliefs, because no action can take place without belief based on *the final accountability on the Day of Judgement, and the angels [who are the functionaries of Allah in the universe], and the Divine Scriptures and all the divine Messengers who came...* (2:177). It also entails articles of faith, without which a worldview or social philosophy is not possible. Here is where the human heart tries to become an obstruction:

$$\text{وَآتَى الْمَالَ عَلَىٰ حُبِّهِ ذَوِي الْقُرْبَىٰ وَالْيَتَامَىٰ وَالْمَسَاكِينَ وَابْنَ السَّبِيلِ وَالسَّائِلِينَ وَفِي الرِّقَابِ وَأَقَامَ الصَّلَاةَ وَآتَى الزَّكَاةَ}$$

> *Spending of your wealth for no other reason except for the love of Allah, for your kith and kin, the orphan, for those who are destitute, for the wayfarer who may be in trouble whilst on his journey, for those who ask for help, for the emancipation and abolishment of slavery all over the world...*[6]

(2:177)

Different categories of people who might need your help and service,

---

[6] ... Then he will be of those who believe, And enjoin patience and enjoin deeds of kindness and compassion (90:17). Ansari provides the gist and meaning of the verse to convey the theme of his lectures. In several instances, a verse is quoted and a segment of its meaning given. In the course of his lecture, the gist and meaning completes the rest of the verse.

have been mentioned here. Then only comes the mention of the establishment of prayer. Why have social virtues been mentioned first and prayer afterwards? Prayer is accepted by Almighty Allah only from those who practice social virtue and not from others. Praying to Allah is a 'selfish' act on my part for I'm praying for myself. I'm not doing anything for others when I am praying. So, Islam has placed social virtue before personal virtue which is clear from all the verses in the Holy Qur'ān, as well as the verses mentioned earlier. All the wealth spent is voluntary spending and thereafter we have been told about *zakāh*, or compulsory spending.

Then Islam comes to the personal virtue of the personality culture: This is a social virtue. The Qur'ān continues:

$$\text{وَالْمُوفُونَ بِعَهْدِهِمْ إِذَا عَاهَدُوا ۖ وَالصَّابِرِينَ فِي الْبَأْسَاءِ}$$

> *Those who keep their promise when they make a promise. Those who are steadfast in their faith in Allah and who face every trial of this life with dignity and grace.*
>
> (2:177)

Those who possess integrity of personality and face the challenges of life. Then the Qur'ān says:

$$\text{وَأُولَٰئِكَ هُمُ الْمُتَّقُونَ ۞}$$

> *They are true in their proclamation that they are believers and they alone are pious – they have taqwā.*
>
> (2:177)

All these verses belong to the early part of the revelation. Furthermore, we read in the Qur'ān about sacrifice, about the fundamental, unavoidable characteristics of a Muslim's way of life:

وَيُؤْثِرُونَ عَلَىٰ أَنفُسِهِمْ وَلَوْ كَانَ بِهِمْ خَصَاصَةٌ ۚ

It is impossible to find a person who is genuinely a Muslim - that he will not sacrifice everything that he can afford for the benefit of others, even though it may cause him hardship.[7]

(59:9)

So the principle of Muslim unity is governed by these principles. Unless a community follows these two principles, it will be merely lip service. Examples of disunity are numerous, but I will not go into that now. However, let me relate one example of Muslim unity born of love for fellow beings. During the battle between the Muslims and the *kuffār* (disbelievers), several Muslims were seriously wounded and there were others who nursed the wounded soldiers. A voice was heard from one quarter: "I am thirsty, I am dying!" The person in charge of wounded ran towards the thirsty person to offer him water. By the time he reached the wounded soldier, another voice called: "I am thirsty, I am dying." The first soldier refused to drink water unless the second person drank first. When the water carrier reached the second soldier another called out. This second soldier also refused to drink water unless the third one drank. When the water carrier reached the third soldier he was dead, so was the second and the first. This is the act of selfless service to our fellow Muslims and to human beings in general, which was inculcated into the followers of Islam by the Holy Prophet (SAW).

This unbounded, overflowing love by the Muslims became a unifying force and what was the consequence? It was that the greatest miracle in the history of mankind took place: Muslims were able to meet the greatest challenges from the Roman to the Persian

---

[7] Shibli's *Seerat al-Nabi* (vol. 2) covers authentic portayals of the spirit of self-sacrifice by the *Sahābah*. Ansari's extensive study of the sírah literature in his early years at Aligarh Muslim University stands out in his writings and lectures. See also, Ansari, Muhammad *The Glory of the Ages* completed in 1933.

empires, from within and without, in the most glorious manner. Not only did they become the sole superpower in the world but taught the highest morals and spirituality. They also promoted the advancement of technology and industrial knowledge. This was born of unity.

As time passed, disunity came. As we very well know, wealth corrupts and power also corrupts and Muslims had both wealth and power. After some time, the original spirit began to wane and they became entangled in the materialistic pursuit of life and adopted that outlook. And what was the result? All our defeats or setbacks in the latter times and which are taking place in greater tempo nowadays, have been due to one great factor-disunity. An example is the decisive battle that took place between Europe and Muslims in the heart of France.

The Muslim army was led by the great 'Abd al-Rahmān, the Umayyad *khalifah* of Spain. The non-Muslim armies constituted of the French, Germans and neighbouring territories. The battle took place at Portiers near Paris. The Muslim army routed the combined might of Europe. But after the victory, disunity arose regarding the booty and fighting started amongst themselves during the night after the victory. When the retreated forces of Europe heard this, they returned and attacked the Muslim forces. Eventually the Muslims were forced back to Spain, and were ultimately expelled from Spain in the most ignominious manner. Later on, the enemies ruled over them in Morocco, Tunisia, Mauritania, Libya and Algeria.[8]

Another example in history is the powerful Mughal Empire in the Indian subcontinent which established its rule in 1526. Why did this great empire fall? Disunity was the cause! The provincial powers wanted to be separate from the central government of Delhi, so Muslim India became divided into different states. A small group of merchants from the British East India Company could snatch from the Muslims, the Muslim empire and establish their own.[9] This was

---

[8] Likewise, the dissolution of the powerful Ottoman Caliphate was caused by betrayal, intrigue and disunity among Muslims. Colonialism consolidated the process of Muslim disunity. See *The Beacon Light*, 232-43. Ansari refers to it as the 'political ferment.'

[9] The Mughal Empire, founded by Babur came to an abrupt end after the First War

possible only through disunity.

Therefore, in spite of the enthusiasm and love Muslims have for Islam with one of the finest Muslim communities in the world, their problems only multiplied. Things have taken a very ugly shape and now they are worried about the future of their youth. What will happen to Islam when the youth become adults? Problems multiplied because of disunity.

The only solution for this small Muslim community in South Africa is to drown all differences for the sake of Allah and love for the Holy Prophet (SAW) who is our only leader and to whom we owe a pledge of loyalty. Then only can we play a very glorious role for Islam and the country at large. Every Muslim will then be a flag bearer of the Holy Prophet (SAW). *This is the only way.*

Carry the message to every Muslim home: *United we stand, divided we fall* and the fall will be such that the very name of Islam will be wiped off the face of this country. Finally, adopt the motto in which Islam started and flourished: "Love for Allah and love for fellow human beings." And Almighty Allah will bless you in a manner that you cannot imagine.

---

of Independence in 1857. Its last Emperor Bahadur Shah was banished to Burma (Myanmar) by the British Rulers. See Francis Robinson, *Islam and Muslim History in South Asia* (New Delhi, 2001).

PART 3

DYNAMICS OF THE SUNNAH

The Prophet (SAW) has been commissioned for this purpose and this is the goal of Islam-transformation of the personality. Rituals are only a means to an end. The moral laws are also not the goal, but means to an end. The goal is the attainment of holiness and to come into contact with Allah, for He is All-Holy. That holiness that is to be acquired is conferred through the dynamic personality of the Holy Prophet (SAW). As the Holy Qur'ān confirms that the Prophet (SAW) will continue to perform this function which he performed for his Companions and all those of the Muslim community until the day of Qiyāmah.

7

The Inner Dimensions of the Sunnah

There is great misunderstanding about the *sunnah* of our Beloved Prophet (SAW) especially about the dimensions of the *sunnah* and the implication of the word *sunnah*. As I mentioned at a previous occasion, we have reduced Islam to a cult and consequently we have fallen prey to dogmatism (accepting without question) and ritualism. The *sunnah* such as a certain type of dress, wearing of a beard, and having more than one wife, is viewed in the same way.

Sunnah means 'way of life'[1] which implies that which the Holy Prophet (SAW) practised. The ritualistic approach is responsible for our lack of understanding of what Islam stands for. All human activity, individual or social, consists of an inner and outer side of life. I am wearing a particular type of dress, which places me in the category of 'ulama. Therefore, people are inclined to think that I am a holy person. They may not know me or my character or inner aspects of my life. They may kiss my hand, which is fine, but, is this what Islam stands for? Islam has emphasised the spirit first and the body next. In the human personality itself the primary importance belongs to the spirit or the soul. It is the soul which sees, hears, talks and which the body is only a medium for it. In the same manner the inner aspects of life are fundamental. Islam has come to build up those inner dimensions of life.

The inner and outer aspects of life must harmonise, therefore the outer aspects of life have also been emphasised – not as such by Islam, but by the later *fuqahā'* or jurists. For instance, the Holy Prophet (SAW) said that you can wear any dress as long as you do not violate the principle of *hayā*, (modesty, decency) and you do not imitate the religious dress of any other community.

---

[1] Ansari defines the *sunnah* as the dynamics of the Holy Prophet's personality. See *The Qur'ānic Foundations*, vol. i.

Now, examine this principle. Look at the fact that the Holy Prophet (SAW) would wear the same type of dress that Abu Jahl or Abu Lahab wore. Why? If there had to be sanctity in dress then why did the Holy Prophet (SAW) not prescribe a new dress for the Muslims? Why, as Allah's Prophet (SAW) did he continue to wear the same dress that he wore before and the same that was worn by the *kuffār* of Arabia? Why? This is a very important point to bear in mind. When people came to see him and presented him with Roman and Yemenite gowns from Christians and Jews, he put them on and made use of them. Why?

Present day Muslims cultivate an uncommitted attitude towards Islam. In my country, Pakistan for example, some religious people say that if you wear a quadrangular *kurta*, a triangular pyjama and a two pointed or hexagonal cap[2] then you are following a *sunnah*. I am amazed by this saying because the Holy Prophet (SAW) never wore any such dress and neither did the *Khulafā al-Rāshidīn* (Righteous Caliphs). Where did they get this *sunnah* from? It is quite alright that when we wear an English or Western suit then we are damaging our own dignity. There is no doubt about it, but this is not a distinctive point between Islam and *kufr*.

If all the English people were to embrace Islam would you want them all to wear your pyjama? Therefore, distinctions ought to be there, but all factors have to be taken into consideration. Similarly, in the case of the beard. The Holy Prophet (SAW) had a beautiful beard, but Abu Lahab also had a beard, most Christians and pagans of Arabia also had flowing beards. So, if the Prophet (SAW) had a beard and a person imitates him in keeping a beard out of love for him, it is then an act of piety. But then after that he is walking the razor's edge because after keeping this signboard of love for the Holy Prophet (SAW), he has to be very careful in his behaviour not to insult

---

[2] Ansari refers to the Muslim attire worn in the Indian subcontinent. In many instances, it is considered a marker of Islamic identity and piety. His critique about the Muslim mindset is succinctly expressed in *Islam to the Modern Mind*, 167.

the memory of the Holy Prophet (SAW) by keeping that beard.

Furthermore, our religious thought of today is based on the assumption that as long as the uniform of Muslims is there, no training as Muslims is required. The uniform is regarded as more important than training in our religious thought. If a country distributes uniforms to people and does not train them in military science, what do you think will happen to this army in times of war when only people with uniforms are sent to the battlefront? This is exactly what Muslims are doing everywhere. Uniforms with no training, is like "putting the cart before the horse."

The *sunnah* is an outward manifestation of an inner quality. The inner quality as given in the Holy Qur'ān is *taqwā*. This is the *umm al-fadāīl*, the cardinal virtues, also called *taqwā-Allah*-to fear Allah and to revere Him in His Majesty. The emphasis is to keep Allah always in mind and be conscious of accountability before Him. This is *taqwā*. The word *taqwā* is from *waqa'*-to avoid what is wrong. It is primarily an attitude of negation in order to avoid what is wrong which is the first step towards affirmation as in the *kalimah*. It starts with negation of all else –*Lā ilāha*– no god; "illal-lah" – but Allah!

Similarly in *taqwā*, it is the negative aspect, not to do any evil that is most important. Unless you clean your slate, the writing of the positive actions of your life on the tablet of your heart will not come. It will all be confusion. Imām al-Ghazāli and other great thinkers have said: "The *sunnah* starts by imitating the Holy Prophet (SAW) out of love for Allah and love for fellow human beings." Now, what is the *sunnah* of the Holy Prophet (SAW) with regard to love for Allah? Of course, it is so comprehensive that nobody can describe it, but let us take a few examples:

The Holy Prophet (SAW) used to stand for prayer at one place during the night, while all others were sleeping. His beloved wife, Ā'ishah Siddiqah said that he would sometimes stand still for hours until his feet would become swollen and the capillaries in his feet would burst and blood flowed from his feet. Has anyone of us prayed like this? Is this not regarded as *sunnah* of the Holy Prophet (SAW). When he read from the Qur'ān in the prayer, although he would read it silently, a sound used to come from his chest as if it was a big kettle in which something was boiling. So, he would pray and utter whatever he recited with all his heart and total personality. We perform the *salāh* like an exercise, devoid of any spirit and then we consider it to be the *sunnah*.

Our degenerating attitude deforms and deshapes the original practice and spirit of the *sunnah*. A person who rests in the afternoon claims he is following a *sunnah* of the Holy Prophet (SAW) since he did the same. But remember, the Holy Prophet (SAW) was the most industrious and hard working person ever born in the history of mankind. He used to work the whole day and worship most of the night, and in order to worship during most of the night he would take about half an hour's rest during the day. We sleep the whole night until the *fajr* prayers and we sleep in the afternoon and then claim to be following the *sunnah*. How can we expect a reward from Allah Almighty? It is an insult to Islam and to the practice of the Holy Prophet (SAW).

People also say that the Holy Prophet (SAW) used to like perfumes, so we put on eau du cologne after our baths. *Allahu Akbar*. We have been told in the hadith:

The essence of wisdom is fear of Allah.[3]

If you have the fear of accountability before Allah, you cannot do anything wrong. It is only when we become *ghāfil* or absent-minded that we lose sight of the fact that Allah is watching us and He is going to call us to account on the Day of Judgement. Even here, we are called to account or may see the fruits of our good deeds. This is the starting point of the *sunnah*. Human values are built in your inner- self. Truth, justice, beauty, honesty, progressiveness, dynamism, optimism, courage and wisdom are all the inner values.[4] This is the *sunnah* of the Holy

---

[3] Muslim tendency to accessorise Islam and focus on the *sunnah* of convenience is an alarming phenomenon in our societies.
[4] For an elaboration on this theme, see *The Qur'ānic Foundations*, vol.i, 196-201 The

Prophet (SAW). Once these inner values have been built, then it becomes an obligation of love that a person's inner-self becomes an image of the Holy Prophet's personality. Naturally his outward form will also reflect the outer personality of the Holy Prophet (SAW). But to try to build the outer only is like having a timber wall where the wood is infested with white ants. Painting is only done on the outside and not inside. Subsequently, the wood is being eaten by the white ants and such a structure will not last. If the wood is healthy it will stand even without painting the outside.[5]

If my heart is not *mu'min* it cannot be the repository of the highest human qualities as embodied in the *sunnah* of the Holy Prophet (SAW). Otherwise, I am more concerned about the external adornment and deceive others and myself. That is not the way to follow Islam. We should start from the heart. Islam came to change the heart. We are told in the Qur'ān about the functions of the Holy Prophet (SAW) :

هُوَ الَّذِي بَعَثَ فِي الْأُمِّيِّينَ رَسُولًا مِّنْهُمْ يَتْلُو عَلَيْهِمْ آيَاتِهِ وَيُزَكِّيهِمْ وَيُعَلِّمُهُمُ الْكِتَابَ وَالْحِكْمَةَ وَإِن كَانُوا مِن قَبْلُ لَفِي ضَلَالٍ مُّبِينٍ ﴿٢﴾

He it is who has sent unto the unlettered people a Prophet (SAW) from among themselves, to convey to them His messages and to purify themselves, and to impart to them the Book and the wisdom – whereas before they were indeed in error.

(62:2)

Look at the order of merit. The first is the communication

Integrated Individual: Basic Qualities of a Muslim.
[5] A similar comment is expressed by Ansari in *The Sunnah – The Challenge:* "But Islam is something practical and we should try to understand it on the basis of the life of the Holy Prophet (SAW) in how to *transform human beings*. This process (should be) for ourselves as individuals and communities." *Islamic Intellectual Revival*, 208.

of the message as it comes from Allah. The second is reformation and purification *(tazkiyah)*[6] of the entire personality of his followers and only after that was he in a position to impart to them the knowledge of the kitāb and wisdom, *(hikmah)*. Our institutions of theology[7] have nothing to do with *tazkiyah*. They teach theology to anybody and only emphasise the external. It is putting the cart before the horse.

The *sunnah* is actually the transformation of the heart, on the basis of all those human values which reached their perfection in the Holy Prophet (SAW). The start is from the inner-self and has to be built up first; then the external manifestation of those great qualities will automatically come.[8]

The inner dimensions of the *sunnah* is intimately linked with *tasawwuf* or what is known as sufism. Here a misunderstanding can arise in connection with the word sufi which is not found in the Qur'ān nor in the *hadith*. The implication of the word is Qur'ānic and belongs to the *sunnah* of the Holy Prophet (SAW). A sufi is a Muslim whose ideal in life is *safā al-qalb* or purification of the heart. The word *safā* means purification which is the ideal of the sufi and that of Islam. The term sufi came into existence when the 'ulama became divided into the literalists *(fuqahā)* and those 'ulama who also cared for the spirit along with the letter of the law. So, those 'ulama became known as sufis and the others remained 'ulama. So, if by the word sufi is meant "a spiritually refined person or a spiritually purified person", then the Holy Prophet (SAW) was the greatest personification of purification of all time.

---

[6] It the central importance of *tazkiyah* in the collective life of a Muslim is discussed in *The Qur'ānic Foundations*, vol.i, 348-58. *Fazlur Rahman Ansari: Life and Thought:* 253-6.

[7] Reference is to the dār-al-'ulums. For an assessment on the theology institutions, see Ansari, *The Present Crisis in Islam and our Future Educational Programme* (Karachi, 2017).

[8] Ansari reinforces this observation in the following words: "If shari'ah is followed superficially, there is a tendency to emphasise externals at the expense of inner dimension of Islam." *Islam to the Modern Mind,* 316.

The spiritual perfection which was granted to him by Allah is greater than what was granted to anybody in the entire creation.

Certain teachings were given to certain Sahābah like Sayyidinā Abu Bakr and Sayyidinā 'Ali, but here again there is a misunderstanding amongst some people. The Holy Prophet (SAW) has given the teachings of Islam complete in the Qur'ān. Nothing has been left out. The goal of this spiritual pilgrim is higher than a person who wants to lead a good worldly life only. And the dimensions of his quest are different. That person's experiences are of a higher level or dimension and are called the transcendental dimension. The quest of those who are pilgrims of eternity is the transcendental dimension. The dimension of religious experiences of ordinary people who do not take that special quest, are at the mundane level.

The experiences of the transcendental dimension[9] cannot be explained in human speech which is limited to sensory reality. The transcendental reality is beyond the experience of human language. Therefore, if the Holy Prophet (SAW) had to speak about those realities to the common people, they would not have been able to understand them. Those who were in the category of the transcendental dimension, were guided by the Holy Prophet (SAW). Experience of the transcendental dimension is always communicated from soul to soul and not mouth to mouth. Consequently, it has been communicated through the *silsilah* (chain) of the sufis.

Another point is that sufism today is mostly perverted and rotten because 99% of those who are pretending to be shaykhs of sufism do not know the ABC of sufism. It is a sort-of business or trade carried from father to son. Shrines are built and business and money is made.[10] That is not sufism for sufism is

---

[9] See the footnote for an explanation of transcendental dimension as provided elsewhere in the volume. In the language of *tasawwuf*, the inner dimensions of Islam are transmitted and embedded through a *silsilah* (chain).

[10] Mawlana Abdul Aleem Siddiqui, the spiritual guide of Ansari, was unsparing in his criticism of shrine-based Islam. Hereditary claims to spiritual succession (*khilāfah*) sapped the dynamic spirit of Islam and Muslim decline could also be attributed to this practice. Too often shaykhs would appoint their sons to the

Islam. The Law of Islam has a body and a spirit and sufism must remain within the bounds of the shariʻah. The inner aspect of the shar`iah is emphasised after which a person develops internally and travels in the transcendental dimension.

The goal of Islam is to build up a vibrant, living, dynamic relationship with Allah which is the start and end point of Islam. Teach the young Muslim male or female not only the principle of decency which is of the external side, but also that Allah is the source of all blessing, that the only and greatest benefit lies in establishing a living relationship with Allah[11]. And that can be done even though he's clean- shaven or wears an English suit. It depends on the attitude of the heart towards Allah. Once this flame or love for Allah is kindled in a person's heart then everything, even the proper external behaviour, will come by itself.

After interaction with other people I have come to this definite conclusion as a humble and spiritual teacher. Whenever I asked a person to start with the external qualities such as growing a beard, I failed to build his personality on Islamic lines. But, when I started with values that person became an excellent Muslim and I can point them out to you. Jalaluddin Rumi[12] says: "The body came into existence because of my soul. I am not from the body."

The essential human personality has been given a temporary vehicle in order to function in this world – this body. Therefore, build up the human personality and you will become reformed automatically. Don't start from outside to within, but the reverse way. The thought comes into your mind and then the act takes place. Not the act on the outside world first with the thought into your mind next. No!

So action comes from within first and then without. Preach

---

exclusion of worthy and capable murids. See *Fazlur Rahman Ansari*, 79.

[11] According to Ansari, the *sunnah* "is a living, concrete and shining illustration of Islam, and has ever been the mainspring of Muslim progress." *The Beacon Light*, 208.

[12] Interest in the life and thought of Rumi has seen a steady growth in European languages. See, Afzal Iqbal, *Life and Works of Jalal-ud-din Rumi* (Lahore, 1976).

love for Allah and the Holy Prophet (SAW) alone - that is the message. Let every young man and woman take this up first. Don't talk about *kurta*, beard, etc. If people do not follow this method or way, you can only remind them:

Remind the followers what their duties are.[13]

(51:55)

If others preach their way rationally, do the same. If there are young men who have taken to the external *sunnah*, commend them and then encourage them to start with the inner dimension as the real starting point. There should be no question of a conflict or hatred towards anyone. Even if we see a person not following any principle correctly, our attitude should be that of love, not of hatred or contempt.

---

[13] But remind: For reminding benefits the believers. (51:55).

8

Philosophy of Worship ('Ibādah) in Islam[1]

The concept of worship in Islam is unique among the religions of the world. The word which the Holy Qur'ān has used for worship is *'ibādah*, which means submission to Allah and service to Him. The term worship conveys the meaning of adoration in the English language. In Arabic, the word *'ibādah* denotes the act of becoming *'abd,* namely, slave. Consequently, the full connotation of this term refers to an *'abd* who negates himself entirely and affirms the supremacy and absolute authority of Allah in all aspects.

Worship forms only a part of human life in other religions. In Islam it is meant to cover the whole gamut of life. Other religions are dualistic. They divide the world between two water-tight compartments i.e. bearing two different labels of the religious and the secular. For instance, Christianity preaches with all the force at its command: *Give unto Caesar what is Caesar's and unto God what is God's.*

Similarly, Hinduism, Judaism, Buddhism and Zoroastrianism teach an irreconcilable conflict between the physical and the spiritual. Hence, the acts of worship in all these religions are purely devotional and ceremonial in the same way as they are in Christianity.

The fact is that all the non-Islamic religions are basically committed to the doctrine of dualism,[2] and consequently they stand for condemning the worldly relations as outside the scope

---

[1] This extempore lecture was delivered at the Al-Rashid Mosque in Edmonton, Canada. Ansari's presentation of the concept of *'ibādah* (worship) is a testament to his profound knowledge of Islamic sources and their spiritual dimensions.

[2] The dualistic nature of Christianity and Buddhism, for example, creates a 'perpetual conflict' for humanity. It opposes the concept of tawhid in Islam. *The Beacon Light,* 79.

of religious life. Therefore their notion of worship is of a partial type and is confined to rituals and ceremonies. Islam, on the other hand, refuses to acknowledge dualism and affirms monism or a unitary outlook toward life. It teaches that because Allah is absolutely good, all His actions must always be good, whether they pertain to the domain of the spirit or to the realm of matter. The universe is the act of Allah. It is Allah's creation. Hence it is essentially good.

Believing the world to be essentially evil, the great non-Islamic religions teach escape from the world and the obligations of worldly life as the way to attain saintliness. Islam, on the other hand, teaches the fullest utilisation of physical situations and guiding the social life to its maximum potential. According to Islam, it is an insult to Allah for man to despise as worthless anything that He has created, and to refuse to bring into play the different faculties and powers with which He has endowed man.

Now, the different faculties which Allah has given to us fall under five categories:

- Physical
- Mental
- Moral
- Aesthetic
- Spiritual.

Islam wants us to live a life wherein all these different faculties and the corresponding aspects of human activity are optimally realized.[3] This is so because Islam does not regard the worldly life as evil. It is essentially good and can become evil only if it is pursued for its own sake or in obedience to one's passions and appetites. But if the worldly life is led in obedience

---

[3] 'As a self-contained culture and self-sustained civilisation Islam is conceived on the principles of knowledge and *taqwā* (Allah- consciousness). See Ansari, *Which Religion?* (Karachi, 1976), 19-20.

to the commands of Allah, every worldly act becomes an act of worship ('*ibādah*).

Side by side with teaching this philosophy of transforming the whole life into one of worship, Islam also outlines the ceremonial acts of worship because they too play a vital role in building up the human personality. Such ceremonial acts of worship have been given to us in Islam in the form of the following three institutions:

1. Obligatory institutional prayers (*salāh*)
2. Fasting (*sawm*)
3. Pilgrimage (*hajj*)

Zakāh is also included among the '*ibādah* or devotional acts because it entails sacrifice of money at regular periods and according to a fixed rate in submission to the command of Allah. It is, however, distinguished from prayers, fasting and pilgrimage in as much as it does not involve any ceremonies. In fact, strictly speaking, there are only two devotional institutions in Islam which involve ceremonies, and they are prayers (*salāh*) and pilgrimage (*hajj*). It may be remarked in passing that the Muslim jurists have also included marriage among ceremonial devotions. We are not, however, concerned with that here.

We may now take up the rationale behind prayers (*salāh*), fasting (*sawm*), *zakāh* and *hajj* (pilgrimage).

Prayer (*Salāh*)

إِنَّ الصَّلَاةَ كَانَتْ عَلَى الْمُؤْمِنِينَ كِتَابًا مَّوْقُوتًا ﴿١٠٣﴾

Verily the prayer is prescribed to believers at definite times...

(4:103)

Islam has been built up on five Pillars—one of faith and four of action - and prayer (*salāh*) forms the most important pillar of action. The question arises here as to what is the need of Prayer? It is an age-old conviction of humanity that the human personality is constituted of three factors, body, mind and soul. It is also an established fact that it is the nature of human personality to develop and evolve. The law of evolution has been universally acclaimed as the true principle underlying the existence of all organisms. All of us know that the human body is an evolutionary phenomenon. We are told in Biology that the earliest form of every human baby that comes into this world is that of a life-germ, which is just an infinitesimal speck and unnoticeable by the human eye. This speck evolves in its embryonic stage by acquiring more and more developed forms, until it develops into a full-fledged human personality and comes into this world to play its role in the life of humanity. We also know that when a human being enters the world, it has all the human features and human limbs; but it is not yet fully grown. Rather, its physique has to undergo a continuous process of development day in and day out, for years and years, and then alone it acquires maturity of physique—although even then its physical possibilities are not completely exhausted.

Similar to the physical evolution is the process of the evolution of human consciousness. There are three levels of consciousness- instincts, reason and intuition while there are five forms of consciousness- physical, theoretical, moral, aesthetic and spiritual consciousness.[4]

When a human baby comes into this world, its reason and intuition are dormant. Even all the instincts are not active. In fact, the only instinctive activity present at the time of birth is in connection with the sense of taste. The eyes of the baby open only a day or two after birth, but even then the sense of sight is in a very simple and vague form. For instance, the child does not seem to distinguish between different objects, which capacity develops only gradually. In the same way do all other senses develop. Thus human reason starts functioning only when the

---

[4] Ibid., 87. The moral and spiritual values make up the evolution (growth) of the human personality.

primary senses have developed to an appreciable extent. This occurs when the child has learnt to talk and begins to ask questions. Then begins his education in which he gets the opportunity of developing his intellect. This situation continues for some time when the third stage is reached: the moral consciousness starts asserting itself. It continues to deepen and widen as life progresses. Moral development, in its turn, leads to two further realms, firstly of aesthetic and then of spiritual consciousness.

It must be clear at this stage that it is not only the human body which evolves from a life-germ into a full-fledged state, but the human consciousness also evolves through a continuous process.

Now, the human body cannot develop and evolve without being fed and taken care of. Similarly is the case of human mind and human soul.

We feed the human body with physical food. We feed the human mind with ideas or mental food. Likewise, we must feed the human soul with spiritual food.

There is a whole science of dietetics and nutrition concerning the human body. There is a whole system of education for the cultivation of the mental faculties and for feeding the mind. What should be our attitude to the human soul, then? The only rational and natural answer to this question, is that, just as we try to feed the body with different types of food, and just as we try to feed the mind continuously, it is also our duty to feed the soul uninterruptedly.

We have already pointed out that the food for the body is physical in its nature while the food for the mind is mental in its approach. Therefore, the food for the soul should be spiritual. We have been told in Islam that the food for the soul is the remembrance of Allah (*dhikr*).[5] It is to be performed in a state of communion, with similar prerequisites that we observe in the administration of physical and mental foods.

The first prerequisite in connection with the physical food is

---

[5] *Dhikr* involves *ihtisāb* (self-introspection) and to bring into focus Allah-consciousness. See, *Islam to the Modern Mind*, 262-3.

to eat it with preparation and care. Mental food too has to be received with dedication and the fullest attention. Likewise, spiritual food must be administered after preparation, which Islam prescribes in the form of pre-prayer ablution (*wudhu*), establishing the intention (*niyyah*) and withdrawing the thought from everything and concentrating it upon Allah. This form of devotion refers to the act of remembering Allah with both heart and soul.[6]

The second pre-requisite in connection with the physical food is that it should be of a healthy type. Likewise, is the situation with mental food: the ideas which can ensure the healthy development of the mind are always those which are sound and good. As regards our spiritual food, our remembrance of Allah should be centred on the One and True Allah and not on man-made deities and idols. Thus Islam has laid the most profound emphasis on the avoidance of polytheism (*shirk*) and believing in the One and Only Allah as alone worthy of worship.[7]

The third pre-requisite in connection with the physical food is that it should be administered at regular intervals during the day and the night; otherwise the physical organism will not grow properly or may not grow at all. A similar regular routine is essential for feeding the mind. Training must be consistent in order to build up the human mind in a healthy state and on a sound pattern. Likewise, the third prerequisite of feeding the soul should be regular and consistent feeding, and this Islam has provided in the most natural form by prescribing the five obligatory prayers during the day and the night, or, during one cycle of night and day. The *fajr* (morning) *salāh* is observed before sunrise when the day is about to begin and we have to plunge ourselves wholeheartedly into our major engagements. It forms the spiritual breakfast and is timed to act as a

---

[6] In respect of spiritual health, *salāh* should cultivate "[more] and more a living and dynamic relationship with Allah." *The Qur'ānic Foundations*, vol. i, 199-200. Ansari's meticulous observance of *nawāfil* (optional) prayers is illustrative of remembering Allah with both heart and soul.
[7] Islam teaches the purest form of *tawhid* (monotheism) and regards *shirk* (polytheism) as the deadliest sin. See *What is Islam*, 3.

forerunner of the physical breakfast. Then there comes a lull in our physical stamina at noon when we have to replenish our energy by having lunch. Islam prescribes that we should revitalise on that occasion our spiritual energy also by offering the *dhuhr* (mid-day) *salāh*. Later in the day we again need a cup of tea or some light refreshment. Islam desires us to have a spiritual stimulant also at that time in the form of *'asr* (afternoon) *salāh*. Again, when the sun sets and the night begins and a new phase starts and the time for dinner comes, Islam wants us to reinforce our spiritual energy also by means of the *maghrib* (sunset) *salāh*. Later on comes the time for going to bed when healthy and strong people like to take some nutrient in order to pass the night in radiant sleep. Islam desires us to strengthen ourselves spiritually through the *'ishā* (night) *salāh* and to go to bed while we are in a state of spiritual harmony.[8]

Fasting (*Sawm*)

شَهْرُ رَمَضَانَ الَّذِي أُنزِلَ فِيهِ الْقُرْآنُ هُدًى لِّلنَّاسِ وَبَيِّنَاتٍ مِّنَ الْهُدَىٰ وَالْفُرْقَانِ ۚ

"The month of Ramadān : in it was sent down the Qur'ān, a guidance to mankind and with evidence...."

(2:185)

We know that the human body needs not only nutrition in the form of food but also medical treatment whenever it loses its balance or any function of the body gets impaired. Similar is the case with the human soul: Islam has taken the greatest care to ensure that it obtains not only the spiritual food but also the appropriate spiritual medicine which has been prescribed in the form of obligatory fasting during the month of Ramadān and

---

[8] The state of harmony is explained by Ansari: "*Salāh* is not merely gymnastics. [It] is much more; indeed it is communion with Allah where the *'abd* (sincere servant) comes into contact with Him. This is not ritual... ritual is like a dead body. Unless the spirit is there, it has no value." *Islam to the Modern Mind*, 107.

optional fasting at other periods during the year.

Although fasting is essentially spiritual medicine,[9] it is also a great remedy for medical defects and ailments, so much so that even the most serious diseases can be cured through certain types of fasting without the aid of medicine.

Reverting to the spiritual aspect of life: the greatest enemies of man are those that reside within his own person as, for instance, greed, lust and passion which pertain to the lower self (*nafs al-ammārah*).[10] It is because of these baser appetites that human beings have the overpowering desires to commit crimes of intemperance against the body, the mind and the soul; and they wrong others by committing different types of injustices against them. It is again these baser appetites which cause human beings to deny spiritual values and to forget Allah.

Now, the only way to subjugate the lower self is to constantly perform psychological and spiritual exercises.[11] In this way acts of aggressiveness are brought under control and they start obeying the dictates of reason. He whose life is governed by the baser self is worse than beasts. He whose life is governed by reason is really man. He whose life is governed by spiritual aspirations and enlightenment based on the love of and obedience to the One True Allah, undoubtedly, he is pure gold because he rises above the angels in stature. This is the goal which Islam has set for every Muslim and for this purpose Islam has prescribed the obligatory and the optional fasts.

---

[9] Ansari refers to Ramadān as a month of 'self-discipline' and 'spiritual rearmament' that blends man's life with the higher objectives as outlined in the Qur'ān and *sunnah*. See *Islamic Intellectual Revival*, 187-8. Cf. *The Beacon Light*, 211-2.

[10] According to Abdul Aleem Siddiqui, the shari'ah has prescriptive methods for controlling the *nafs al-ammārah*. The institution of fasting (*sawm*) brings the animal appetites under control and to a large extent suppresses the evil tendencies. See *Abdul Aleem Siddiqui and His Mission*, 197.

[11] "Fasting acts as [a] dynamic struggle for cleansing the self from all forms, and types of moral and spiritual impurities." *The Beacon Light*, 211.

Zakāh

Zakāh is one of the pillars of Islam and, as such, stands next in importance only to institutional prayer (*salāh*). While *salāh* is an obligation towards one's own self and towards Allah, *zakāh* is an obligation towards others. The Holy Prophet (SAW) has laid down the law about *zakāh* saying: "It is to be taken from the rich and given to the poor." This means that *zakāh* is a tax[12] which is levied on those who can save after satisfying their basic needs, and is utilised for those who do not possess the means of fulfilling their basic needs.

Zakāh has been conceived in Islam as a state-institution. It is meant to be collected by the Islamic state and to be deposited in the state bank as a social welfare fund. In Islam, it is the obligation of the state to guarantee the basic needs to all the citizens, which are fulfilled through the institution of *zakāh*, as the Holy Qur'ān says:

إِنَّمَا الصَّدَقَاتُ لِلْفُقَرَاءِ وَالْمَسَاكِينِ وَالْعَامِلِينَ عَلَيْهَا وَالْمُؤَلَّفَةِ قُلُوبُهُمْ وَفِي الرِّقَابِ وَالْغَارِمِينَ وَفِي سَبِيلِ اللَّهِ وَابْنِ السَّبِيلِ ۖ

> *Verily, charity is meant for the destitute and those who are short of means, and the officials (of the department of zakāh), and those who are converts and their financial difficulties entitle them for help, and for the emancipation of slaves, and for extricating the people from the burdens of their bad debts, and for the defense of Islam, and for assisting the stranded travelers...*

(9:60)

Since some time a social insurance tax has been levied by certain Western governments and it is said that that step is a

---

[12] Not a tax in the conventional sense, but as "economic ideal of the Qur'ān to eradicate poverty and multifaceted evils associated with excessive wealth by individuals." *The Qur'ānic Foundatons*, vol. ii, 386.

landmark in the history of social welfare. But it was Islam which instituted the department of social welfare and guaranteed the welfare of all its citizens for the first time in the history of mankind.[13] This department was inaugurated and organised by the Holy Prophet (SAW) himself and it continued to develop as the Islamic economic order. During the rule of Caliph 'Umar, it assumed its full-fledged organisational structure. He established the Diwān, i.e. the Bureau of Statistics,[14] wherein the particulars of every citizen were recorded and as a consequence everyone who required help was assisted financially without any hardship and to the fullest extent. Those who were incapable of earning, namely, the elderly people, the crippled, the orphans and the widows were granted pensions and stipends. Those who were capable of earning but were unable to enter into trade because of a lack of financial resources were provided the fullest assistance. The positive results through such sustainable development projects[15] were that within thirty years after the advent of Islam, and more particularly during the rule of Caliph 'Umar, not a single family could be found who would accept *zakāh*. This meant that every Muslim had become so rich or self-sufficient that he or she was paying *zakāh* rather than being in need of accepting it.

Pilgrimage to Makkah (*Hajj*)

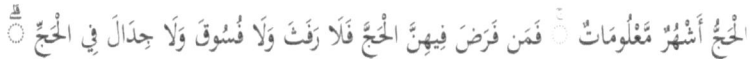

The season of Hajj is the months known; so whoever

---

[13] Ibid., 385-90.
[14] Ansari proposed a review of *zakāh* disbursement in context of the geopolitical changes in the twentieth century. See, *Islamic Intellectual Revival*, 891-91.
[15] Ansari was profoundly influenced by the writings of 'Allāmah Shibli Nu'mani who was actively associated with the Aligarh University. See *Omar the Great*, vol. ii (Lahore, 1971) regarding Caliph Umar's system of administration.

enjoins upon himself the hajj therein there is to be no lewdness nor wickedness nor disputing during the hajj...

(2:197)

Pilgrimage to Makkah (*hajj*) is one of the five pillars of Islam and enjoys an eminent place among Islamic religious institutions. We might mention here certain spiritual and social benefits which it confers on the pilgrim:-

- A Muslim is a person who is meant to be Allah- conscious in all the actions of his life and this higher consciousness is cultivated in Islam by means of different Islamic institutions like prayers, fasting and *zakāh*. It is in the *hajj*, however, that it assumes its highest form, for the pilgrim is required not only to give up his regular work for a number of days, for the sake of journey to Makkah and the participation in congregational communion with Allah there, but he must in addition, sacrifice many other amenities and comforts of life. Cut off from worldly pursuits in this manner, he undergoes a spiritual experience of the highest type.[16] Every member of the great assemblage at Makkah sets out from his home with this object in view. He discards all those comforts of life which act as a veil against the inner spiritual experience. He puts on the simplest unstitched dress and he is required to avoid all indecent thoughts, all evil talks and all disputes. All the prayers and the symbolisms which he observe during the *hajj* express only one ideal and only one goal: absorption in the love of Allah. It is the same when he runs between the hills of Safā and Marwā and it is the same when, like a moth whirling around a flame, makes *tawāf* (circumbulation) around the Ka`bah.

- The Ka`bah excels all other institutions of the world in its wonderful influence in levelling all distinction of race,

---

[16] "The *hajj* forms the climax of a Muslim's demonstration of devotion to Allah in ceremonial observance..."*The Beacon Light*, 215.

colour and rank.[17] Not only do people of all races and all countries meet together in the House of Allah as members of one family, but they are all clad in the same dress - the same two sheets of seamless white cloth – and there remains nothing to distinguish the high from the low.

---

[17] Ansari states that Islam reforms and transforms the whole society. The *hajj* represents a practical form of universal brotherhood whose beginnings are from the *salāh* in the mosque. It is a dynamic institution that transcends the barriers of race and geography. *The Beacon Light*, 216-7.

PART 4

ISLAM AND KNOWLEDGE

Try to rediscover yourself and your foundations. Otherwise, remember that if you remain for long in this confusion and ignorance of the Holy Prophet (SAW)'s contribution to knowledge you would be lost and ruined. So, be true to yourself; be honest to yourself and find out to what is the message of Islam for everyone of you.

Thus a person cannot walk the way of becoming beloved of Allah without becoming a slave to the personality of the Holy Prophet (SAW). We are pygmies and therefore we wish to measure the Holy Prophet (SAW) with our dwarfish status. We know that charcoal is pure carbon and diamond is pure carbon. It is only the frequency of the vibration of the molecules that makes them different. The Holy Prophet (SAW) is like a diamond and we are charcoal.

9

The Holy Prophet (saw)'s contribution to Knowledge[1]

Those who are students of history of religion and philosophy are well aware of the fact that there can be a perpetual war between the demands of faith and reason. There has been a general belief that a dichotomy exists between these two dimensions of human consequences. Even among Muslims, due to a lack of knowledge, there is a tendency to equate the realms of faith and knowledge as two water-tight compartments. Consequently, the demands of faith and the findings of knowledge have been drawn into a battlefield of confusion.

What is the contribution of the Holy Prophet (SAW) in this realm? He resolved first of all, the conflict between faith and reason.[2] This implied that faith without reason is superstition. Faith is primarily subjective whereas knowledge is objective. What is the criterion to judge the faith of three persons, for example when it is divergent in concepts and in consequence? To draw an analogy: three diametrically opposite views are associated with particular colours: white, yellow and red. Can these colours be reconciled to express a unitary response? In other words can they be at one and the same correct?

The first rule of the law which the Holy Prophet (SAW) laid down was that faith should be acquired on the basis of reason. Of course, faith is integral to the human personality and human life. Even an atheist who does not believe in God or in the higher values and whose outlook in life is purely materialistic possesses a certain faith. A Communist who pursues the Marxist

---

[1] The article is an adapted version of an extempore lecture at St. Patrick's College (Karachi) in 1972. The broad sweep of Ansari's knowledge is a testimony to his remarkable scholarship.
[2] "A Muslim has to walk this path right here and to acquire knowledge at all levels..." See *Dr. Fazlur Rahman Ansari*, 214.

philosophy champions the cause of the proletariat (working class) so that social justice may be established and guided by a peculiar form of faith or the righteousness of the cause.[3]

These human beings express their faith in different forms and in response to different circumstances. The human psyche is a repository of feelings. Actions are generally based on feelings. Reason serves as handmaid for actions. What distinguishes human beings from animals is creative reason. In this regard, the Qur'ān states categorically about the function of reason in relation to the Holy Prophet (SAW)'s mission:

لِيَهْلِكَ مَنْ هَلَكَ عَنْ بَيِّنَةٍ وَيَحْيَىٰ مَنْ حَيَّ عَنْ بَيِّنَةٍ ۗ وَإِنَّ اللَّهَ لَسَمِيعٌ عَلِيمٌ ﴿٤٢﴾

That he who would perish might perish by clear proof and he who would live might live by clear proof....

(8: 42)

In Arabic the word *bayyinah* used in this *āyāh* refers to logical argument. Therefore belief in the mission of the Holy Prophet (SAW) is based on clear logical arguments. Furthermore, the Qur'ān states that those who opposed the Holy Prophet (SAW) were not threatened with curse or damnation. Rather they were asked proof on certain knowledge either to contradict or refute his claim to Prophethood.

The first message on proclamation that the Holy Prophet (SAW) received must be understood in a historical context. The Holy Prophet (SAW) was unlettered[4] because he did not attend any

---

[3] Marxism confines itself purely to the problem of 'Man and Society, which is in sharp contrast to Islam's comprehensive code. In a similar vein, Communism has been rife with [unlimited] exploitation and unbridled oppression of man by man leading to widespread misery and frustration and finally man giving birth to the fire of vengeance and revolt. Cf. Ansari, *Communist Challenge to Islam*. (Karachi, 2018). See Ansari, *Islam versus Marxism* (Karachi, 1980), 9-11.
[4] Ansari makes interesting comments on the term *ummi* (unlettered) based on specific Qur'ānic verses. See, *The Qur'ānic Foundations*, vol.i, 349.

institution or sat at the feet of any teacher. Among the Arabs there were very few people who had acquired education. They were a community who disdained knowledge and instead prized military pursuits. Before the advent of Islam countries like India, China, Greece, Rome and Egypt were seats of great civilisations. The general decline in knowledge was glaringly evident before the advent of Islam.

It was during this age (of decline) that a great man appeared in the arid wasteland of Arabia among a community of illiterate people who did not acknowledge the merits of the pursuit of knowledge at all. And the first message the Holy Prophet (SAW) gave was:

اقْرَأْ بِاسْمِ رَبِّكَ الَّذِي خَلَقَ ﴿١﴾ خَلَقَ الْإِنسَانَ مِنْ عَلَقٍ ﴿٢﴾ اقْرَأْ وَرَبُّكَ الْأَكْرَمُ ﴿٣﴾ الَّذِي عَلَّمَ بِالْقَلَمِ ﴿٤﴾ عَلَّمَ الْإِنسَانَ مَا لَمْ يَعْلَمْ ﴿٥﴾

> Read! In the Name of your Lord who created, created man from a clot. Read! And thy Lord is the most Bounteous, Who taught by the pen, taught man that which he knew not."
>
> (96: 1-5)

These are five short verses (*āyāt*) which form the content of the Message revealed to the Holy Prophet (SAW) by Allah. A brief analysis of the message deserves mention. Firstly, the emphasis of the pursuit of knowledge forms the cornerstone of Islamic civilisation. Secondly, mention is made of the Lord of the universe who brought human beings into existence from a world of non-entity. Lastly, *imān* (faith) is interlinked with knowledge. In these verses the psychology for the quest and promotion of knowledge through the pen (*qalam*) is emphasised.[5]

Knowledge can be of two kinds: oral knowledge which is

---

[5] Cf. *Islam to the Modern Mind*, 31.

transmitted from generation to generation, and formal knowledge which in its institutional forms leads communities to the path of progress. Again, these Qur'ānic verses unambiguously promote the institutionalised pursuit of knowledge. Hence there is no room for forklore or hearsay in Islam. Another dimension to this revelation is the function of the Muslim community to unearth all the treasures of knowledge, systematise, classify, refine and promote its cause. This is the message which the Holy Prophet (SAW) gave to the Muslim community.

The following Qur'ānic *āyāh* supports the Prophetic mission:

يَرْفَعِ اللَّهُ الَّذِينَ آمَنُوا مِنكُمْ وَالَّذِينَ أُوتُوا الْعِلْمَ دَرَجَاتٍ

Allah exalts and Honour those who cultivate Faith and cultivate Knowledge.

(58: 11)

The fusion of faith and knowledge has important implications for the Muslim community. In contrast, the modern youth of the West and in their imitation, the modern youth of the East, are under the spell of unchannelised knowledge: a knowledge which they want to divorce from the highest apex of human emotion. The emotive conviction (emotion) they say should be set aside and only the cognitive conviction (reason) should be taken into consideration.

I had the opportunity of visiting Europe and the USA several times. I also had the opportunity of working among the youth who disenchanted with religion had become hippies, beatles and teddies. In the course of our conversation I asked them: "What do you want?" They replied "We want to escape." I asked again: "Escape from what?" They said: "Escape from all that we find around us because we don't feel satisfied." And in utter confusion they take to heroin and LSD and any other drug-fuelled intoxicants which can transport them from the ugly realities they face to the illusory, utopian realms of this life.⁶

I wish to emphasise this fact that unless you harmonise emotion with reason you will not be able to build a holistic personality. This is the Message of the Qur'ān. This is the Message of the Holy Prophet (SAW). While he emphasised the primacy of reason in human life, he consistently pointed out to the development and evolution of an integrated personality.⁷ Equilibrium produces a balance in all composite aspects of human life; and departure from it engenders conflicts which result in the split personality syndrome. This term is used by psychologists whereas Moralists describe this condition as hypocrisy. A person suffering from a split personality attempts to sail in the two boats which are heading in opposite directions. This split reaches the recesses of the social life of communities with bleak prospects for meaningful progress. In contrast, the blending of the human personality is an important contribution of the Holy Prophet (SAW).

Another unique contribution is that the Holy Prophet (SAW) laid down the blueprint for the pursuit of knowledge. The methodology which he advocated was knowledge which is from observation and verifiable. Logical categories or abstract thinking are not equivalents of observation. To put it simply, a logical deduction does not have the same value as observation. In the following *āyāh* of the Holy Qur'ān, we are told:

أَفَرَأَيْتَ مَنِ اتَّخَذَ إِلَٰهَهُ هَوَاهُ وَأَضَلَّهُ اللَّهُ عَلَىٰ عِلْمٍ وَخَتَمَ عَلَىٰ سَمْعِهِ وَقَلْبِهِ وَجَعَلَ عَلَىٰ بَصَرِهِ غِشَاوَةً فَمَن يَهْدِيهِ مِن بَعْدِ اللَّهِ ۚ أَفَلَا تَذَكَّرُونَ ﴿٢٣﴾

Have you not seen such a one who takes as his god

---

⁶ Ansari's extensive visits to the West in the 1960s sharpened his focus on the failings of materialism. The youth were exposed to pseudo- religious cults which offered them an illusory sense of spirituality and liberation from worldly trappings. Cf. *Islam to the Modern Mind*, 291.

⁷ Ansari devotes a detailed chapter on the Integrated Individual in *The Qur'ānic Foundations*, vol.i, 196-201.

his own vain desires? Allah has, knowing (him as such) left him astray and sealed his hearing and his heart and put a cover on his sight...
(45:23)

Man cannot see the Truth. The lens of subjectivity gives him another vision of observation. Consider the case of Sigmund Freud, the father of psychoanalysis. Had he not lived the life of a debauch then he would not have formulated the theory of libido or 'pan-sexuality'.[8] Likewise, Karl Marx who lived in abject poverty revolted against the strictures of the Church in Europe by advancing the theory of *Dialectic Materialism*. His theory creates a labyrinth of confusion and fallacies which are diametrically opposed to the teachings of the Holy Prophet (SAW). Again the subjective feelings confounded Karl Marx to formulate his theory with serious repercussions in countries which embraced Marxism.

The Holy Prophet (SAW) emphasised that the pursuit of knowledge should be anchored on observation and acceptable scientific methodology. The mission of the Muslim community in this context is three-fold: conquest of the self, conquest of the social environment and conquest of nature. The spirit of conquest is the distinctive hallmark of the Islamic ideology. And the Qur'ān is replete with āyāt (verses) urging mankind to study the phenomena of nature.[9] In fact more than three hundred verses relate to realms of astronomy, geology, astro-physics etc. The Qur'ān directs man's attention to the study of these phenomena as the following āyāh reveals:

﴿٢٨﴾ إِنَّمَا يَخْشَى اللَّهَ مِنْ عِبَادِهِ الْعُلَمَاءُ ۗ إِنَّ اللَّهَ عَزِيزٌ غَفُورٌ

---

[8] Sigmund Freud (d. 1939) is generally recognised as one of the most influential thinkers of the twentieth century. His theory of psychosexual development is in direct contrast to the moral values endorsed by the Qur'ān and *sunnah*. See *Islam to the Modern Mind*, 211-6.

[9] The pages of the Qur'ān abound with passages which invite our attention to an empirical study of the natural phenomena and emphasise the conquest of nature by man. See *Islam and Christianity in the Modern World*, 208.

> *Those who truly fear Allah are among His servants who have knowledge: For Allah is exalted in Might, Oft-Forgiving.*
>
> (35:28)

Islam emphasises the realisation of God (*ma'rifah*). It has combined the pursuit of knowledge with the realisation of God. Allah is Supra-rational therefore man realises His Majesty through His Creation: the exquisitive patterns of law, the exquisite beauty and symmetry found in the diverse natural phenomenon attest to the Majesty Wisdom of Allah who created the entire universe.

Apart from the theory, psychology and quest of the pursuit of knowledge given by the Holy Prophet (SAW), the Muslim community is reminded that the entire universe has been subjugated by Allah for the service of mankind:

وَسَخَّرَ لَكُم مَّا فِي السَّمَاوَاتِ وَمَا فِي الْأَرْضِ جَمِيعًا مِّنْهُ

إِنَّ فِي ذَٰلِكَ لَآيَاتٍ لِّقَوْمٍ يَتَفَكَّرُونَ ﴿١٣﴾

> *It is God Who has made subservient to you, as from Him, whatever is in the heavenly bodies and on the earth and in this are guidelines for those who use their reason.*
>
> (45: 13)

Thus the Holy Prophet (SAW) not only stated that it was an act of *'ibādah* (worship) for his fellowmen but he also chartered the course of science. If you read the works on the history of science which are largely written by non-Muslim scholars you will note their pertinent remarks that physical science before the advent of the Holy Prophet (SAW) was pre-scientific. The deductive method of was already known to do the Greeks who organised, systematised and channelised knowledge. In contrast to this form of enquiry, the inductive method was unknown to the Indian, Greek and Chinese civilisations. In fact, the history of science acknowledges the contributions of the

Holy Prophet (SAW) and his fellowmen for promoting the inductive method of enquiry. It is an indisputable fact that the advancement of science during the last three hundred years owes its genesis and development to the contributions of Islam.[10]

The Qur'ān was revealed as a guidance to mankind. It is not a book of science, geology or mathematics - it is a book of life encompassing comprehensive guidance for mankind. Scientific discoveries have merely confirmed the revolutionary theories explicitly mentioned in the Qur'ān. Consider the following *āyāh*:

سُبْحَانَ الَّذِي خَلَقَ الْأَزْوَاجَ كُلَّهَا مِمَّا تُنبِتُ الْأَرْضُ وَمِنْ أَنفُسِهِمْ وَمِمَّا لَا يَعْلَمُونَ ﴿٣٦﴾

> *Glory to Him who has created in pairs all things, from what the earth brings forth as well as from their own (human) kind and in those things which they have no knowledge.*

(36: 36)

The principle of parity discovered in the twentieth century is discussed. Students of botany perhaps know that in the scientific world this was not known until the nineteenth century; and it was finally put on the anvil and projected properly by an eminent scientist in 1921.

The Qur'ān in a single verse lays down in categorical terms the principle of parity which has been established in modern physics. The atom, for example, contains within its structure this principle. In fact the different phenomena of nature also reflect the principle of parity. Thus the term *az- wāj* is expressive of the pairs created by Allah and unfold the Majesty of Allah through his creation.

The prevalent knowledge of the cosmos before the advent of Islam deserves mention. The Greeks, for example, conceived the universe is a pre-scientific way. The earth was considered flat; the sky was a canopy studded with lamps. The Qur'ān repudiates this theory by stating that the heavens with the earth are a planet. They are spherical in shape and possess a

---

[10] Ibid., 209-11.

movement both in their orbits and axis. It was to the credit of Muslim scientists that they made accurate measurement of the circumference of the earth, sun and moon and also measured the distance between the moon and the sun. Their quest for scientific observation was guided by the following *āyāh*:

وَكُلٌّ فِي فَلَكٍ يَسْبَحُونَ ﴿٤٠﴾

..And each (of these) swims along in (its own) orbit.

(36: 40)

The movement of rotation and revolution in the planetary systems were meticulously studies in the field of astro-physics. It was therefore hardly surprising that Muslim scientists prepared the first globes.

About the movement of the sun, the Qur'ān says:

وَالشَّمْسُ تَجْرِي لِمُسْتَقَرٍّ لَّهَا ۚ ذَٰلِكَ تَقْدِيرُ الْعَزِيزِ الْعَلِيمِ ﴿٣٨﴾

The sun is moving towards its destination...

(36: 38)

The Qur'ān refers to the horizontal movement of the sun. I read at one place that somebody had to deliver one lecture on the manuscript of a Muslim scientist which had been translated into Latin. It is interesting to note that Kepler who enjoys an eminent position in the field of astronomy had studied the manuscript and did not fully understand it. He argued that the above verse contradicted their findings that the sun is stationary and the other planets revolve around it. Their findings according to Kepler, were irrefutable proof that the Qur'ān is not the Word of Allah. Of course, Muslim scientists who preceded Kepler and Copernicus affirmed through their extensive study and observation that the sun moves in a horizontal manner and is a constant state of movement. In the works of modern astronomy, galaxies and the entire universe are moving. And the sun along with the planets are moving towards the Dog Star. Who gave this clear-cut explanation to the Qur'ān and the Holy Prophet (SAW)?

Space travel has assumed important dimensions today. Who could have thought of space travel 1400 years ago? The following *āyāh* mentions it in categorical terms:

يَا مَعْشَرَ الْجِنِّ وَالْإِنسِ إِنِ اسْتَطَعْتُمْ أَن تَنفُذُوا مِنْ أَقْطَارِ السَّمَاوَاتِ وَالْأَرْضِ فَانفُذُوا ۚ لَا تَنفُذُونَ إِلَّا بِسُلْطَانٍ ﴿٣٣﴾

> *O company of jinn and men! If you are able to penetrate the strata of the heavens and the earth then penetrate. But you will not penetrate except with authority (acquired on the basis of knowledge of the secrets of Nature).*

(55: 33)

Remember the style of the Qur'ān is based on its divine guidance and in no way is a book of science. But here in a single verse it opens up the possibility of space travel and probing into the bowels of the earth which are covered with layers (strata) of immense potential.[11]

In sum, the contributions of the Holy Prophet (SAW) in the realm of knowledge are immense. I therefore appeal to my young Muslim friends that you are the inheritors of a very great heritage. Try to rediscover yourself and your foundations.

---

[11] Exploration of Mars is one example of man's conquest of the planetary system.

10

Islamic Theological Education[1]

Heart of Muslim Society:

History reveals that different human groups have been coming into existence on different foundations. Some have sought the bond of integrity in common geographical boundaries, others in the affinities of race and colour, and still others in the possession of a common language. But, whether it is geographical boundaries or race or colour or common language, the bond of group-integrity thus created, remains materialistic and non-ideological.

The concept, on the other hand, which Islam upholds and gives, is that of an ideological community (*ummah*). The Muslim community of the world, is thus, a community which is through and through ideological in character, having come into existence on the basis of the ideology of Islam, which in its turn, is constituted of a distinct system of belief and a comprehensive code of life based upon it.[2]

As regards the Islamic system of belief, again, it is founded on spiritual verities and its function is to orientate the entire human life in spiritual values. Thus, every cross-section of Muslim life, both on individual and collective levels, is determined by spiritual norms and is to be pursued in the service of spiritual ideals.[3] Again, because Islam forms the

---

[1] The article was written in 1943 in response to Qua'id-e-Azam's (Muhammad Ali Jinnah) historic appeal for planning a National System of Muslim Education. Ansari's incisive analysis about the problem of Muslim education evolved during his first tabligh tour in 1938. His presentation is firmly grounded in his dynamic formulation of the Islam and Knowledge paradigm. See Ansari, *The Present Crisis in Islam and our Future Educational Programme* (Karachi, 2017).
[2] For a detailed discussion about Islam as a comprehensive code of life, see Ansari, *What is Islam?* (Karachi, 1985).
[3] Ansari elucidates the relationship between ideals and Islamic values in *The Qur'ānic Foundations*, vol. ii.

ideological basis of the Muslim community, Muslims can prosper and progress harmoniously only if they submit each and every aspect of their individual and collective life to the eternal Guidance of the Holy Qur'ān and the *sunnah*.

The above-mentioned truth is accepted not only by the 'ulama but also by all genuine lay-Muslims. But neglect of the logical implications of this acceptance is as universal as the acceptance itself.

One of the most important of these logical implications is that the 'ulama constitute the heart of the Muslim society. This is so because Divine Guidance in the form of the religion of Islam has not only given birth to the Muslim community but also forms its basis of activity and source of sustenance; and the function of the 'ulama is that, equipping themselves with this Guidance, both academically and practically, they have to serve the Muslim community and humanity at large as the representative of the Holy Prophet (SAW), as we read in the *hadith*:

> *Verily the 'ulama are the successors of the Prophets (in the mission of delivering the Message of Allah).*[4]

Combined with this there is another truth which has been stated by the Holy Prophet (SAW) in the following words:

> *Verily, there is a piece of flesh in the body of man which if diseased, the whole body is diseased: while if it is healthy, the whole body is healthy. And behold it is the heart.*

This law which relates to individual personalities has also a direct bearing on collective life. It means that if the "heart" of the community is healthy and strong, the community is basically healthy and strong: while if the heart is weak or diseased, the community is bound to suffer from all types of

---

[4] Ansari's balanced approach on the status and role of the 'ulama is succinctly expressed in *Islam to the Modern Mind*, 185-90.

collective ailments.
Muslims of the world are suffering today not only from weakness on the international plane but also from collective diseases of different types. This is a fact which has been accepted by social reformers, in fact, by all thinking Muslims. However, no proper attention seems to have been concentrated on the root-cause, namely, the deficiencies and the diseases that have found their way into the ranks of Islamic religious leadership.

Sad story of the Dark Period of Muslim History:

There was a time when Muslims surpassed all communities of the world in every field of human activity - in spirituality and morals, in intellectual and aesthetic pursuits, in economic and social organisation, in commerce and industry, in military science and state-administration. Then came the time when, after the destruction of Baghdad and the fall of Cordova (*Spain*),[5] they (Muslims) withdrew from the intellectual *jihād*, which assumed later on such permanence that until today they have not been able to recapture their eminent position in the intellectual field. The political front also suffered a setback. But it was short-lived, because of the conversion of the Ottoman Turks who, taking over the leadership of the Muslim world, a new glorious chapter in the history of Islam. Muslims with added thus able to maintain their political supremacy all over the Islamic world. This included Muslim Indo-Pakistan for a further appreciable length of time.

Unfortunately, however, during that period of renewed political strength and stability, nothing tangible was done to reinvigorate Muslim society on other planes of activity, with

---

[5] The destruction of Baghdad in 1258 by the Tartars became known as the Scourge of God. Another tragic event in Muslim history was the fall of Cordova in 1492 – a traumatic experience for the Muslim world. The Inquisition by the Spaniards led to either the coercive conversion of Muslims to Christianity or expulsion from Andalusia (Muslim Spain).

the consequence that it continued to degenerate and debilitate, so much so that finally its life became infested with different types of ailments. The Muslim social order was menaced by the existence of the privileged classes who destroyed the vitality of the Muslim world through their luxurious and effeminate habits.

The ideal of conquering the world spiritually for Islam was made subservient to the ambitions of worldly gains and material ends. The scholars of Islam fell prey, with few honourable exceptions, to intellectual stagnation, while many of the rulers sold their hearts away to the satisfaction of baser desires. The greatest crime against their own selves which the Muslims committed was, however, the neglect of the of the cultivation of physical sciences - a task which had been sanctified by Islam, a task which their forefathers had pursued with glory ultimately to become the inaugurators of the modern scientific era, a task without which the maintenance of political greatness and material prosperity was impossible.[6]

Historically viewed, the neglect did actually pave the way for backwardness in the realms of technology, industrial production and economic organisation. It kept the Muslims back from developing better weapons of war and it finally culminated in making the Muslim world politically vulnerable, and as a consequence thereof, economically and intellectually conquerable.

Even before the close of the 18th century, cracks began to appear in the magnificent edifice of Islamic civilisation which the sacred hands of the Holy Prophet (SAW) had built; and the cracks continued to grow wider until the Christian nations of the West, who owed their Renaissance to none else but the Muslims, but who were in spite of that, their bloodthirsty enemies, entered in those cracks from all sides equipped, as they

---

[6] *The Beacon Light*, 181-200. Ansari reiterates the cultivation of sciences in the following words: "With the advent of the Holy Prophet (SAW) the Muslim community should unearth all the treasures of knowledge systematise, classify, refine and promote it." Cf. *The Holy Prophet's Contribution to Knowledge*.

were, with superior military weapons, intellectual achievements (especially) in physical sciences, industrial techniques, economic production, social organisation and democratic political ideals.

As regards the Muslims, they had already given up *jihād* to a great extent in the spiritual, social and intellectual fields. Now when occasion came to meet the biggest collective onslaught of Christendom on the battlefield, they found it impossible to achieve victory in their military *jihād;* even though they had formerly routed Christendom during the Crusades. Muslim countries fell to the enemy one after the other until a large part of the world of Islam from the Atlantic to the Pacific and from the islands of the Indian Ocean to the frontiers of Siberia was enslaved by the Christian powers of the West before the close of the nineteenth century.[7] The only exception was the Turkish Empire which could cross the nineteenth century with some of its dominions intact. But Turkey was herself sick and had, therefore, to surrender those dominions to the enemies of Islam even before the first quarter of the twentieth century ended.[8]

The slavery which started gripping the Muslim world more than a century ago was not purely political in character. Along with that came two other and more terrible forms of slavery, namely, economic and mental slavery. Then a fourth form of slavery was also born as a result of the above-mentioned three forms – social slavery.

As to political slavery, it has gradually disappeared by Allah's Grace. Most of the Muslim countries have regained their freedom in the wake of the Second World War. The economic

---

[7] Colonialism and Communism conspired to bring about the enslavement of Muslim countries. The nineteenth century may be regarded as the darkest period of Muslim subjugation to the reincarnated Crusader hostility in both military and intellectual fields. Western colonialism and Western-dominated politics created a servile leadership syndrome in Muslim countries resulting in a total surrender to values antithetical to Islam. Ansari, *Islam and Western Civilisation*, 3-9. Cf. *Fazlur Rahman Ansari*, 23.

[8] The dissolution of the Turkish Caliphate was the last semblance of Muslim unity, albeit, in a fragmented form.

emancipation of the Muslim world is also taking shape and the chains of economic slavery are becoming progressively weaker in response to the progress in scientific education and better organisation of economic resources.

The situation is, however, different in respect of mental slavery and social slavery,[9] wherein the grip has continued to become more and more severe and there are still no signs of our emancipation, in spite of certain measures adopted by certain Muslim governments for promoting the cause of Islam and in spite of the fights waged against these evils by certain powerful Islamic organisations in particular and by the 'ulama in general.

Evaluating their adverse effects, mental slavery is by far more dangerous because it is this which really brings about and perpetuates social slavery. The fact is that the acceptance of mental slavery of the enemy by a community gives birth to such a deadly social poison as can kill that community from within, however great and glorious its past history might have been. This acceptance (of mental slavery) is not possible without loss of faith in its own values - an adverse factor which is even more injurious than political slavery. So says Dr. Muhammad Iqbal:

> *Faith consists in forsaking one's ego and living in the ecstasy of Divine Presence*
> *Faith consists in accepting the ordeal of fire like Abraham.*[10]
> *Listen O you who have been enthralled by (the materialistic values of) modern civilisation*
> *Lack of faith (in your destiny as Muslims) is worse (in its injurious effects) than political slavery.*

From North to South and from East to West the above-

---

[9] The mental slavery may be expanded to the intellectual stagnation prevailing among Muslim societies. See *Islam to the Modern Mind*, 181-93.

[10] The *Ordeals of fire like Abraham* refers to the blazing fire in which the Prophet Ibrahim was thrown. "They said burn him and protect your gods, if you did anything at all! We said: O Fire! Be you cool and a means of safety for Abraham"(21:68-9).

mentioned social poison has been penetrating into the ranks of the modernist Muslim intelligentsia.[11] And not only that, the greater calamity is that those who brand conformity with the principle of historical continuity in Muslim thought and belief as slavery regard the mental slavery of the West as freedom. Thus, giving to evil the place of good and to vice the place of virtue is bound to land every community in a situation where its very foundations are sure to be destroyed. But, even the consciousness of this heart-rending consequence is getting lost in the ambition for false freedom.

It may be emphasised here that this ugly situation is the result of a long-drawn historical process. When Muslim scholarship proved deficient in fulfilling the intellectual needs of the community and the non-Muslims became the custodians of all the sciences and arts, it was only natural for the Muslim to become votaries at the non-Muslim shrines of learning. It was thus basically our own neglect of intellectual *jihād* which caused the present ugly situation.

Islam has invited its followers through the Holy Qur'ān and the hadith of the Holy Prophet (SAW) to a comprehensive intellectual *jihād*. Had we not kept ourselves aloof from it for centuries, especially in the fields of physical and social sciences, it appears in the light of philosophy of history that neither would the Muslims have fallen prey to mental slavery nor to political, economic and social slavery.

The fact is that whenever any community tries to accommodate two conflicting and mutually hostile systems of thought and action within its body-politic, disintegration is always the result. This disintegration causes a shake-up in the realm of beliefs on the one hand, and double-facedness in character, on the other. Besides that, mental slavery of the

---

[11] Ansari makes a rigorous analysis of Muslim intellectual trends which had assumed alarming forms in the nineteenth century. His prolonged study at Aligarh Muslim University (AMU) provided him the opportunity to make a systematic and rigorous study of this movement. The 'intellectual dishonesty' of framing Islam through the lens of Western scholarship is modernist Muslims' salient trait. See *Islamic Intellectual Revival*, 214-5.

opponents gives birth to inferiority complex. The inferiority complex, in its turn, tends to create petty-mindedness and meanness. And the final result is that life is pushed further and further from moral excellence and closer to moral degradation.

Unfortunately, most unfortunately, the Muslim world of today is confronted with the same ugly situation. We are not only weak politically, economically and intellectually, but even our moral life is not what Islam wanted it to be.[12] Morally we have been caught in a whirlpool and signs of moral degeneration are manifest everywhere.

Islam's weak Intellectual front in the Modern age:

This unfortunate situation is there. But more unfortunate than this is the situation which obtains in the ranks of religious leadership. It is more unfortunate because it is the religious leadership which forms the real spearhead of reform and its failure means a basic failure.

The invaluable intellectual (as also spiritual) services which the genuine and respectable members of this most respectable group have rendered during the different epochs of Islamic history are too well-known to be recounted here. But the point which demands and deserves full emphasis in connection to the present discussion is that deterioration has manifested itself in the ranks of this group in proportion to the deterioration of conditions in the Muslim world. Or might it not be more true to say, that conditions in the Muslim world deteriorated in response to the deficiencies and weaknesses that gripped the group of the 'ulama. Their standard and scope of knowledge and practice has been gradually deteriorating for some centuries past, so much so that even that standard of knowledge and piety that existed among most of the 'ulama a hundred years ago is rarely to be met with today.[13]

---

[12] In response to the moral decline that set in Muslim collective life, Ansari's *The Qur'ānic Foundations* is a refreshing effort to define Islam as a comprehensive code of life.

[13] The 'ulama's legacy in Islamic intellectual thought receives a brief mention in

There is no doubt that the hardships that the group of 'ulama has endured in preserving and defending Islam and the contributions which the individual 'ulama have made everywhere in accordance with their respective capacities, during the past one hundred years of unprecedented trials and tribulations, deserve all praise. May Allah bless all those who have served, and are serving the cause of Islam genuinely and truly. In spite of that, however, the weakness that had entered their ranks have continued to grow, so much so that we find today the prestige of the group of 'ulama shattered considerably.

The emergence and growth of group-weaknesses among the 'ulama have not only damaged their prestige but have also inflicted a severe injury on Islam and, consequently, on humanity. This could not have been otherwise, because knowledge of Islam forms the only ideological nourishment and, therefore, the only source of ideological survival for the Muslim community. Therefore, the only vehicle of the transmission of this nourishment are the 'ulama. Consequently if the 'ulama are not highly equipped intellectually and truly dynamic and powerful in their spiritual leadership, it would be futile to expect a radiant and healthy ideological life within the Muslim community and a proper transmission of the message of Islam to humanity at large.

Now just as Islam does not base its conception of worship on the separation of the religious from the secular, similarly, in its concept of education, it does not exclude "secular" knowledge from the curriculum of "religious" studies in the manner in which the one-sided religions and cultures of the world do it.[14] This is the reason why, during the age of glory of the Islamic

---

Ansari's lectures contained in *Islam to the Modern Mind*. Ansari wanted to see 'ulama as religious as well as socio-political leaders of the *ummah* who were equipped intellectually and possessed a dynamic spiritual leadership. See Siddiqui, *Dr. Fazlur Rahman Ansari: The Ghazali of His Age* (Karachi, 2016), 212.

[14] For example, the overemphasis of *fiqh* (Islamic jurisprudence) is deplored by Ansari. It is a formalistic Islam that disregards the higher objectives of the shari'ah. However, Ansari qualifies this statement in response to Muslims who reject *fiqh* in its entirety. *Islam to the Modern Mind*, 315-6. Ibid., 212.

civilisation, the educational system of the Muslim world was unitary, being based on the fundamental Islamic principle of *tawhid*. In that system, theological sciences were taught together with all other so- called "secular" subjects, e.g. natural sciences, mathematics, philosophy, etc. The result was that every Muslim scholar of that age used to be a comprehensive scholar. Again the formal system of examinations and award of formal certificates which are prevalent today were not in vogue at that time. Hence none could obtain a certificate without genuinely acquiring the necessary knowledge and the requisite intellectual and spiritual discipline. *In fact* everyone got an individual certificate in accordance with the actual intellectual stature he had acquired and this fixed up his place in society. Moreover, spiritual discipline[15] and character-building also formed a vital part of education side by side with academic achievements, and thus aptitude, labour and piety, all were fully coordinated, harmonised and rewarded.

But when, in the nineteenth century, the enemies of Islam succeeded in enslaving a large part of the Muslim world, they planned and adopted different schemes for crushing and annihilating the religion of Islam itself; and unfortunately they succeeded in causing colossal damage to Islam. One of the most far-reaching and disastrous among these schemes was the establishment of an educational system which snatched away from the hands of Islam the resources and the opportunity of educating the Muslim in accordance with its norms and ideals; and this has resulted in the slow but steady alienation, or, at least, indifference of a powerful section of western-educated Muslims from the Islamic ideals and values.

Side by side with that, another and more terrible consequence also emerged - theological education was devalued almost to the limit of zero; *hence* it could no more attract, beyond a few students from among the intelligent and well to- do Muslims, virtually all of whom went in for modern education. Gradually,

---

[15] Spiritual development is synonymous with *tazkiyah* – pursuit of a spiritual culture within the ambit of the Qur'anic and *sunnah* guidelines.

the institutions of Islamic theology were filled up with students many of whom were backward and below the mark in different respects. Its natural result was that the courses of theological education had to be made lighter [scaled down], causing the standard of religious training to suffer. And as a consequence, the standard of religious leadership degenerated.

Day by day the situation has continued to deteriorate in these respects, until it has reached a point today where, because of their one-sided education, the 'ulama have become confined to the mosque while all the departments of thought and action have passed on solely to the charge of those who have received purely secular education.[16]

Inside the mosque itself, the leadership of the 'ulama, is largely confined to the uneducated or the less-educated Muslims.

Surely, in the ranks of the 'ulama there are even today such personalities, although very few, whose intellectual calibre or standard of piety can be a source of satisfaction to the Muslim community. The majority however, consists of those whose shortcomings and deficiencies stand in the way of the 'ulama fraternity[17] in achieving its rightful role in Muslim society. Regrettably the 'ulama have become incapable of leading modern humanity.

In this connection, it is very significant that they could not produce in the present century a dynamic thinker like Iqbal who could inspire the Western-educated Muslim youth with love for Islam, or a leader like Jinnah who could unite the Western-educated Muslims, the 'ulama and the Muslim masses for achieving Pakistan. By contrast the best among them were forced to play only a subservient role in the national struggles of Muslim countries.

As regards the creation and the continuation of

---

[16] Ansari's critique of the 'ulama must be read in context of the events leading to the Partition of India in 1947. The views expressed in the booklet were written in 1944.
[17] Reference is to the dār al-'ulums.

shortcomings, and deficiencies among the 'ulama, it is the Muslim community as a whole which is responsible for them, and not merely the 'ulama. It is, therefore, the obligation of the Muslim community to remove those shortcomings and deficiencies.

The only genuine and correct method of resolving this ugly situation is through the creation and adoption by all Muslim countries of a system of education which should harmoniously combine the "religious" and the "secular".

However, until this most vital step is taken, an urgent demand of the situation is that:

> Our theological institutions should adopt a comprehensive course of education wherein high level knowledge of Islamic theological subjects may be combined with a critical study of other religions and of modern thought,[18] so that it may become possible for our 'ulama to guide and inspire all sections of the community and all the cross-sections of humanity with proper insight and in keeping with the dignity of true religious leadership.

This point needs some elucidation. A critical study of other religion and of modern thought, is necessary for the 'ulama, for three reasons: Firstly, they cannot preach Islam successfully to the non-Muslims unless they possess a proper knowledge of the ideologies which they follow. Secondly, they cannot inspire the modern-educated with the love for Islam without establishing rationally the truth of the Islamic teachings and their superiority over the teachings of other religions and ideologies. Thirdly, the latest advances in knowledge assist in understanding the Holy Qur'ān and the *hadith* better.

---

[18] The missionary activities of Ansari reinforces the need for 'ulama to study the dynamics of tabligh and comparative religions. See Siddiqui, *Maktubāt i-Ansari* (Karachi), 2016.

- Spiritual discipline, character-building and social service should receive recognition in our theological institutions similar to that extended to the acquisition of knowledge.
- For those who qualify from our theological institutions and wish to devote themselves to missionary work, an academic career or skill is also necessary whereby they may be able to earn their livelihood in an honourable way and independently of their missionary work and may thus, save themselves from financial and moral suffering.

In this way shall it be possible to have those 'ulama who may be the possessors of comprehensive knowledge on the one hand, and of a genuine and high-class Islamic character and personality and the mission of social service, on the other?[19] The fact cannot be over-emphasised that it is only the creation of such 'ulama which can form the first sure step towards the revival of our lost glory. Indeed all other reformative efforts seem to be futile without this most basic step.

Generally speaking, the acquisition of the available comprehensive knowledge has been our tradition during our age of glory. Among the jurists, the historic achievements of Imām Abu Hanifa, Imām Shāf'i, Imām Mālik and Imām Ahmad bin Hanbal could not have been possible without profound comprehensive scholarship.[20] Among the philosopher-

---

[19] The establishment of the World Federation of Islamic Mission, for example, aimed to establish an Islamic institution of higher learning through which 'ulama were trained "[to] meet the challenge of understanding and interpreting orthodox Islam in the light of the latest advances in human thought..." *The Beacon Light*, 435.

[20] Ansari lauds the achievements of the founders of the *fiqh* schools and pre-eminent philosophers like Ghazāli who represented a synthesis of faith and reason and knowledge and action. They also served as the bedrock for raising up the mighty edifice of our distinct (Islamic) civilisation. *Islamic Intellectual*

theologians, we may cite the example of Imām Abu Hāmid Muhammad al-Ghazāli who, as the possessor of comprehensive education, shattered the aggressive and hostile forces of alien philosophies and thus wrote a new glorious chapter in the intellectual and religious history of the Muslims.

Similarly, Muslim history abounds in such personalities in whom intellectual and spiritual greatness had been harmoniously blended. Their spiritual leadership was crowned with miraculous success both among Muslims and non-Muslims and the spiritual service they rendered was of such a high order that their names have become immortalised in history. Here we might cite the example of that august personality Sayyid Abdul Qādir Jilāni of Baghdad.[21] He rose to a high stature in the field of intellectual attainments. But more than that, his greatness lies in spiritual development with which his personality was crowned. He shone out as the sun of righteousness and spiritual splendour amidst a night of storms. His radiant personality broke the dark spell of confusion, his efforts for the revival of spiritual fervour among the Muslims were crowned by Allah with glorious success. Indeed, his services to Islam and to humanity form a landmark in our history, and his spiritual blessings have been immortalised in the constitution of Muslim society. Likewise, there is the refulgent personality of Qutb-al-Aqtāb Khawājah Mu'inuddin Chishti of Ajmer.[22] The harmonious blending on a high level of intellectual and spiritual attainments and his dynamic spiritual leadership has made him once for all one of the greatest

---

Revival, 71.

[21] The illustrious personality, Shaykh Abdul Qādir Jilāni changed the course of history, by his aura of holiness (*ruhāniyah*). This 'miraculous success' was attributed to his intellectual prowess and total devotion to the *sunnah*. *The Qur'ānic Foundations*, vol.i, 359-60.

[22] Likewise, Ansari pays glowing tributes of Khawājah Ajmeri: "[He] alone with his spiritual dynamism and without any army of political thrust, pitched the banner of Islam in the heart of an inimical and alien population, changing the course of history in South Asia permanently." Ibid., 360.

spiritual luminaries of Muslim history. It was none else than he, the sword of whose spiritual personality conquered the fortress of *kufr* in India and laid the foundation stone of Pakistan centuries before the emergence of the latter state.

Among the 'ulama of the present century also, there have been several spiritual luminaries who have shone out with distinction through the combination of academic and spiritual attainments. The work of all such 'ulama has been more effective than the work of those whose sole focus was academic. An illustrious example in this connection is that of the renowned spiritual leader and missionary of Islam, His Eminence Mawlana Siddiqi.[23] He combined modern education with the theological and possessed a magnetic and radiant spiritual personality. With these qualities of head and heart he rose to be a distinguished international Muslim missionary of his time and the services he rendered to humanity through Islam form a glorious chapter in recent Muslim history.

---

[23] On Siddiqui's life and thought, See *Abdul Aleem Siddiqui and His Mission*. The global influence of Mawlana Siddiqui is best illustrated by the *Abdul Aleem Siddique Memorial Lecture*, an initiative by Harmony Centre in Singapore.

11

Our Intellectual Emancipation and Islamic Reconstruction[1]

Progressive Musulman[2]

Of all the evils which Western domination has brought to the Muslim world, the greatest and the most dangerous, in view of the present writer, is that of the "slavery of the mind" and the transfer of power into the hands of those who have succumbed to it. These so-called "progressive" Muslims[3] seek the justification of their existence and their ideology in the shortcomings of the technique of conservatism.[4] But, actually, they are the product of gross ignorance of the beauties of Islam and true Islamic life, on the one hand, and of the spirit of intellectual defeatism which, followed fast upon the heels of Islam's political decline in the nineteenth century. For them Islam is just a religion among religions and deserves respect, if it ever does, merely as a social symbol or as a historical legacy. It is at best a personal faith, meant to comfort and sustain the individual, and capable of being set in any cultural framework they choose. They are vehemently opposed to the idea that Islam is a discipline, a way of life, a self-contained culture, and

---

[1] The article forms an important chapter of Ansari's *The Present Crisis in Islam and our Future Educational Programme*. The courses and programmes outlined illustrate Ansari's profound understanding of the dynamics of Islamic renaissance. Mahdie Kriel's *Islamic Intellectual Revival of the Modern Mind* is a significant contribution to Ansari's multidimensional contribution in this regard.
[2] The word Musulman is generally used in the Indian subcontinent. For the sake of clarity and uniformity, the word *Muslim* is used in the chapter.
[3] Progressive Muslims refers to the emergence of modernist Muslims who under the spell of Western civilisation, attempted to recast Islamic culture and civilisation into new moulds of interpretation. For Ansari's critique, see *Fazlur Rahman Ansari*, 141-4.
[4] Conservatism has been exploited by modernist Muslims to support their arbitrary interpretation of Islamic belief and practice. By contrast, Ansari's formulation of dynamic orthodoxy steers away from the extremes of conservatism and liberalism. *Islam to the Modern Mind*, 182.

a self-sustained civilisation.

This 'progressive' view of Islam is not the product of any intellectual appreciation of the Qur'ān and the *sunnah*, but of the spirit of slavish submission to Western norms and ideals. It began in the adoption of Western dress and manners and the creation of the pseudo-rational apologetics[5] of the nineteenth century and has culminated today in the cultural and intellectual apostasy of a fairly large section of Muslim intelligentsia. And in truth it could not have been otherwise. The new current of Western thought was not confronted with the vigorous and dynamic Islam of the Qur'ān and the *sunnah* but with a narrow, static and formalistic scholasticism, which, under the stress of circumstances, had divorced itself from the practical problems of life.

Few of us, however, realise the tremendous havoc which the multifaceted impact of Western culture has caused to the Muslim world. Still less do we realise the doom which must inevitably befall Islam if the present self-complacency and senselessness of its upholders continues. It is a fact known even to the man in the street that the majority of our rising intellectuals are not only ignorant of Islam but, because of this ignorance and the powerful impact of anti-Islamic influences, also positively antagonistic towards its ideals. The phenomenon of some of our best youths succumbing to the fashionable materialistic sociopolitical creeds of the West, as for instance Marxism,[6] is now of daily occurrence. It may be a transitory phase; but it is there all the same.

It is not, however, individuals only who are deserting our cause. The poison has percolated into the very heart of our

---

[5] In simple terms, 'scholars' who seek to promote Western civilisation uncritically in Muslim countries. India and Egypt were the forerunners in advancing the cause of the West. *Islam and Western Civilisation*, Cf. Fazlur Rahman Ansari, 142-3.

[6] The essay, *Islam versus Marxism* was written for the Muslim – Christian Convention held in Lebanon in 1954. Ansari makes a cogent presentation of the dangers inherent in Marxism. In his submission, Ansari briefly presents Islam as an alternative to Marxism.

body-politic. Typical in this respect is the case of modern Turkey, where a radical divorce from the Qur'ānic ideals was effected by Ataturk and his party not only in the externals of culture, in social outlook, in political policy, but also in intellectual and religious life. The last links with the Islamic cultural past were brutally broken by abolishing the Islamic code of law and the Arabic script[7]- the script which enshrines the Islamic past of the race and which is the international script of Muslim Asia, Africa and Europe. Instead, they adopted the German, Swiss and Italian codes and the Latin alphabet, forgetting in the blind fury of revolutionary spirit that nothing is more national than the law and the history of a people.

Importance of The Intellectual Factor

- Who is responsible for this deterioration of Islamic religious life and disintegration of Islamic cultural order? The enemies of Islam attribute the responsibility to Islam itself.
- The Muslims, in their turn, generally refer it to Islam's political breakdown - to their political servitude in the recent past and in the present.

The first is at best a contention and collapses as soon as it is brought to face the evidence of the Qur'ān, the *sunnah* and Islamic history.

The second contention is a half-truth. It is true in the sense that political subjugation does bring in its wake a sort of intellectual inferiority complex - a spirit of intellectual defeatism[8] - especially when the intellectual level of the ruling

---

[7] The noted philosopher – historian Arnold Toynbee echoed a similar view regarding the change of alphabet (with particular reference to Turkey): "Nowadays there is no need to burn books or huge libraries. The change in alphabet of a nation is sufficient to put the house of knowledge out of currency."

[8] Intellectual defeatism is a euphemism for Muslim surrender to Western values and secular worldview. In fact, Ansari is emphatic about Islamic identity built on a 'self-contained culture and self-sustained civilisation.' *Islam and Western Civilisation*, 23.

nation is higher than that of the subject race. It is more than true in the positive sense that complete and perfect political freedom of all the Muslim peoples is an essential condition for the ultimate dissolution of the anti- Islamic world-order.

However, the restoration and consolidation of political power in several Muslim countries has not in itself contributed in any appreciable degree to a revival of the Islamic world-order. In fact, in certain cases, as for instance in Turkey and Iran, quite the contrary happened and political consolidation and evolution only brought greater opportunities to the anti-Islamic forces.

To seek a solution of our present tragedy in the political resurgence alone, would, therefore, be a blunder of the first magnitude. And those who might take an exclusively political view of our destiny may be reminded that in the very midst of the struggle our youth have been forsaking our hope and the ghost of scepticism haunts the impregnable fortresses of our faith.

Consequently, while acknowledging that our political weaknesses and shortcomings have been contributing greatly to the present crises, we should not blind ourselves to the importance of other basic factors, among which the most fundamental is our intellectual collapse, which snatched away from the hands of Islam the right to educate us and to transform us into supermen and soldiers of the Kingdom of God. Our national existence has in consequence come to resemble a tree whose roots have been washed bare by the mighty torrent of Western civilisation: and the tree is slowly withering, decaying and collapsing for want of proper nourishment.

Confusion and Chaos

All of us probably realise the intellectual backwardness of the Muslim world, particularly in the field of natural sciences, but few of us have cared to evaluate our horrifying ignorance of

Islamic values and our intellectual bankruptcy in the creative realm.

A majority of our old school seem to have forfeited all creative genius. They have been mostly employing and considering as final a technique evolved centuries ago in an atmosphere and under circumstances in many respects different from our own.[9]

The reaction against it has given rise to an ever- increasing loose-thinking and scepticism. The modernised educated Muslims, with few honourable exceptions, learn their faith and their past national history from Western orientalists- Goldzihers and Nicholsons and Margoliouths and Macdonalds[10]- who paint Islam in the blackest colours. Even when they venture to come out of that vicious circle, the bias for Westernism persists and the demi-gods of Western thought continue to keep them in thrall.

The confusion thus created has landed us intellectually at the crossroads.

- On the one hand, there is a new-fangled trend of modern materialism and scepticism which is leading us straight into the arms of apostasy.
- On the other hand, there is a trend which seeks to steer a middle course between Islam and modern Western ideals, thus assuming that black and white are the same colour and consequently grey. Hence there is alarge proportion of this "grey" belief in the ranks of the westernised Muslims.
- There is a third trend less vigorous than the rest

---

[9] It is only the 'dynamic orthodoxy' a term coined by Ansari that can save Muslims from the challenges of Western inclusion and the loss of creative genius that was the pride of Islam's intellectual legacy. *Dr. Fazlur Rahman Ansari: The Ghazali of His Age*, 215-6.

[10] Ansari's *Muhammad The Glory of the Ages* first published in 1936 is a rejoinder the Orientalists' biased and often hostile writings on the Qur'ān and the sīrah literature. His subsequent writings are an elaboration of the Orientalist project against Islam and its foundational sources. Cf. *Islam and Christianity in the Modern World* (Karachi, 1965).

of the two, but quite alive among the general masses - the trend, which refuses to come out of the intellectual atmosphere of five hundred years ago and disdains to forms contact with modern problems.[11]

All these three trends will lead us to disaster, have actually landed us in disaster. The storm in the world of Islam is in full swing!

Towards an Intellectual Renaissance

The storm of un-Islamic and anti-Islamic forces is in full swing in the world of Islam, creating confusion and chaos all around and penetrating even in the most hidden recesses of Muslim national life.

But shall this be our end? It should not be; it must not be; it cannot be.

It should not be because an immense majority of Muslims all over the world still retain an absolute faith in the redeeming powers of Islam.

It must not be because Islam still possesses those infinite potentialities which can avert the mightiest catastrophe.

It cannot be because humanity, in spite of all her progress in science and philosophy, has not yet outgrown Islam. What is needed today is an ardent faith, a firm resolve, an intelligent move, in the direction of the reconstruction of the basis of our intellectual life. An instance in point is al-Ghazāli who tried to accomplish (this reconstruction) to a certain extent in his own day.

By thus emancipating our intellect from the serfdom of the West and all other un-Islamic and anti-Islamic influences, we shall be able to lay the foundations of the Islamic intellectual

---

[11] Ansari uses the term *integration approach* to explain the comprehensive moral code of Islam. See *The Qur'ānic Foundations,* vol.ii for details from a Qur'ānic perspective, its ethical teachings.

renaissance, which in its turn will contribute to our moral regeneration. And, moral regeneration will form a genuine guarantee not only for the restoration of our political power but also against the repetition of the present tragedy.

Instruments for Bringing About The Islamic Intellectual Renaissance

In laying down a programme for our future intellectual struggle, a distinction must be made at the very outset between two different concepts, namely, Islamic intellectual revival and revival of Muslim learning. The first concept is fundamentally 'religious' and consequently comprehensive. The second is fundamentally 'secular' and consequently partial. The foregoing analysis of the intellectual aspect of the present crisis makes it clear that our effort should be based primarily and essentially on the first concept.

The idea in undertaking such a task should be four- fold:

- To eliminate all anti-Islamic elements from our intellectual life
- To impart to the intellectual aspect of our national existence a true and positive Islamic character by creating a distinct and powerful Islamic thought which may fundamentally cover all branches of knowledge
- To ensure and conserve our intellectual self-sufficiency
- To bridge up the gulf and resolve the conflict which exists today between theological and 'secular' education as our ancestors did in the heyday of Islamic civilisation. This (approach) will allow Islam the opportunity for its full and rich expression in our intellectual life, which should finally become the bedrock for raising up the mighty edifice of our distinct civilisation.[12]

---

[12] The guidelines for an Islamic renaissance are expressed in the following

Verdict of Muslim History

Here I wish to respond to an important objection. Some might protest that my idea of adopting a long-range policy and of completing an elaborate work of research before attempting to plan and introduce a sound system of Muslim national education[13] is too far-fetched to deserve any serious consideration.

I would say that the alternative policy of adopting popular remedies and short-cuts cannot pay in the long run and has actually proved to be the ruin of Islam and Muslims in the past. And this view of mine is not only negatively grounded in the verdict of the last five hundred years of the history of our decadence, but is also positively supported by the voices of our great reformers.

- Khairuddin Barbarossa (D. 1546), whose plea for reforming the house of Islam on the basis of a long- range policy, made at the fateful hour when the Christian flood, gathering at the gates of Islam, was preparing to sweep off the Muslim countries of Europe, Asia and Africa. He failed in penetrating the sterile brains of a corrupt Muslim administration.

- Mustafa Fazil Pasha (d.1875), whose Reform Manifesto, submitted to the Sublime Porte[14] for checking the Western tide with a comprehensive, constructive programme, was dynamited by the reactionary forces of the lethargy of an indolent people under the smoke-screen of a false plea for protecting the rights of

---

words: "[The] function of this *ummah* will be to unleash all the treasures of knowledge that are buried in the different civilisations of the world: to preserve, to classify and to rectify all the different types of knowledge and advance the cause of knowledge." *Islam to the Modern Mind*, 188.

[13] The detailed scheme of planning a Islamic research institution appears in the original chapter. Our focus is about the contemporary significance of Ansari's broad outline of the Islamic renewal project. See *Islamic Intellectual Revival*, 72-84 for details on the national educational system.

[14] The central government of the Ottoman Empire.

conservatism.
- Syed Jamaluddin Afghani (d.1897)[15], whose masculine efforts for administering the antidote against disruption and for revitalising the body-politic of Islam by a constructive process, were undermined by the self-seeking Muslim exploiters of Islam.
- Prince Saeed Halim Pasha (d. 1921), whose clarion call for the Islamisation (*Islamlashmaq*) of the collective life of the Muslim peoples under the Caliphate,[16] at a time when the sapping influences of Turkish nationalism were still in their infancy and could be nipped in the bud, fell on the deaf ears of a self-conceited scholasticism[17] and was lost.

A Final Appeal

I wish every Muslim to remember one heart-rending fact once for all:
The Muslim world has already forfeited much of its individuality and now stands in danger of losing its destiny.

I further wish every Muslim to realise, and realise finally, that the impending danger *cannot* be averted either by sticking to the old conservative technique, or by means of theological

---

[15] Afghani introduced the concept of Pan-Islam and was a political activist. Ansari draws a parallel between Afghani and Mawlana Siddiqui on the following counts: restoring unity of the *ummah* under a politically charged climate and presenting a progressive approach to Islamic faith and practice. *The Beacon Light*, 474-5.
[16] The *Islamlashmaq* like his other work *Reform of Muslim Society* sought to harmonise Islamic teachings in a changing geopolitical world. Ansari showed a deep admiration for Pasha's work of Islamic reform. Ibid., 470-2.
[17] The 'ulama's conservatism was resistant to any positive changes resulting from the encounter between the West and the declining political fortunes of the Turkish Caliphate.

patchworks, or by building up our national programmes on the shifting sands of expediency.

Only a scientific approach to our present peril, a rational analysis of the shame and misery that surrounds us, a research in the ever-fresh and fertile fields of the Holy Qur'ān and the *sunnah* for finding out the possibilities of the revival of Islam as a world-policy, can save us from our inevitable doom.

Indeed, unless Islam wages a determined, final and all-out war against the thought-forces of modern materialism and scepticism, and triumphs in establishing its own world-order, Islam it must suffer the fate which is overtaking all other faiths. And if knowing the infinite resources and strength of Islam in this respect, we Muslims of the present day shirk our duty and thus deprive ourselves and humanity of the blessings of Islam, we should be regarded as the greatest criminals of all history.

PART 5

ISLAM AND MODERN CHALLENGES

Therefore, the message to the Muslims and all the rest of humanity is: **Return to Allah genuinely.** And obtain from Him the light to dispel darkness. Otherwise, this darkness will continue and consume wherever you will find it. Materialism has spread its tentacles all over, covering every facet of human life. Perhaps it is not too late; so let us act now, otherwise it will be too late. The impact of materialism may lead to a worldwide nuclear war; and the atom bombs and hydrogen bombs (nuclear weapons) will be blind to the race or community they are aimed at.

12

The Challenge of the Twentieth Century[1]

The twentieth century is a challenge to Muslims in particular. This challenge can be understood in terms of politics and philosophy of life. I shall focus my lecture on the latter aspect of belief and culture. What challenge does the twentieth century present to us as Muslims? The basic factors involved are the systems of values and culture. Initially, when Islam came, spiritual ideologies had emerged in different communities. The main idea common to all these ideologies was the concept of other-worldliness. One had to forsake one's worldly occupation and renounce this world as in mysticism. Life appeared as something mystifying. Buddhism considers this world to be an illusion; and to Christianity it is evil. These outwardly religions represent the *ideational culture.*[2]

However, Islam came with a positive outlook on life that God Almighty is Absolute Good. Thus, whatever Allah created is also good and its misuse makes it evil. Islam changed the outlook of humanity and gave belief a unique character, as is mentioned in the hadith:

Islam began as something unique.

Islam says that true religious life is to spiritualise the life here on earth. Instead of tribal gods and idols, people should believe in the one true God, Allah, who is above all human conception for as we are told in the Holy Qur'ān:

---

[1] The issues raised in the chapter have contemporary relevance for the *ummah* in the twenty first century.
[2] Refer to *The Qur'ānic Foundations*, vol.i for an exposition on the ideational culture.

there is none like Him.

(42:11)

It was a revolutionary idea even to those who claimed to be monotheists for it combined the notion of *"this-worldliness"* with *"other-worldliness."* As we have been taught to pray since childhood:

﴿رَبَّنَا آتِنَا فِي الدُّنْيَا حَسَنَةً وَفِي الْآخِرَةِ حَسَنَةً وَقِنَا عَذَابَ النَّارِ ۝٢٠١﴾

O' Lord! grant us the good of this world as well as the hereafter.

(2:201)

This philosophy of life reforms this world, establishes (here) the kingdom of God[3] between the good and virtuous and eradicates all evil. The idea of Islam was not to renounce the world but to conquer it as a servant of Allah who establishes all that is good. Thus, Islam provides a comprehensive way of life with clear-cut directions to Muslims. The Muslim community – which started in the most glorious manner – was confronted by the Roman and the Persian Empires.[4] These empires were destroyed, both politically and ideologically. Islam was therefore a challenge to the world, as the Qur'ān tells us:

﴿هُوَ الَّذِي أَرْسَلَ رَسُولَهُ بِالْهُدَىٰ وَدِينِ الْحَقِّ لِيُظْهِرَهُ عَلَى الدِّينِ كُلِّهِ وَلَوْ كَرِهَ الْمُشْرِكُونَ ۝٣٣﴾

Allah sent the Messenger (and Islam) with guidance

---

[3] The term has a broader definition than used in the Bible. It does not have a restrictive meaning as expounded by the Prophet Jesus.

[4] In the subsequent years after the demise of the Holy Prophet (SAW). the Roman and Persian Empires were defeated by the Muslim armies. *Muhammad The Glory of the Ages*, 132.

based on truth and that this way of life may overpower other systems that are not true, even though the unbelievers may detest it.[5]

(9:33)

The mission for the Muslims as we are told in the Holy Qur'ān is:

كُنْتُمْ خَيْرَ أُمَّةٍ أُخْرِجَتْ لِلنَّاسِ تَأْمُرُونَ بِالْمَعْرُوفِ وَتَنْهَوْنَ عَنِ الْمُنكَرِ وَتُؤْمِنُونَ بِاللَّهِ

You are the best of peoples, evolved for mankind, enjoining what is right, forbidding what is wrong and believing in Allah.

(3: 110)

Those who understood the meaning and mission of Islam projected a challenge to the rest of the world. The world saw a comprehensive revolution by a small group of Muslims, trained and inspired by the Holy Prophet (SAW) and took the challenge to the farthest regions of the world. The Muslims became pioneers on all fronts; they became the teachers in all branches of knowledge and personified the highest moral standards and spiritual values. They were respected for it because they took the lead in spiritualising culture to an extent that many countries became "Arabicised"[6] like North Africa. This was the impact of Islam which came with such beauty that people not only loved Islam, but also its followers.

Islam even penetrated Spain, where Muslims built up a civilisation and culture that will remain the envy of all peoples. When the Muslims built universities, hospitals, observatories, and educational institutions, Europe was still in a state of medieval barbarism. The Church in Europe fought against the

---

[5] It is He who has sent His Messenger with guidance and the religion of truth, to cause it to prevail all other religions. Even though the pagans (*mushriks*) may detest it (9:33).

[6] Egypt, with its rich legacy was Arabicised and became the citadel of Islamic culture and learning.

forces of enlightenment and the Europeans were compelled to study under the Muslims. The basis of this antagonism was two-fold:

- Knowledge came to Europe through the Muslims, the Church hating the Muslims, and
- Christianity was built on the conflict between faith and reason.[7] It based its philosophy on faith only. The philosophy and scientific knowledge that evolved and followed was considered against the Church. Hence, the saying of the Church fathers," The blood of the martyr is the seed of the Church."

Subsequent history evolved a philosophy that was based on materialism and atheism. Thus, the philosophy of modern civilisation is atheistic and materialistic in the realm of belief; sensualistic and hedonistic[8] in the domain of morality; exploitative in the field of economics and expedient (what is good for themselves) in the political arena.

This modern civilisation has branched into two camps, namely: philosophical materialism or capitalism and scientific materialism or communism.[9] Do not be fooled by the difference in terminology, both ideologies are materialistic through and through. When we look at the world today, we find that it is controlled by political forces and not ideological forces. In terms of politics in this century, it is the politics of the superpowers. No

---

[7] The forces of enlightenment and progress were considered satanic by the Christians. Moreover, the purge of Enlightenment as opposed to ignorance and superstition was followed by widespread persecutions against those who dared to promote different views from the Church.

[8] Ibid., 114-8 In philosophy it refers to pleasure (in the sense of satisfaction of desires) which is the highest good and proper purpose of life.

[9] Communism has benefitted a selected few and rejects spiritual moral values envisaged by Islam. Like other western countries, it is Islamophobic. The persecution of Muslims in the Soviet Union (which included Muslim autonomous states) makes chilling reading. See *Communist Challenges to Islam: An Exposition of Communism vis-a vis Islam*. This scholarly work written by Ansari was published by the Makki Publications (Durban, South Africa) in 1951.

one else matters. Their religion is pure and fanatical materialism. These are their pillars and their ideology is built on that.

No wonder – to the materialist – if you believe in God today, you are considered reactionary and if you do not believe in God, you are considered to be progressive and modern. If you do not believe in morality, you are modern, but if you believe in truth, goodness, moral integrity and chastity then you are outdated. If you do not believe in ethical principles or moral foundations in business, you are prosperous. This is the real challenge!

Remember, Islam came as a challenge and thus brought into existence a counter challenge – and if you cannot withstand it, you will be destroyed. Consequently, Islam taught the Muslims principles of greatness in this world through virtue – power is virtue and weakness is vice. As Almighty Allah says in the Holy Qur'ān:

$$وَأَعِدُّوا لَهُم مَّا اسْتَطَعْتُم مِّن قُوَّةٍ$$

Keep your powers at the highest pitch against them.

(8:60)[10]

If you do not do it, you will suffer very badly. The time is going to come when the forces against you are going to become greater. Therefore, acquire knowledge in the realm of technology, commerce, economics, military science and spirituality. Unless you maintain that status for all time, as soldiers of Allah, you will be in trouble. This is the challenge for us because Islam teaches us to obtain all the good of this world as well as of the hereafter. When our enemies overpowered us on the battlefield, we were enslaved and at a loss as how to balance ourselves.

The challenge is not an ordinary challenge. Most of us are still asleep. The theory of the pendulum clock is an example of

---

[10] Against them make ready your strength to the utmost of your power... (8:60).

regression of the Muslim community. When the 'Abbasid caliph sent its first delegation to Europe, he sent a pendulum clock, first made by a Muslim in Syria, as gift to the Emperor Charlemagne. When the clock was presented to Charlemagne his advisor said to him, "These Muslims are very clever, they have put a ghost inside it and this is going to cause great damage to us." But, the situation is reversed in the nineteenth century. When the Bedouins used to rob the pilgrims, they would find a clock in the dead person's pocket, listen to it, throw it on the ground and shouted: "It is a devil!"

Modern civilisation with all its glamour is alluring to our youth and they imitate the glamour only, which is natural. The Holy Qur'ān says:

﴿إِذَا جَاءَ نَصْرُ اللَّهِ وَالْفَتْحُ ﴿١﴾ وَرَأَيْتَ النَّاسَ يَدْخُلُونَ فِي دِينِ اللَّهِ أَفْوَاجًا ﴿٢﴾﴾

When comes the help of Allah and victory, and you see the people enter Allah's religion in crowds.

(110:1-2)

The opposite is happening now. This is the challenge.

This is not politics. This is religion! How is this challenge to be met? Reformers arose in many countries and they tried to cure the disease which inflicted the Muslims, but conditions have degenerated. This community has been divided into more sects because we are not producing thinkers like Imām Ghazāli, Imām Shāf'i, Imām Fakhr al-din al-Rāzi,[11] and many others. We are producing charlatans, very ordinary persons including myself. We don't understand and are like the blind men from India who went to see an elephant. We do not have that wisdom therefore matters are becoming worse! The one blind person says that the elephant is like a thick rope, another says that it is like a pillar. Are we not doing the same? Why are we becoming more divided and not progressing like the early Muslims?

---

[11] Imām Rāzi (d. 1209) was a celebrated *mufassir* (commentator) of the Qur'ān and an accomplished philosopher. He is best known for his rational approach to Islamic beliefs and teachings..

That healthy spiritual and intellectual climate does not exist anymore. Neither do the conditions for a healthy, moral pattern of life.

Can this be our end? No, it cannot be! Even if one spark remains, it can be converted into the biggest fire that can burn out all the evil within us. This is the same spark our Prophet (SAW) placed in the hearts of his companions. This spark is that genuine *imān* in Almighty Allah. If we can only understand that *imān* is not a mere ritual or formal exercise, but something real and alive which must be cultivated. This force made our forefathers great and this *imān* became the real challenge. But this *imān* was not for any racial or political aggrandisement, nor for causing any harm or evil to anyone. This *imān* was a challenge only for the establishment for all that is good and eradicating all that is evil for all of humanity. We shall have to return to that *imān*.

When we read the Qur'ān and the life of the Holy Prophet (SAW) and his Companions, we will discover that we are very different, even those amongst us who are representatives of Islam. Read the Qur'ān and try to think about the qualities of a genuine Muslim:

وَعِبَادُ الرَّحْمَٰنِ الَّذِينَ يَمْشُونَ عَلَى الْأَرْضِ هَوْنًا وَإِذَا خَاطَبَهُمُ الْجَاهِلُونَ قَالُوا سَلَامًا ﴿٦٣﴾

The servants of Allah -The Merciful Lord- are only those who walk on this earth with humility. If the ignorant people want to drag them into fights and quarrels, they say: "Our ideal in life is peace"

(25:63)

How many of us are like that and have it as our watchword to be humble? Try to judge for ourselves – and judge others silently – for the sake of understanding only.

وَالَّذِينَ يَبِيتُونَ لِرَبِّهِمْ سُجَّدًا وَقِيَامًا ﴿٦٤﴾

> *Those who spend their nights standing in front of their Lord and prostrating.*
>
> (25:64)[12]

Are we doing it? Where will that spiritual and moral fibre come from if we don't practise it?

Today, our enemies have no need to destroy us, for Muslims kill and damage [other] Muslims best![13]

This is our condition. This topic requires volumes, but whatever has been said it is not to become frustrated, for Allah says:

$$\text{وَلَا تَيْأَسُوا مِن رَّوْحِ اللَّهِ ۖ إِنَّهُ لَا يَيْأَسُ مِن رَّوْحِ اللَّهِ إِلَّا الْقَوْمُ الْكَافِرُونَ ﴿٨٧﴾}$$

> *A Muslim, however weak in imān he or she may be, can never allow frustration to overpower him or her except those who have no faith.*
>
> (12:87)[14]

$$\text{قُلْ يَا عِبَادِيَ الَّذِينَ أَسْرَفُوا عَلَىٰ أَنفُسِهِمْ لَا تَقْنَطُوا مِن رَّحْمَةِ اللَّهِ ۚ إِنَّ اللَّهَ يَغْفِرُ الذُّنُوبَ جَمِيعًا ۚ إِنَّهُ هُوَ الْغَفُورُ الرَّحِيمُ ﴿٥٣﴾}$$

> *Proclaim to these servants of mine who have been cruel to themselves (by damaging themselves and transgressing) – do not despair of Allah's mercy, for Allah forgives all sins; for He is Oft-forgiving...*

---

[12] Those who spend the night in adoration of their Lord, prostrate and standing (25:64).

[13] The civil wars orchestrated by the West and Russia in the Middle East are grim reminders of Muslim blood soaked in dividing the *ummah*.

[14] ... And never give up hope of Allah's soothing mercy: truly no one despairs of Allah's soothing mercy except those who have no faith (12:87).

$$\text{وَأَنِيبُوا إِلَىٰ رَبِّكُمْ وَأَسْلِمُوا لَهُ}$$

Turn to your Lord, approach Him, come near Him and bow to His will.

(39:53-54)

Try to imbibe godliness in the manner it should be done and the miracle that happened fourteen hundred years ago, is bound to happen again. It is bound to happen for all time. But the condition is: *anibu ilā rabbikum wa aslimu lah*. To carry the label of a Muslim only will not do. Half-hearted action does not help. Doubting which is right and wrong will not do. *Al-yaqin* - an indomitable faith - that alone will help us, and this faith cannot be acquired by sermons only.

Every Muslim should study Islam and the Qur'ān. Study the message. Let us investigate for ourselves and we'll find that Islam today is the only panacea (universal cure) for the ills and problems of mankind. Islam is that alchemy that can turn base metals into gold. Islam can benefit us in this life and in the Hereafter. The seeker will acquire real *imān*. Islam did not come to wage war, but to advise positive living, to invite others with love and affection, with sympathy and the best of goodwill. Understand Islam in the light of the demands of this modern age and do not be affected by any group or sect. If there is any good in any group, that good must be acknowledged, if there is any bad, that bad should not be admired for that would be *sabilah al-Jāhiliyyah*[15] - to follow the way of the days of Ignorance.

Allah is Truth, Islam is the way of truth and we have to learn that we should be true to ourselves, true to our fellow beings[16] and

---

[15] *Jāhiliyyah* or pre-Islamic Ignorance has a specific historical context. It was a religious and moral corruption that included the social evil of burying girls alive and perpetuating tribal wars for trivial reasons. *Muhammad The Glory of the Ages*, 43-51.

[16] True brotherhood is inspired by values that seek to promote goodwill and love for humanity. This is embodied in the following Qur'ānic verse: I only desire your

true to Allah. The threat to our value system and culture is a challenge we can and should face with the weapons of virtue, godliness and sacrifice. The challenge can be met with the weapon of glory and greatness which comes through humility and godliness and not through arrogance and vice.

My dear brothers and sisters, some people think that this is the end. The conditions that exist are not the conditions of the termination of our existence. The conditions are the throes (the pains) of a re-birth.[17] The community is the womb out of which the new forces are to emerge and the community (womb) is experiencing those throes so that every member of the community feels it. But, blessed are those who can understand, feel and realise the challenge that has come through our beloved Prophet (SAW).

Almighty Allah has set it as a challenge:

يُرِيدُونَ لِيُطْفِئُوا نُورَ اللَّهِ بِأَفْوَاهِهِمْ وَاللَّهُ مُتِمُّ نُورِهِ وَلَوْ كَرِهَ الْكَافِرُونَ ﴿٨﴾

> *The forces of evil want to extinguish with their mouths the light that Allah has sent, but He is going to perfect this light even though the unbelievers detest it.*
>
> (61:8)

The question is, who will be selected by Allah to play this role? Let every one of us aspire to be one of those through whom Allah will accomplish His design, of making Islam the dominating force on the face of the earth. Almighty Allah says:

> *O' Believers, if you are slack in your duty towards your dín, then Allah will bring others in your place, those whom He will love and they will love Him genuinely.*

---

betterment to the best of my power. (11:88). *The Beacon Light*, 148-53.

[17] Throughout his lectures and writings Ansari offers effective solutions to the predicament Muslims face. The analogy of rebirth is associated with Islamic renewal which he fervently upheld and exemplified in his message to the *ummah*. Cf. *Dr. Fazlur Rahman Ansari*, 100.

They will have goodwill towards the believers and strive against the unbelievers, they will struggle and strive and exert to establish goodness, justice and piety on this earth, without any regard (fear) for themselves.
(5:54)

The invitation from Allah is there and it depends upon us to take up this challenge. May He inspire us and all the Muslims of the world to understand the nature of this spiritual challenge. May He enable us to conquer this challenge for in that lies the good for humanity at large.

13

The Age of Doubt

The issues raised are comprehensive and relate not only to the Muslims of South Africa, but to the whole world, even where majority Muslim communities are to be found. Certain fundamental factors have come into existence in this modern age and have influenced the Muslim community. The present-day thinkers all agree that the previous age was the "age of faith" and the present age is the "age of doubt". What are the reasons that this age should be called the "age of doubt"? What caused humanity to follow the path of faithlessness?

The Muslim community, especially the rising generation of Muslims, is in a state of doubt and confusion. Our Muslim youth are caught in the crossfire of ultra- conservatism and ultra-modernism. Conservatism is a virtue, but when it is taken beyond limits, it becomes a vice.[1] The entire universe is conservative only fundamentally and it is changing all the time. Even humanity, though it remains fundamentally the same throughout the ages, has to undergo changes. The philosophy of change is based on the pursuit for knowledge – to fly on the wings of knowledge to even greater heights, the quest for discovery, and to probe all those resources which are here. Consequently, the material life of mankind changed because of the ambition of the human being. This ambition which is physical in its foundation has resulted in changes in the economic pattern. People adopted one type of economic pattern and replaced it with another.

---

[1] In other words, religious conservatism remains static if its resists the dynamic spirit of knowledge *('ilm)* as proclaimed in the iqra paradigm (96: 1-5). As an alternative, Ansari formulated dynamic orthodoxy which steers away from conservatism and modernism. This has emerged as the salvation of Muslims and of humanity at large. Preface to *The Qur'ānic Foundations,* vol. i, xvii.

The pursuit of knowledge has led to inventions or discoveries of material things and instruments, which have now changed the lives of human beings. When the first human beings invented the sled to carry their belongings from one place to another, it was a big step forward. Then the wheel was invented and used in the car. This process continued until today when the human is able to build spaceships and travel to the moon.

Human probing brings about technological changes. Modern sociologists say: "Technological changes bring about a change in cultural mentality, and this brings about a psychological change." This change in the psyche brings a change in focus towards the metaphysical reality until the very beliefs of human beings are changed. Religion is changed on the basis of change in the technological pattern. That has been the process.[2]

Consequently, conservation is a virtue, but taken beyond its limits, it is a very big vice! The world in which we live is conservative – it has conserved its fundamental characteristics but it has also changed and is continuously changing. Therefore, there has to be the harmonious blending of preserving the fundamentals and always being ready to change the secondaries.[3] If you want to conserve everything, then this "caravan of life" which is moving all the time and its law will become "everyone to himself and devil takes the hindmost."

Those who are efficient, who have the energy to go ahead and the will to move, they move ahead. Those who want to remain stationary, they are trampled under the feet of the crowd!

Life is movement and everything in this universe is moving all the time. But in our Muslim community the pietists have decided that we should remain stationary and become negative and proclaim everything to be *harām*! The narrow-minded pietists believe that we should live in a shell and remain

---

[2] Technological advances are directly linked to the religious outlook of man.
[3] The fundamentals are non-negotiable. However, matters that fall under *furū'* (secondary importance) may be adapted or reviewed by 'ulama specialists. This point is best illustrated in Ansari's article *The Sunnah – The Challenge*. See *Islamic Intellectual Revival*, 192-209.

stationary! We have lived in this shell for the last one hundred and fifty years and the consequence is that although we are seven hundred million in terms of numbers,[4] we are not worth seventy cents in the international affairs of the world. Despite the fact that Muslims are in strategic positions all over the world, it is the most impotent community in the world![5] It has no say in international affairs and other communities are planning all the time how to swallow us. We have become like the ostrich which buries its head in the ground and feels that all is well. We have built up superstitions and shells around ourselves and around Islam so that the light of Islam may not penetrate those false barriers. We have changed Islam into a cult.

A cult is a combination of certain dogmas, rituals and some ethical principles. We do not go beyond that cult. Even an ethical principle like morality[6] has been divorced from religion in our society. I don't know about your community, but I know about the Indian community where I was born in and the Pakistani community where I live. For a good Muslim, morality has no meaning today. Pious Muslims with all the paraphernalia of a good Muslim: long beards with long flowing robes called *hājis* hold the whole market of Pakistan in their hands. If one wants to buy pure honey, for example, one rather buys the imported honey to get the real thing, although it is also produced in Pakistan. But one cannot get pure Pakistan honey! I mention things that are very simple but far-reaching. Go to the matrimonial courts in Pakistan and see what Muslims think of their religion now. Compared to the Qur'ān and *sunnah*, religion to them has nothing to do with morality.

For instance, a traveler may be pious and marry two wives

---

[4] The 2017 statistics indicates 1.8 billion Muslim population from the world. This exponential increase since 1970 (Ansari's first lecture series in South Africa) is a reaffirmation of Islam's rapid spread.

[5] The establishment of the Organisation of Islamic Cooperation (OCIS) was founded in 1969. It was in its early stages and therefore did not play an effective role in Muslim world affairs. Recent geopolitical developments have changed the landscape of Muslim communities.

[6] The theory of morality forms the basis of *The Qur'ānic Foundations*, vol. ii.

who will each live in a different town, but none of the two wives will know about each other. He will have children by both wives and none of them will know that they are sisters and brothers of one another. The father dies and these children meet and marry one another – of course, not knowing that they are brothers and sisters![7]

We can go on and probe what this malady is that we are suffering from. The parents, even well-meaning parents, have time only for earning money and counting it. This has been cursed in the Qur'ān and such people are condemned as people of hell.[8] They go five times a day to the *masjid* (mosque) to perform their *salāh*, but when they come home, they have no time for their children and their wives. I have seen good hardworking Muslims who become multimillionaires through business.

But the children receive no affection nor teachings from their parents. The father thinks that everything can be purchased with money.

In my community, you get *zakāh* from the rich *hāji* but when you tell him that *zakāh* cannot be spent for the madrasah teachers or for constructing the madrasah building, he would say; "Take it or leave it! I have only *zakāh* to pay."

Ramadān is the month of charity and these so-called "wealthy, religious, pious Muslims" will calculate their *zakāh*. They will let their managers get ½ and ¼ rupee pieces, one and ten rupee notes.[9] In Karachi and Colombo, these wealthy merchants will sit at a table with this heap of money in front of them. Then a whole army of undignified Muslim beggars in dirty and tattered clothes will swarm the market places of Karachi and Colombo.

---

[7] The risk of an incestuous marriage is therefore not far-fetched.
[8] Ansari shared the concern of Mawlana Siddiqui in his assessment of parental neglect to Islamic morality. He issued a stern warning – a declarative announcement of divine punishment. "[Parents] will definetly taste the severest torment of the wrath of the Almighty Allah in the tight chamber of the grave and the deep dungeons of Hell." *Abdul Aleem Siddiqui and His Mission*, 104.
[9] Pakistan denomination.

This scene continues for the whole month.

When a beggar comes to them, he will be given a ½ rupee; if the beggar complains, he is given a one rupee note. If he does not move, finally he is given a ten rupee note. The merchant considers it *harām* to pay beyond ten rupees! This is the way we treat *zakāh*, which was the social welfare tax of Islam! The Holy Prophet (SAW) established for the first time in known history, the welfare state. No Muslim community can be called an Islamic community or state unless that community or state undertakes to guarantee the basic needs of every member of that community. This is the welfare community that was founded! It was not a community of Qāruns[10] on the one hand and the dumb-driven cattle of the dumb-driven masses on the other hand. It was not that community which we find in Pakistan and elsewhere!

The community which the Holy Prophet (SAW) built was on the basis of social justice.[11] He said that everything which a Muslim possesses belongs to Allah and not to that person. The Holy Qur'ān states:

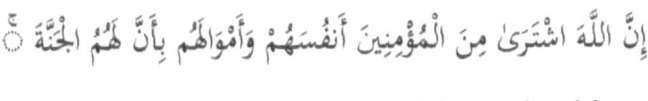

Allah has purchased from the believers their life

---

[10] Qārun lived at the time of Prophet Musa and had accumulated wealth beyond description. The Qur'ānic account describes his obsession to his wealth, bloated arrogance resulting in his dreadful fate: "Then We caused the earth to swallow him up and his house; he had not (the least little) party to help him against Allah, nor could he defend himself." (28:81).

[11] Ansari summarises the function of the Islamic welfare state and the distribution of *zakāh* in the following words:
"The economic ideal of the Holy Qur'ān is the eradication of poverty and the multifaceted evils to which the possession of excessive wealth by individual leads... [The] spending of the wealth by the wealthy freely and at the highest level for the benefit of their unfortunate fellow beings has been proclaimed as the characteristics of every wealthy Muslim. " *The Qur'ānic Foundations*, vol. ii, I 386-7.

and their wealth, in lieu of deferred payment, jannah.

(9:111)

Whatever good you do now, you will receive the jannah. No businessman would like to do that kind of business here! In the first instance, Allah is the Real Owner, Creator and Maintainer of everything. The secondary ownership that we acquire has to be surrendered to Allah in order to be a believer. How many of us are there who are doing this? In Pakistan, if a wealthy man gives you something for a madrasah or anything else, he will give it with *zakāh* money only. And beggars cannot be choosers!

These are the spiritual leaders, behind whom we pray! They have made their 'ulama (in Pakistan) beggars. If an 'ālim wants to open up an institution, he has to go from door to door and if the merchant wishes, he will see the 'ālim – otherwise not.

With all this charity that they do they have sunk to the lowest and deviated from the Holy Qur'ān and *sunnah*. For example, they do business with human beings in this way: the lower the investment, the higher must be the profit or dividend. Consequently, they conduct business this way with Allah also. They would say: *"Mawlana* Saheb, if I give so much for such a cause, how much *thawāb* (blessings) will I get?" And the *Mawlana* Saheb, who is under the thumb of the merchant, tells him all sorts of nonsense to please him. He doesn't tell him outright: "You can't do business with Allah like that and whatever you have been entrusted with is an *amānah* (trust). Do you want to use Allah's *amānah* and make business with Him?"

Another aspect of trading with Allah is: make so much tasbîh on a particular night and get so much *thawāb*. Obtain the jannah with zero investment![12] -To read certain things a thousand times a night is easy. But we cannot build Islam's prestige and glory on this basis. What is the real Islam?

---

[12] Ansari's sarcastic comment has resonance among segments of Muslims who continue with this malpractice of reciting tasbîhs of baseless Islamic formulae designated as *dhikr*.

Let me tell you about the lady saint, Rabi'ah al-Basri. She was absorbed all the time in the remembrance of Allah. One day she was seen running along the road, a bowl with fire in the one hand and a container with water in the other.

When *Sayyidinā* Hasan al-Basrí, her spiritual companion, asked her what the problem was, she said: "People worship Allah either out of desire for *jannah* or out of fear for *jahannam*. I wish to burn that *jannah* with this fire and extinguish that *jahannam* with this water, so that people may worship Allah out of love for Him and no other reason." This is Islam! Not this debit, credit business, because the Holy Qur'ān says:

$$\text{وَالَّذِينَ آمَنُوا أَشَدُّ حُبًّا لِلَّهِ}$$

The believers are those who are strong in their love for Allah.

(2:165)

This love is the real connection that has to be established between the believer and Allah. I am sad to learn that the conditions here are probably the same as in my country, Pakistan, where our errors have brought the evil day to us. If in your minority community, conditions are what they appear to be, then allow me to say as a humble servant of Allah that things can only worsen and we will remain at the mercy of the superpowers.

If any one of the *kāfir* powers wants to annihilate a Muslim community any day, it can do it. We are at their mercy for we have no answer to their atom bombs. Consequently, you'll find that in the politics of Muslim countries, i.e. those which have Muslim governments, are not free to do as they want. The superpowers always come forward and give a command. The Soviet Union wanted East Pakistan to be taken from West Pakistan, and it had to happen. The superpowers want the state of Israel to remain as a dagger in the heart of the Arab world,

and Muslims can't do anything.[13]
Why? What is wrong with the Muslims? Muslims may worship Allah more than other communities worship their God, but their religiosity has absolutely no meaning where material forces are concerned. We may worship as many times as we want but it is no antidote for our slavery to the superpowers! I am referring to Muslim governments who are slaves of superpowers because they have to obey their orders. The main fault with Muslims is that they have lagged behind in the field of science and technology. Disunity is there in other communities as well. Lack of good morals is to be found in other communities too, but there is one thing which Muslims lagged behind to the extent that they are now considered to be a primitive community. Japan, China, Europe and America are considered to be advanced communities. Are they advanced in spirituality, humanity or morality? No, but they are advanced in the material instruments of domination. Why has it happened?

Here, the most tragic thing has taken place. If you study the history of physical science, you will find that the founder of the modern scientific era is the Holy Prophet (SAW).[14] He is the founder, not the West or anyone else. Let me refer you to the history of science by R. Briffault. In his book, *The Making of Humanity* he says: "Science before Muhammad was pre-scientific ..."[15] It was he who gave the scientific method of inquiry, without which no advance in the field of science would have been possible. Of course, this may sound unbelievable, but let me explain further. The methods of inquiry are two: deductive logic and inductive logic. Before the advent of the Holy Prophet (SAW) humanity knew only the deductive method – and on the basis of this method, no progress is possible in the field of physical science. It is the inductive method of inquiry which brings progress in the field of physical science. This

---

[13] Pakistan was established in the name of Islam. Ironically East Pakistan (Bangladesh) was dismembered in the name of nationalism in 1971.
[14] *The Beacon Light*, 122-4.
[15] Robert Briffault, *The Making of Humanity* (London, n.d.), 190.

inductive method was given for the first time by the Holy Prophet (SAW), as given in the Holy Qur'ān and *hadith*.

In our conception of an 'ālim or Mawlana, there is even no resemblance between, for example, Imām Abu Hanifa, Imām Ghazāli, and so on. Returning to the point in question, read any book on philosophy of science and you'll find that there are the three principles on which physical science is based: unity of mankind, unity of nature and unity of knowledge.[16]

The Holy Prophet (SAW) taught these principles! What is the first message he gave because there must be a system in the divine scheme, it cannot be meaningless. The first message from the Holy Qur'ān:

اقْرَأْ بِاسْمِ رَبِّكَ الَّذِي خَلَقَ ﴿١﴾ خَلَقَ الْإِنسَانَ مِنْ عَلَقٍ ﴿٢﴾ اقْرَأْ وَرَبُّكَ الْأَكْرَمُ ﴿٣﴾ الَّذِي عَلَّمَ بِالْقَلَمِ ﴿٤﴾ عَلَّمَ الْإِنسَانَ مَا لَمْ يَعْلَمْ ﴿٥﴾

> Read in the name of your Lord who created – created man out of a germ-cell. Read – for your Lord is the Most Bountiful One who has taught the use of the pen – taught man what he did not know!
>
> (96:1-5)

These five verses deal with two things – the psychology for the quest of knowledge and the technique for the quest of knowledge.

The first message came for *'ilm*. The message given to Muslims is that the function of this *ummah* will be to unearth all the treasures of knowledge that are buried in the different civilisations of the world: to preserve, to classify and to rectify all the different types of knowledge and advance the cause of knowledge. This is the function of this community as laid down in the first message that came. Unfortunately, now this

---

[16] The unity theme is articulated in *Islam and Western Civilisation*, 14-6. According to Ansari unity is associated with the integration of values within an Islamic framework.

community is a community of illiterates. In Pakistan the Muslims are 85% illiterate; the 15% who are literate only 2% of them are educated.[17] To be literate is one thing but to be educated is another. And this is supposed to be one of the most advanced Muslim communities of the world.

If I come forward and deliver the message of Islam, people regard it as nonsense, although it is based on the truth! Why did Allah send the first message about the psychology for the quest of knowledge and the technique for the quest of knowledge? It means that the foundation of this *ummah* was being laid and its basis is *'ilm* (knowledge). At another place in the Holy Qur'ān we are told:

يَرْفَعِ اللَّهُ الَّذِينَ آمَنُوا مِنكُمْ وَالَّذِينَ أُوتُوا الْعِلْمَ دَرَجَاتٍ

> *Allah will elevate those who cultivate faith and knowledge.*
>
> (58:11)

Here the Qur'ān mentions *'ilm* -all knowledge- not only the knowledge of a few books of *fiqh* or *tafsīr*, but also mathematics, physics, chemistry, medicine, etc. The cultivation of all knowledge is *'ibādah*, the real mission of this *ummah*. None of the founders of faith said what the Holy Prophet (SAW) said:

> *The superiority of a person who pursues knowledge over a person who remains engaged in devotional exercises, is like my superiority over the meanest amongst you.*

Here is the teacher of real religion. Islam is *dīn* 'the way of life' and the concept of Islam is different to what we'll find in other religions. The emphasis in other religions is dogma or rituals

---

[17] In many Muslim countries the plight of illiteracy has not been seriously addressed.

but in Islam it's the contrary. Read the Qur'ān and find out what *dín* is.

$$\text{فَأَقِمْ وَجْهَكَ لِلدِّينِ حَنِيفًا ۚ فِطْرَتَ اللَّهِ الَّتِي فَطَرَ النَّاسَ عَلَيْهَا ۚ لَا تَبْدِيلَ لِخَلْقِ اللَّهِ ۚ ذَٰلِكَ الدِّينُ الْقَيِّمُ وَلَٰكِنَّ أَكْثَرَ النَّاسِ لَا يَعْلَمُونَ ﴿٣٠﴾}$$

> To live your life according to the nature which Allah has made you and the nature around you. To live your life in conformity with nature, that is the right religion, but most human beings do not understand this.
>
> (30:30)[18]

There is a wrong notion that *dīn* consists of rituals and dogmas, but the Qur'ān negates this assertion. The way of life is to live life according to nature, the nature on which Allah constituted the human being. Therefore, we should not be amazed if we hear that the Holy Prophet (SAW) gave this importance to the pursuit of knowledge which he did not give to optional devotional worship when he said:

> The ink of the scholar is holier than the blood of the martyr.

No founder of religion ever said these words, for the place of the martyr in religion is very high. He also commanded his followers:

> Every piece of wisdom or knowledge is the property of the believer.

---

[18] So set your face truly to the religion being upright. The nature in which Allah has made mankind: No change there is in the work by Allah: that is the true Religion: But most among mankind know not (30:30).

Every believer should get hold of whatever knowledge and wherever he may find it. However, we are living in a shell and the consequence is that our rising generations all over the world are revolting against Islam because our Islam solves no problem at all, according to them. If the love that the elders have for Islam is not transmitted to the youth and if we remain in that shell, we will lose our generation – our Muslim youth. I have been informed about what is happening in some towns of South Africa: how the madrasah students are starving and the manner in which the elders, who have lots of money, but cold-shoulder their duties. Another point is that the youth also earn a lot of money and don't care about their lowly paid teachers. If ten teachers are required only one is employed because money is not to be spent for this job.[19]

Problems are emerging in this township and we are simply sleeping over the issues as to what is going to happen tomorrow. If a girl wears a mini-skirt, the *fatwā* goes out immediately. But it does not work because the poison has gone into the minds and there is no cure![20] Remember, prevention is better than cure. What you have to do is to build up the fortress for Islam amongst the youth so that they may develop into better human beings than the youth of other communities and be able to show the torch of guidance to others. But, we don't want to do our duties, we don't want to work for the cause of Islam. Money is more important. If we die as millionaires, we feel that it is good while we just give a pittance to Islam as it is given to a beggar! Islam is a beggar at our door! People do not have the mind, nor the heart to understand Islam and to serve Allah. They do not stop to think that whatever they have, have been given to them by Allah only and that He who gave it also has the power to take it away. They don't understand that if this community is not

---

[19] It will be worthwhile to note that Mawlana Siddiqui made a clarion call for reconstructing the madrasah system and facilities for the professional growth of 'ulama. *Abdul Aleem Siddiqui and His Mission*, 158.

[20] Not only is faith (in the case, Islam) a challenge, but there is a justification to dress immodestly at these tertiary institutions. Thus the essence of *hayā* (modesty) is lost by our youth.

built into a proper Muslim community with the highest ideals and in the noblest fashion, then this community will not survive as a Muslim community.

It is a minority community and will be swallowed by other more dynamic ones. I do not know why people do not see to the problems of madāris and why it is at such an inferior level in this country. Obviously, the first problem is to teach our young children. The more important problem is what to teach them when they go to the college and are exposed to many secular theories which create doubt in their minds such as the theory of Darwin. There is no arrangement at this level in this country. There is not even a single person who can tackle this problem. What I observed during my tour of South Africa is that what should be done, is not being done.

It is only a half-hearted measure and in the meantime, we are gradually losing our youth. We are presenting Islam to the youth in a manner in which he finds that most of his problems remain unsolved. Consequently, he has to beg at other doors while the only way open to him is that of western education. If you don't give the youth western education, you are going to kill them materially. If you give them that education they might deviate. So your community is between the devil and the deep sea! And you'll have to answer for it. Those who have the money and the influence will have to answer on the Day of Judgement!

My dear brothers and sisters, the Islam that was given by the Holy Prophet (SAW) is dynamic and revolutionary. Islam in the fashion we have it today, in the form of a cult, is something meaningless. Allah has laid down the law for Muslims, that they should try to build this world first and the next world after. We have been asked to pray:

رَبَّنَا آتِنَا فِي الدُّنْيَا حَسَنَةً وَفِي الْآخِرَةِ حَسَنَةً

Our Lord, give us the best of this world and then the best of the next world.

(2:201)

But we put the cart before the horse. If we become religious, we think only of the other world. The other world is real and we must work for it because the spiritual life is the highest life, but we must keep the logical sequence intact. We must build this world first and then the next. The Holy Qur'ān tells us:

كُنْتُمْ خَيْرَ أُمَّةٍ أُخْرِجَتْ لِلنَّاسِ تَأْمُرُونَ بِالْمَعْرُوفِ
وَتَنْهَوْنَ عَنِ الْمُنْكَرِ وَتُؤْمِنُونَ بِاللَّهِ ۗ

You are the best community that has been raised for mankind and you enjoin what is right and forbid (eradicate) what is evil and you believe in Allah.

(3:110)

Think about this verse, for this is the mission of this Muslim community. Are we doing this job? For to establish good and eradicate evil from all over the world is a much greater job than eradicating evil from our own community. Even of this we have no consciousness because we suffer from this malady and remain in a state of "piety complex."

Very ordinary things in Islam, we are told, are the most important. We look down upon one another. If a man does not grow a beard he is labelled a *fāsiq*.[21] Growing a beard for the sake of the Holy Prophet (SAW) is a sacred act, but there is an added responsibility. After keeping the beard, never commit the slightest crime or sin, otherwise you'll be insulting the memory of the Holy Prophet (SAW) and that is something Allah will never forgive you.

We should turn our backs on all this sophisticated foolishness in the name of Islam, and go back to that original Islam of the

---

[21] According to Ansari, growing a beard is a signboard that implies a commitment to lead a righteous life. It does not suggest a pietest appearance or following the shari'ah superficially. *Islam to the Modern Mind*, 162, 316.

Qur'ān and the life of the Holy Prophet (SAW).
That is the only way. Here Islam is dynamic, progressive and such that Muslims are born to be supreme.

$$وَأَنتُمُ الْأَعْلَوْنَ إِن كُنتُم مُّؤْمِنِينَ ﴿١٣٩﴾$$

You will be superior if you are believers.
(3:139)

And if we are not superior in this world, then we are not real believers. This is a clear proclamation of Allah. You will be superior in technology, science, art, peace and war, politics and economics and in every other branch of knowledge! But, Muslims today are the most inferior! Are we believers?

We should take stock of the entire situation and teach our youth and create those agencies whereby they can acquire that real Islam. And the real Islam is so fascinating, charming and beautiful, that if it is offered to anyone, that person will never refuse it. That is our duty and the only cure for our present malady. At the moment we are at the crossroads. We are at the stage of being annihilated as Muslims. Persons by the name of Ya`qub, Hasan and 'Umar may walk on the roads, but there will be no Islam if we don't wake up in time.

May Allah enable us to be true to Him and His Beloved Prophet (SAW) and the Qur'ān and leave all our foolish ideas wherever they collide with what is given in the Qur'ān and hadith. Turn back to that source of life, and *inshā-Allah* this small community in South Africa will be a beacon of light and provide guidance to other communities. Our function is to be a beacon of light towards a higher life: godliness, absolute justice, truth, beauty, wisdom and holiness. We have to become this! We have the money and manpower in the community, we only need to rediscover ourselves as to *what* we are and *what* we ought to become.

14

Westernised Muslims

Muslims all over the world are faced with the problem of re-adjustment to the environment. We are unable to find a solution to our present decline and degradation, whether we belong to South Africa, Pakistan or the Arab world or anywhere else. Muslims find themselves in critical conditions and are even insulted. A Muslim poet asked: "What has happened to us, that today we are looked down upon by the other communities of the world? We have become like international mercenaries and outcasts." Despite the fact that we are seven hundred million (now 1.8 billion: 2017) in the world and the inheritors of the glorious history of Islam, we enjoy no status in the international affairs of the world.

Although we take pride in the fact that we are the *muwahiddun*- the believers in the One God – we generally have a wrong notion of Allah. This sounds like an amazing statement for we are believers in the One True God and His Unity but unconsciously, we believe that He is capricious[1] and not a righteous God! Let me explain further. The Holy Qur'ān says that Allah created this universe with all the laws that govern everything in it, but He has imposed it upon Himself to follow His Law. The Qur'ān says:

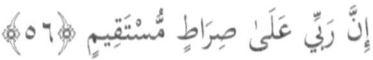

Say, my Lord is on the straight path.

(11:56)

---

[1] Ansari makes an important point that is worthy of reflection. Allah's laws and divine qualities are manifested through His creation. The Guidance is exemplified in the message of His Messengers.

Like we have been asked to pray, Allah is saying about Himself that He is also on the straight path. He is not unjust and does not indulge in favoritism. Here, Islam negates the concept in the Bible that the children of Israel are the chosen people of God. Allah has made the Law and sent the Guidance. Whoever follows the Guidance is dear to Him, conversely whoever does not follow the Guidance whether a Muslim or anything else has absolutely no status in the presence of Allah. Unfortunately, we proclaim that our God is Righteous but we unconsciously believe He is not because we believe He has chosen heaven for us and hell for others.

This ugly theory has no basis in the Qur'ān, nor the *hadith* and this point of view has brought calamity to the Muslims. If only they remembered that *dunya* is *dār al-'amal* (house of action)- the place where a person earns heaven on the basis of faith and action. And not on the basis of superstition, ceremonialism, ritualism or petty bickering about theological issues. Salvation is not on the basis of formalism and externalism but on the basis of the transformation of the human personality, on the human social order, and on the basis of the spirit of *imān billāh* (faith in Allah). It is also based on the spiritual orientation of life:[2] to follow the Divine law and the commandments given by the Holy Prophet (SAW).

The Qur'ān says:

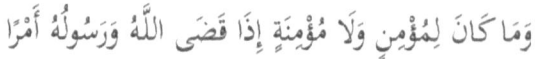

It is not possible for a true believer, whether male or female, to have his or her own freedom of choice

---

[2] It is a perpetual conscious struggle (*mujāhadah*) for the sake of establishing a more living relation with Allah. In other words the religious quest is grounded in the love of Allah. *The Qur'ānic Foundations*, vol.i, 155,158.

after he or she has been given a command by Allah and His Prophet.
(33:36)

Islam means discipline which must be followed: Islam is not merely a signboard. Imagine a shop with signboards but without commodities. Can there be any business? The Muslims– especially those who claim to be religious – seem to believe that only signboards can do the entire job!

Travel to the East or the West as I have, and observe the different communities whether they are majorities or minorities and you will notice a crisis of moral character in the Muslim world. Muslims are not what they claim to be, they tend to be hypocritical, whether consciously or unconsciously.

Why do we shed crocodile tears because we have fallen so low? We are going to fall lower and Allah Almighty is not going to forgive us, because He is the Righteous God and not capricious. He has to run the entire cosmos with everything in it, and remember that He created all human beings. You and I can take pride that we are Muslims, but remember that we are Muslims by accident.

How many of us devoted ourselves to acquiring education about Aristotle, Plato and Kant,[3] but ignored Islam? Therefore, we remain Muslims because our parents were Muslims. Bear in mind that Almighty Allah has not promised anything to this category of Muslims. Promises have only been given to the believers – the *mu'minun*. History bears testimony to it. During the Makkan period of the Holy Prophet (SAW)'s life, when the handful of Muslims were being persecuted, Almighty Allah's promise came to them:

وَعَدَ اللَّهُ الَّذِينَ آمَنُوا مِنكُمْ وَعَمِلُوا الصَّالِحَاتِ لَيَسْتَخْلِفَنَّهُمْ فِي الْأَرْضِ

---

[3] Reference to ancient Greek philosophy and the nineteenth century study of science and philosophy advanced by Immanuel Kant. See, *The Beacon Light*, 114-21.

Allah promises to those who cultivate imān and who lead lives of purity, of moral integrity and the grandeur of character, He promises that they will be the greatest dominant force in this earth.[4]

(24:55)

The infidels of Makkah jeered at them and said that: "Your leader wants to boost your morale and holds out false promises." But history tells us that this small group of Muslims became the master force in the world and remained the supreme political and ideological power for centuries! This was the promise that was fulfilled, and the Holy Qur'ān says:

وَلِلَّهِ الْعِزَّةُ وَلِرَسُولِهِ وَلِلْمُؤْمِنِينَ وَلَٰكِنَّ الْمُنَافِقِينَ لَا يَعْلَمُونَ ﴿٨﴾

Honour belongs to Allah and His Prophet (SAW) and to the believers...

(63:8)

to those who possess a dynamic, loving and vibrant faith in Allah. To them belong the honour and if we do not have any honour in this world, then we are not *mu'minin*. The promise came, but not to the Muslim, not to those who pay lip service, not a mere intonation, nor a spiritless proclamation of the *shahādah*.

Shall we remain in this state? Is it really worthy of a human being to stay in this abject condition? Do we realise that we have reached the rock-bottom of our degradation? The proof of it is that the most persecuted, the most hated, the smallest ideological minority[5] in the world, the Zionist Jews, snatched away your *qiblah al-awwal* (Jerusalem) surrounded on all sides

---

[4] Allah has promised to those who among you believe and work righteous deeds, that He will of a surety grant them in the inheritance (of power...) (24:55).

[5] The ideological minority is the Jewish nation. Of course, ideology in a political sense refers to Zionism that has not only deprived Palestinians of their land but through systematic measure of persecutions dispossessed them of their national identity.

by so-called Muslims! Those Muslims are helpless in spite of the fact that they are begging for help from the Soviet Union, China and elsewhere but still cannot do anything! What a contrast between that handful of Muslims in Makkah, to whom that promise was made and fulfilled against the heaviest odds. What a pity for us that we are seven hundred million[6] and we cannot do anything!

This hopeless apathy is a measure of our *imān*. We have no *imān*! And we still believe that the system of guidance, the Qur'ān and *sunnah*, is true! That is the biggest tragedy. We have no *imān* but we believe; hence we cannot say on the Day of Judgement that we did not know. We will be told: *"You knew it, but you did not follow My guidance, instead you followed your hawā al-nafs, your baser or lower self! You followed the devil."*

Allah has promised and proclaimed:

> *Whoever revolts against the devil and establishes his loyalty towards Allah, he obtains a support which will never fail him.*
>
> (2:256)[7]

Why is all the support failing us? Don't we think? Don't we have minds? Have we become so foolish and ignorant not to understand this at least?

My dear brothers and sisters, Islam is the alchemy that transforms all base metals into gold, and it has proved itself to be the alchemy. It was sent by Allah to the most backward people in the world – the Arabs of those days. Thomas Carlyle in his book *On Heroes, Hero-worship and the Heroic in History* says:

"They were a people who made no mark in known history, those nomadic Arabs, a handful in number, filthy and barbaric in character. To them was sent Allah's greatest Prophet (SAW), and within twenty years, this crowd of barbarians was

---

[6] 1.8 billion Muslims (2017 estimates).
[7] Hence who rejects the evils ones and believes in Allah has indeed taken hold of the firm, unbreakable hand-hold (2:256).

transformed into a group of supermen!"[8]

And they challenged the entire world of *bātil* (of all that was false) and they conquered the world and they established the truth! What are we doing? If my remarks sound bitter I ask pardon. But ask the doctors – a patient who suffers from malaria should not be given anything that is sweet – the remedy for malaria is bitter quinine!

Another important point raised was that the Muslims in the Republic of South Africa are living in a Western- oriented country. They are a minority and living under a non-Muslim majority. This problem is not confined to South Africa only. It is to be found in every Muslim community, even in Pakistan, which is a country with an overwhelming Muslim majority. The Muslims are leaving the old culture and running after the new, to whatever country you may go. It is not a case of being a minority. They are doing the same things in Pakistan and on a stupendous scale in Turkey, Iran and in the Middle East.

If you go there you will find that they are more Westernised than the Western people. There are people who condemn them – fortunately or unfortunately, I don't condemn them because there are certain laws of the historical process called in the philosophy of history – the principle of historical compulsion. And this principle claims that however much a community may try to behave in a certain manner, the historical forces that are around it, compel it to do as they want it to do.

A community can make itself immune to outside influences only when it is definitely superior and more virile than those other communities that are there in the environment.[9] But if the community is docile, if the community has no law to govern its life, if it is bankrupt in respect of its character and its ideals, then it is, as the saying goes: "The devil occupies the vacant home."

---

[8] Cf. *Muhammad The Glory of the Ages*, 49.
[9] Ansari provides a sociological perspective of communities that surrender to 'superior and more virile' communities. The West is representative of the historical process to which Ansari alludes.

A community which has no positive idealism and is not struggling to achieve the goal of that idealism, is a passive community. And the nature of Allah's Law is (the Sociological Law) that all human beings are moving ahead like a caravan. This caravan of humanity is moving all the time and whatever portion of the caravan becomes stagnant or stationary, or those who do not want to move, the law is that they will be thrown back. They will not be allowed to be stationary but will be trampled. This is the law.

What we have been doing is that we have left the mission of Islam long ago. We were not inspired by the Islamic idealism anymore. Our plans were not what the Holy Prophet gave us. We were indulging in all sorts of un-Islamic activities even before these Western powers came to wrest away our sovereignty in Africa and Asia. After they came, they tried their best to de-Islamise us. It was a duty to themselves that their potential enemies should be crushed. They did just that and we cannot complain.

In the meantime, another tragedy has happened. Islam, like every other religion or system, comprises certain components.The first being the values of Islam, from which emerge the norms, and then the laws.[10] Then follows the rules and regulations such as etiquette – personal, religious and social.

What do we find in the Muslim world of today? The concept of values and norms have been forgotten. We stand by the Law. Our 'ulama also study only the Law, the *fiqh*. This Law is given to the people and when that Law degenerates among the people, then only etiquette is left. How far have we gone in this?

Last year (1969), in New York, I had the opportunity of addressing a group of new converts to Islam. As I entered the hall, I thought that all the people present were villagers from

---

[10] Values and norms, according to Ansari, are ingrained for believers (*mu'min*) striving towards truth, justice and beauty. Instead, expedience and religious opportunism have displaced the universal message: *Return to God genuinely.* See *Islam to the Modern Mind*, 294.

Pakistan. I could never dream that the Afro-Americans could dress and behave like that. I inquired from the chairman and he confirmed that they were all Americans and none were from Pakistan. After the lecture, I invited all those people to me and asked them to explain why they were wearing that type of dress. They replied that it was the symbol of piety. They said that great Islamic workers came there and taught them that if they wanted to be really good Muslims in the eyes of God, they should wear a triangular pyjama, the quadrangular kurta and the hexagonal cap![11]

It took me a long time to convince them that they were committing a crime by wearing that dress in America. Firstly, no dress has been prescribed by the Holy Prophet (SAW). He only prescribed rules of decency about dress. Secondly, if you wear this strange type of dress then you are a walking propaganda against Islam among the Americans. If the condition to become a Muslim is to wear those clothes, then the other Americans would refuse to become Muslim.

The problem is not unsolvable. If we go to the Qur'ān and *hadith*, we'll find that many things we think are compulsory are in fact not compulsory. Islam is a universal religion, which has come for all ages. Students of sociology know that the cultural pattern changes with the industrial pattern. The change in the cultural pattern leads to a change in the psychological pattern. The Holy Prophet (SAW) was aware of all that. He did not give this type of religious outlook that we have developed. It is we who are responsible for it.

Islam begins with the values and the moral life is the basis. Of course, the moral life is built on the spiritual orientation of life, in order to acquire the purity of motive, as the Holy Prophet (SAW) said:

---

[11] The problem of a Muslim dress code has become a contentious issue. In many instances it has become a religious marker in Islamic circles. The paraphernalia of outward piety is much entrenched in Muslim society. The following *du'ā* is revealing on this matter: 'O Allah! Make my inner-self better than my outer-self, and let my outer-self be virtuous.' (Tirmidhi).

The higher the morals of a person, the better is his imān.[12]

The measure of a person's *imān* is his moral integrity and his behaviour. It is the moral life that is the foundation of the Islamic life. The moral life - as prescribed by Islam - can be followed and practised fully in every society, whether that society is South African, German, or American. This is what makes a Muslim!

The other external factors vary from community to community. The dress, for example, varies from Indonesia to Morocco and Nigeria. We cannot object to the national dress of a people. Our 'ulama raised objections to the English suit because it was imported from another community. They are correct in that to adopt the dress of another community corrupts one's outlook and creates a sort of inferiority complex. But the English suit has now been accepted by the upper strata of Muslim society all over the world. So, the problem of imitating foreign dress out of inferiority does not apply. Islam emphasises the spiritual and the moral culture and if we follow those moral and spiritual teachings of Islam properly then that is what matters.

In Pakistan, for example, we find certain people who regard themselves alone to be Muslims. They behave in a strange way, for example, a Muslim merchant grows a long beard, wears a kurta, a triangular pyjama and wears the haji's cap - showing himself to be a person who is dedicated to Islam and Allah. He makes a survey of the market and Muslim business all over Pakistan.

Go to Karachi, which is a Muslim town, and try to buy pure butter (prescribed by a doctor). You will find different brands of butter, but you will not find pure butter. These people who adopt all this paraphernalia of piety who own all those dairy farms and factories earn their money in this manner.

In Pakistan people have been caught so many times adding

---

[12] The *hadith* on morality filters through virtuous manners. In a Prophetic *du'ā*, it is linked to *imān*. (Mustadrak Hakim).

impurities to their dairy products. Once, a well-known hāji was caught red-handed. He installed a factory in an underground cell where he manufactured butter from grease and that butter inflicted polio on about forty children! This is the type of Islam of those so-called religious people! Which Islam is this that has to be adjusted to a particular age and area? And mind you, these people go to Makkah four times per year with *harām* money and when they come back they are welcomed, praised and garlanded by all their friends that so-and-so has performed the *hajj* seven or seventeen times.[13]

The sores on the body of the Muslim community are so many. It seems as if we have lost completely our grip on what Islam stands for. We have coined our own Islam. Certain portions of Islam have been taken, like prayers, fasting, charity and pilgrimage and given a certain organic unity, and this is the Islam we carry.

Islam can adjust itself anywhere; in a capitalist country or a communist country. It is adjusting itself under Jamaluddin Nasser,[14] Turkey, Pakistan, etc. Why can't it adjust itself here? Why all this hue and cry about it? But as far as the original Islam of the Qur'ān and *sunnah* is concerned, we have been told:

كُنْتُمْ خَيْرَ أُمَّةٍ أُخْرِجَتْ لِلنَّاسِ تَأْمُرُونَ بِالْمَعْرُوفِ وَتَنْهَوْنَ عَنِ الْمُنْكَرِ وَتُؤْمِنُونَ بِاللَّهِ

You are the best ideological group which has been raised and chosen by Allah for the purpose that you will establish all that is good and eradicate all that is

---

[13] The Holy Prophet (SAW) emphasised the immense importance of *hajj* in the task of spiritual reformation and transformation. Only, those who perform it conscientiously can earn the spiritual benefits in full measure. The above comment is self-explanatory against the background of hājis with dubious credentials. Cf. *The Beacon Light*, 216.

[14] Nasser's unconditional support for socialism is contextualised in Ansari's critique of Communism. Muslim countries in general cannot respond forcefully to the suffering perpetrated by Russia and the West because "[their] are strings around their necks." *Islam to the Modern Mind*, 209.

evil, as believers in Allah.

(3:110)

If this ideal is not there for us, we won't know how to proceed. If Islam is not a way of life and challenge for all evil, then Islam is only a cult with an otherworldly orientation combined with a few ethical principles.

We treat and accept Islam as a cult and we do not go beyond these requirements. This problem requires a scientific analysis. If this problem is understood fully as to what is the pattern of life, which Islam gives; what are those things that are obligatory and what are optional, then only can we understand!

And if our ideal is to establish those ideals for which Islam came, then this work can be done methodically, like in a scientific analysis. Prioritise one value after the other. If we do that, we will get an Islam that is very dynamic, progressive and enlightened. There will be no difficulty in living here as good Muslims and we'll be able to live Islam in a manner that will attract the non-Muslims!

PART 6

INNER DIMENSIONS OF ISLAM

The world of Islam will have to revive the pursuit of comprehensive *tazkiyah* (spiritual reformation) in accordance with the norms and principles laid down in the Qur'ān and *sunnah*... [in order] that genuine Islamic leadership of the Muhammadan pattern (*uswah al-hasanah*) emerges on a high level and in a large measure, and acts fruitfully for the fulfilment of the mission of Islam.

- It is the spiritual impact of the Holy Prophet's personality that has been prescribed by Allah as the most powerful instrument of *tazkiyah* in the life of a Muslim.
- The Holy Prophet's basic function of bringing about *tazkiyah* in his followers transcends the limitations of space and time.
- The Holy Prophet's spiritual impact was available not only to the Muslims of the period of his physical existence but has remained available ever since and will remain available up to the Last Day.

15

Tasawwuf: Spiritual Pursuit in Islam

Tasawwuf is a very important topic because it deals first of all with the very essence of Islam and secondly there is gross misunderstanding about it.
There are Muslims who give due importance to *tasawwuf* and there are others who condemn it as something foreign to Islam. In this connection, there have been two contributory causes:

- o The Orientalists have tried to misguide the Muslims and damage our loyalty to the Holy Prophet (SAW) so that the enthusiasm of Muslims for Islam will vanish. Therefore, these Orientalists always tried to pick up arguments against the life and personality of the Holy Prophet (SAW).
- o The next target is *tasawwuf*. If we are made to believe that Islam is only a ritualistic code of life, the next step is atheism. Unless we have that inner experience, something that touches the inner self – we will be misled and only become nominal Muslims.[1]

The practice of *tasawwuf* in the Muslim world has degenerated and it is very difficult to find it in its original form as it was given.[2] I know how this noblest of pursuit has been

---

[1] It is practical *tasawwuf* that sought to replace 'mechanistic' religion with 'dynamic' religion. In other words, *tasawwuf* was realigned to the dynamic orthodoxy that Ansari formulated. Dr. Fazlur Rahman Ansari, 103. In recent times, segments of Muslims are inclined to *deism*. In other words, they believe in the existence of a Creator who does not intervene in the universe. This emerging mindset is alarming for the *ummah*.
[2] The following comment of Ansari on *tasawwuf* is revealing: "With the awful

commercialised, ritualised and degraded by many a person who claims to be the *murshid* (spiritual guide) of a certain order. All this is due to ignorance on the part of general Muslims and those who misrepresent this noble pursuit.

The verse from the Holy Qur'ān is unambiguous:

$$هُوَ الَّذِي بَعَثَ فِي الْأُمِّيِّينَ رَسُولًا مِّنْهُمْ يَتْلُو عَلَيْهِمْ آيَاتِهِ وَيُزَكِّيهِمْ وَيُعَلِّمُهُمُ الْكِتَابَ وَالْحِكْمَةَ$$

> *It is He Who has sent amongst the unlettered a Messenger from among themselves, who communicates the message as it comes to him from Almighty Allah. He purifies them and he expounds the Qur'ān and he teaches wisdom.*
>
> (62:2)

Here Almighty Allah defines the functions for which the Holy Prophet (SAW) was sent:

He gives to the people the Law or the divine code of life. He purifies those that accept the message. Therefore, the process of purification is different from learning the shari'ah. He teaches the Qur'ān (*kitāb*) and He teaches the wisdom. Anybody who is serious about his life and its problems, would first question: "Why Religion?"[3] If this question is answered to his or her satisfaction that one should have a religion then the next question arises: "Which Religion?"[4] There are so many and each one claims to be true. When the answer comes that the religion to adopt which is considered to be true is Islam, then arises the third question: "What is Islam?" Here one is faced with

---

degeneration of Muslim society, due to certain factors, well-known to students of Islamic history, the understanding as well as the practice of *tasawwuf* has also degenerated in more dimensions than one. Also its name has been misused for certain wrong notions in certain quarters." *The Qur'ānic Foundations,* vol. i, 168.

[3] See *The Beacon Light,* 42-52.

[4] See *Which Religion,* (Karachi, 1976). This was an extempore (unprepared) lecture delivered at the Tokyo Mosque, Japan, in 1960.

shari'ah– the divine law.

The first two questions "Why Religion?" and "Which Religion?", are covered by *al-hikmah,* the wisdom. Unless one knows why he is a Muslim, it will not lead him to the goal for which Islam came. Another question that follows is "How to be a Muslim?"

For just to know the teachings of Islam does not help, but how to be have as a Muslim, and how to proceed on the Path is vital. In the same surah we have been told about the 'ulama of the Jews:

مَثَلُ الَّذِينَ حُمِّلُوا التَّوْرَاةَ ثُمَّ لَمْ يَحْمِلُوهَا كَمَثَلِ الْحِمَارِ يَحْمِلُ أَسْفَارًا

The example of those who learn the Torah, who learn the shari'ah, but could not assimilate it in their personalities for the transformation of their personalities, is like a donkey carrying a load of books.

(62:5)[5]

Every human being is confronted by obstacles that arise from within the human self, the baser or lower self of man all the time. The *nafs al-ammārah* obstructs the path of the human being in his pursuit to follow his higher nature. There are also obstacles in the environment and within the community where one has to live and interact. One has to fight against all these obstacles and unless one fights successfully, one will not be a Muslim in the real sense of the word.

Consequently, there should be a methodology (through the vehicles of the shari'ah) to answer the question of 'How to be a Muslim?' which can be employed in transforming the human personality in accordance with Islam. Therefore, the word

---

[5] The similitude of these whose who were entrusted with the Torah but who subsequently failed in these (obligations) is that of a donkey which carries huge tomes (but understands them not). (62:5).

ma'rifah actually means methodology.⁶ We have various methodologies through the spiritual orders.

Another question asked by a person who is serious about his life and future is, "If I succeed in becoming a Muslim in the real sense of the word, adopt the shari'ah and follow a methodology, what will be the reward or consequences?" It is human nature to ask about the reward for according to Islam it is to develop the human personality from a lower to a higher level.

Therefore, if you adopt *tariqah* the reward will be *ma'rifah*– Godly knowledge in depth. We have what is called *'Ilm*-knowledge and *'Irfān* which is the superior degree of "knowing" and is higher than the concept of knowledge. The reward is to gain the knowledge of things as they really are and not how they appear to be.

'Irfān has three levels:
- Man should know his "self". Knowledge begins from the self; charity begins at home. When a Muslim cultivates his personality as a Muslim and, adopts the methodology, he gets the knowledge about himself – called *'Ilm-al-nafs*.
- *'Ilm al-'Āfāq* – knowledge of the environment and knowledge of the cosmos.
- Knowledge of Almighty Allah, to know Allah and experience Him, which brings a conviction that cannot be shaken. This is a conviction that transcends the argumentation of logic. About direct experience our Holy Prophet (SAW) said: *Nothing can bring conviction as direct experience can.*

When this experience of Allah comes as the final fruit or

---

⁶ The four tariqas (spiritual orders) represent the core of *tasawwuf*. They are Qādiriyyah, Chishtiyyah, Suharwardiyyah and Naqshbandiyyah. Their respective representatives have projected the inner dimensions of Islam through their important writings. See *Fazlur Rahman Ansari, Life and Thought*, 250-1.

reward of being a Muslim, then arrives the fifth stage, *haqiqah*. The pilgrim of eternity arrives at his goal, as the Holy Qur'ān says:

$$وَأَنَّ إِلَىٰ رَبِّكَ الْمُنْتَهَىٰ ﴿٤٢﴾$$

"Unto your Lord is your goal

(53:42)

Now, Allah is Infinite, therefore the experience of Him has infinite possibilities and this journey is a journey in experience of Allah and to discover what connection "I" have with Him.

So the foundations of Islam are five and the stages through which a Muslim has to pass are also five, namely,

hikmah
shari'ah
tariqah
ma'rifah
haqiqah[7]

Furthermore, about *tariqah*, we find the authority of the Holy Qur'ān:

$$لِكُلٍّ جَعَلْنَا مِنكُمْ شِرْعَةً وَمِنْهَاجًا ۚ$$

To every community Allah has prescribed a divine code of life and a methodology.

(5:48)

And the function of this methodology is what has been said about the function of the Holy Prophet (SAW), that is,

---

[7] These terms are not abstract concepts but refer specifically to the progression of human personality within a *tasawwuf* framework. They are integral to the purification (*tazkiyah*) of the human personality.

purification of the human personality.

In the Holy Qur'ān we are told that every human being was created in *jannah* – the world of purity and bliss – which is very different from our world for it is a spaceless and timeless world.

After the transgression of Adam and Eve (AS), Almighty Allah commanded:

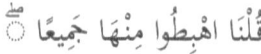

Go from here, all of you. (2:38)

The command was given in *plural* and not in dual.

The fact is that every human is a being of the transcendental world and was created at the dawn of creation in *jannah*. In another verse we are told:

وَإِذْ أَخَذَ رَبُّكَ مِنْ بَنِي آدَمَ مِنْ ظُهُورِهِمْ ذُرِّيَّتَهُمْ وَأَشْهَدَهُمْ عَلَىٰ أَنْفُسِهِمْ أَلَسْتُ بِرَبِّكُمْ قَالُوا بَلَىٰ

Almighty Allah assembled the entire progeny of Adam at the dawn of creation and said: "Am I not you Lord?" They said, "Yes, You are our Lord."

(7:172)

Thus we were all existent there and possessed consciousness otherwise we would not have been able to answer. This further means that the real human being, *al-ruh* – the essential being – in its consciousness is a spaceless and timeless being. Then the command was given:

قُلْنَا اهْبِطُوا مِنْهَا جَمِيعًا

Go from here, all of you.

(2:38)

Consequently, all human beings have been travelling through infinite space and time to emerge here on this earth at the appointed hour as a spatial temporal being. Mawlāna Rumi[8] has said, *"This body is the projection of the essential being"* which is not dependent upon this body.

When this essential being projects itself in terms of space and time, its first projection is in terms of its mind. The mind exists only in time, not in space, and consequently, its final projection is as a spatio-temporal being (in the body).

Think of anything that exists in this world, for example, a flower. At first, a very small microscopic point comes into existence on the twig of the plant and it develops into a small bud and finally into a beautiful flower. Therefore, before its emergence as a point on the twig of the plant, it must have been something finer, for its development has been towards coarser stages of existence. This body of ours, before it assumes the life form – the microscopic sperm is still physical – it must have been "mental" – that is, its first projection in this spatio-temporal world.

The essential being travelled through countless periods of time under the divine command, *"Go from here, all of you"*. When death comes – death does not mean termination of existence– it only means, transfer from one level of existence to another. Before coming here into this world, this human being undergoes numerous changes or numberless births and numberless deaths. And every death is a stage for further evolution. Before every new emergence on a higher plane, this "essential being" has to be incubated. The first grave is in the mother's womb, where it incubates and undergoes numerous changes. The word *qabr*, used in Islamic terminology, actually means a type of shell in which the essential being exists and undergoes changes. When the period of incubation (*'ālam al-barzakh*) in the mother's womb ends, it is ushered into this world

---

[8] Rumi's *Mathnawi* in four volumes is considered a masterpiece is Islamic literature and *tasawwuf*.

and participates in human civilisation as a moral being. After this term, it is again sent to the grave where it will stay till the Day of Qiyāmah.⁹

The word *qabr* stands for the physical grave only secondarily. This is also called *hayāt al-barzakhiyyah*. It remains alive in a process of experience in accordance with what it has done in this world. Then on the Day of *Qiyāmah*, the next stage will come as we are told in the Holy Qur'ān: *the constitution of everything will be changed.* Let us come back to the actual topic.

The Holy Prophet (SAW) said:

Allah created man (Adam) in His image.

It means that Allah placed those qualities, which He possesses infinitely, in the human who is finite. When this essential being arrives here, it is a created being and has a shadow or it is composed of light and darkness. According to the Holy Qur'ān:

وَنَفْسٍ وَمَا سَوَّاهَا ﴿٧﴾ فَأَلْهَمَهَا فُجُورَهَا وَتَقْوَاهَا ﴿٨﴾

Man can pursue the path of good or the path of evil.

(91:7–8)

He is between the angels and Iblis. The purpose for which he has been sent here is to participate in the struggle here on this earth – as a servant of Allah. Allah is Absolute Good, so when He created the human being, originally, is also good. The evil comes as a shadow and is the negative aspect of the human faculty. The Holy Prophet (SAW) said:

Imbue yourselves with divine attributes

In the Holy Qur'ān we are told:

---

⁹ For a detailed discussion, see Ansari, *Beyond Death* (Karachi, 1996).

$$\lqcad{\text{لَقَدْ خَلَقْنَا الْإِنسَانَ فِي أَحْسَنِ تَقْوِيمٍ ﴿٤﴾}}$$

Verily, We have created man in the best form.

(95:4)

Therefore, it is for us to have and develop that *a`māl al- sālih*[10] which was demonstrated by the Holy Prophet (SAW). It is at that level that the human being regains his original purity – for he is born a pure being. According to another *hadith*:

Every human being is born pure and holy.

He does not belong to this world but belongs to the world that is pure and holy.

The journey of the essential being can be conceived as in the form of a circle. When we arrive here, we have traversed half of the circle – *descend!* Then there is the ascent. It has to go back where it came from, as we are reminded in the Holy Qur'ān:

$$\text{إِنَّا لِلَّهِ وَإِنَّا إِلَيْهِ رَاجِعُونَ ﴿١٥٦﴾}$$

We belong to Allah (our existence is only for Allah) and our return is to Him.

(2:156)

for He created us in His "Image". Thus, that part of the journey, which remains, is the journey of *return* at the other arm of that circle. What the Holy Prophet (SAW) meant is that we should try to regain and maintain our original purity and holiness. When we arrived here, naturally we were enticed and fascinated by things of this world which take away from us our innocence and beauty of the inner self, our moral and spiritual purity in terms of being a slave of Allah. Unfortunately, the human becomes a slave of

---

[10] Righteous, virtuous actions. See surah `Asr (103:3) for a brief comment about the relationship between belief (*imān*) and action (`*amal*).

other things and when this happens, he is disloyal to his pledge that was given at the dawn of creation when he said: *Anta Rabbunā-* You are our Lord.

Consequently, man is bound by his pledge and in order to remain loyal to his pledge he has to strive all the time in order to acquire *nafs al-mutma'innah*. A sufi has said, "His outer senses are engaged with things of this world but his heart remains engaged with God." Now the problem arises: "How can this *tazkiyah* be performed?" Remember the verse, "He purifies those who accepts the message." Unless it is performed, unless we are *muzakkah*[11] (purified or in this process of purification) we will be in trouble.

In the early history of Islam, Muslims acquired enormous wealth and power and subsequently became corrupt. When the seat of the empire was transferred from Madinah to Syria and then to Baghdad, the original purity of the Islamic way of life was progressively damaged. Muslims started practising Islam ritualistically. The meaning of prayer was not important anymore and ritualism permeated all actions. Even, the 'ulama became materialistically-minded and conditions deteriorated badly. A group from amongst the 'ulama emerged and started the movement of *tasawwuf*, and their objectives were clearly laid down.

Sayyidinā Hasan al-Basri [d.728] is considered to be the founder of this movement, of which unfortunately no writings of his are available. However, the following works of classical masters in *tasawwuf* have their entire doctrine on the shari`ah. Sayyid 'Abdul Qādir Jilāni said: "The spiritual pilgrim cannot go one hair's breadth out of the shari`ah.

- Abu Bakr al-Kalabadhi (d. 990) *Al-Ta'arruf li Madhab Ahl al-Tasawwuf* (Introduction to the Way of the people of Sufism).
- Abu Tālib al-Makki (d. 996) *Qut al-Qulub* (The

---

[11] *The Qur'ānic Foundations*, vol. i, 154-5 Like *tazkiyah*, the term *ihsān* refers to spiritual excellence that permeates a Muslim's life in totality.

Sustenance of Hearts)
- Abul Qasim Qushayri (d. 1072), *al-Risala* (Treatise)
- ʿAli ibn ʿUthmān al-Hujwairi (d. 1077) *Kashful Mahjub*
- (Uncovering the Veiled)
- ʿAbdullah Ansāri (d. 1089) *Tabaqāt al-Sufiyya*
- (Generations of the Sufis)
- Abu Hāmid al-Ghazāli (d. 111). *Ihyā ʿulum-al-din*
- (Rejuvenation of the Religious Sciences)

There have been mystics amongst the Hindus, Jews, Christians and many of them embraced Islam. Unfortunately, some of them retained some of their former practices and customs. For example, movements like Bātiniyyah or Karāmitah, carried Muslim names only. But Islamic scholars and sufis fought tooth and nail against them! Read *al-Munqid min al-dalāl*[12] of Imām Abu Hāmid al-Ghazāli and you will find the full refutation of these foreign doctrines in these works. Read the works of the ancient masters and you will find them talking about *suluk al-salāh* or *suluk al-sawm* – how to develop a methodology on the basis of the *salāh* and *sawm* which have been prescribed in the shariʿah.

The misunderstanding of *tasawwuf* is highlighted in the following happening. ʿAllāmah Ibn Taymiyyah[13] opposed sufism and his student Ibn Qayyim also challenged the world of Islam to prove that sufism had anything to do with it. His contention was that it was un-Islamic. Ibn Qayyim raised this challenge in Egypt. This intellectual giant was advised to go to Shaykh

---

[12] Translated as *Deliverance from Error* it is considered to be a spiritual journey of Ghazali rather than an autobiography. See Mohamed Al-Musleh, al-Ghazāli, *The Islamic Reformer* (Kuala Lumpur, 2012).

[13] A clarification about Ibn Taymiyyah's position on *tasawwuf* makes interesting reading. The unbiased accounts restate his position clearly: *tasawwuf* that is aligned to shariʿah is commended. However, it is the salafi movement and Orientalists that have distorted his interpretation in order to project his writings as an antagonistic to *tasawwuf*. The *Madārij al-Sālikin* (Ranks of Divine seekers) is arguably Ibn Qayyim's most developed spiritual work. It also is a systematic commentary of Shakyh Ansari's influential work. *The Qurʾānic Foundations*, vol.i, 154-60.

'Abdullāh Ansāri of Herat in (Afghanistan) who taught that sufism was the very essence of Islam and wrote a booklet called *Manāzil al-Sā'irin* (The stations of the spiritual travelers). This book explained *tasawwuf* or the sufi way of life based upon the Holy Qur'ān.[14]

Thus, if we study Islam deeply and understand how and why this movement arose, all our doubts should vanish.

Tasawwuf is nothing else but the effort to fulfil that mission of the Holy Prophet as mentioned in the Holy Qur'ān – *al-tazkiyah*, or as mentioned in the *hadith* as *al-ihsān* – the beautification of Islam. It means to rise and to cultivate one's consciousness in terms of slavery to Allah to a level where the Holy Prophet (SAW) said:

> *Serve Allah as if you are seeing Him and if that is not possible then serve your Allah with the consciousness that He is seeing you and you are worshipping Him.*

---

[14] See *Chapter 16* of this work for the distinction between Mysticism and *tasawwuf*.

16

Mysticism and Tasawwuf: An Overview

Basic Difference between Mysticism and *Tasawwuf*

Lexicologically, the word mystical has two meanings: 'relating to mystery' and involving a sacred or secret meaning hidden from the eyes of the ordinary person, only revealed to a spiritually-enlightened mind.' Similarly, the word 'mysticism' carries two shades of meaning: 'fogginess and unreality of thought (with suggestion of mist)' and 'the habit or tendency of religious thought and feeling of those who seek direct communion with God or the divine.'

- Refined mysticism, as it has emerged in civilised religions, conforms to the second shade of meaning. And in this respect, some superficial affinity might be discernible between Mysticism and the Islamic religious quest (*tasawwuf*). But going deeper we find certain basic differences which are of immense importance. These differences exist in terms of philosophy, technique, function, outlook and goal. In terms of *philosophy*: Islam differs with all the systems of Mysticism, either largely or wholly, with regard to the teachings of God, the World, and Man. It is self- sufficient that that those differences cannot but influence the structure of the quest most vitally.

- In terms of *technique*: All schools of Mysticism employ as their instruments meditation, contemplation, recitation and asceticism. In contrast, Islam employs spiritual devotion to

Allah, and spiritual contact with the Holy Prophet (SAW) and with the spiritual world as such. These involve recitation of spiritual truths as one of the instruments, intellectual grasp of the value system of the Islamic code of guidance, study of nature and history, practice of social morality, meditation, contemplation, and periodic seclusion or 'withdrawal' called *i'tikāf*. Again the element of asceticism in Mysticism makes its quest possible only for a select few. However, in Islam the practice of religion in social life and its religious quest is an obligatory religious routine which makes it possible for every Muslim to undertake according to his capacity and availability of opportunity.

- In terms of *function*: The function of Mysticism is the annihilation of the animal self, the development of psychical powers, and self-realisation in terms of its specific philosophy. The function of Islamic religious quest is spiritual and moral integration and development of the self (*nafs*) through self-purification, ultimately for reforming society.

- In terms of *outlook*: In Mysticism, the outlook is pessimistic as regards earthly existence, and hence, it is passive in relation to it. In the Islamic religious quest, the outlook is optimistic based on the faith in the goodness of the Divine plan under which everything exists and every event occurs. It is dynamic because the world and worldly life, handled in accordance with Divine guidance, are viewed as a means to the attainment of human destiny. The glorious role of the genuine sufis in Muslim history bears testimony to this fact. They and their disciples propagated Islam and contributed to the moral and spiritual fervor among Muslims. Also their heroic struggles in the field of political reform form a very important chapter in the history of Islam.

- In terms of *goal:* The goal of the mystic is personal salvation. The goal of the pursuer of Islamic religious quest (a true sufi) is personal fulfilment at three levels: in his inner being, in human society, and finally in God. This is the ceaseless struggle for transforming human society in terms of godliness.

The term 'Islamic religious quest' is interchangeably used for *tasawwuf.* Ansari makes a candid observation of *pseudo-sufis* who have tarnished the image of *tasawwuf.* They have interpreted it through the lens of Mysticism, which is a violation of the inner dimensions of Islam.

(Adapted from *The Qur'anic Foundations,* vol. i, 166-8.)

17

Discipline in Dhikr

Islam is the religion of discipline. It is not based on any dogmatic mysterious belief, nor on any mystifying scheme of salvation. It is based on very clear beliefs given in the *'aqā'id* (belief system).[1] All of us know what the *aqā'id* of the *Ahl al-sunnah wa al-jamā'ah* are according to Islam. In this connection, the most important point is discipline.

In the Holy Qur'ān we are told:

إِنَّمَا كَانَ قَوْلَ الْمُؤْمِنِينَ إِذَا دُعُوا إِلَى اللَّهِ وَرَسُولِهِ لِيَحْكُمَ بَيْنَهُمْ أَن يَقُولُوا سَمِعْنَا وَأَطَعْنَا ۚ

> The function of a believer whenever he or she is invited towards what Allah and His Messenger orders, their function is only to say: 'We hear and we obey.'

(24:51)

We are also told that whatever is commanded by the Holy Prophet (SAW), there is no choice for anyone.

> It is not possible for the believers whether male or female, when given a command by Allah or His Messenger, to have any choice in the matter.

(33:36)

Of course, Islam has been given to us in such a rational manner, such a natural code of life, that all our hardships have been taken into consideration. For example, we have been taught that we should pray in such a manner – the *qiyām, ruku', sujud*. But if one is sick, one is allowed to sit and read the prayer.

---

[1] Ansari uses this term to refer to *tasawwuf* in its broadest sense.

If the person is more sick, he or she may lie down, and if he or she is very sick, he may do his prayer without reading with his tongue. Thus Islam has taken into consideration all the different situations that might arise in the life of a Muslim.[2] But the spirit that should be there in every Muslim is that of obedience.

A person who wants to be a Muslim in the genuine sense of the word, in its depth and in his inner as well as his outer self, that person is called a sufi. He does not merely believe in only the external or formal manifestation of Islam. He also believes in combining the spirit of Islam and doing everything out of consideration for the spirit behind it and with consciousness. As we have been told in the hadith:

> ...[with] genuine imān and by constant examination of what we are doing.

Ihtisāb (self-examination) has to be there when we are praying, in the manner in which the Holy Prophet (SAW) asked us to pray, or is it just a formality? The real purpose of prayer is to be conscious of Allah and to examine our actions. True prayer involves a change from within, if this does not take place, we have not really prayed.

The prayer should be repeated until a person acquires that change according to his capacity, for everyone's capacity is not the same. One should practise this until one is confident that he has acquired that benefit from praying.

In the sufi way of life, what is emphasised is that we not only have to obey at the formal or external level of obedience[3] but also in terms of real inner obedience. It is only when this consciousness is there that we can obtain those benefits that are there in prayer or fasting or in speaking truth, etc.

---

[2] Refer to *Foundations of Faith*, 59-69, 81-3.
[3] Ansari makes a poignant remark. "Thus our earthly surroundings are not a meaningless projection of the play of blind forces – a mere empty shell with no content. The tiniest particle of sand, the smallest drop of water, the frailest rose-leaf is full of meaning and music and functions under a definite and well-planned Divine scheme." *Islam and Christianity in the Modern World*, 201.

A person speaking the truth, for the sake of people's praise, has lost the real value of it. If the ulterior motive is there, then he has not performed virtues – only the evil effects of speaking falsehood have been avoided. Speaking the truth must be solely with the consciousness that Allah is seeing me and will take account of me, and to speak falsehood is something dishonourable.

The consciousness has to be built up in this manner that "I am a human being and Allah Almighty says that He has made me honourable as His potential *khalīfah*. Thus, I have to build up and develop all those powers which Allah has placed in me, whether they are physical, moral, and intellectual or spiritual, all these have to be cultivated by me."

The entire personality is a unit and all these faculties will have to be developed. If a person pursues spirituality and concentrates only on that and neglects the doing of good, he will not be acting as a balanced Muslim nor will he be able to develop his full personality. The straight path is the moderate path, which requires discipline, otherwise one ends up in mysticism.

Many Muslims pray, fast, and love the Holy Prophet (SAW) and Allah, but they have forgotten that discipline[4] is the condition which will make them good and great. Consequently, it was impossible for any of the Companions of the Holy Prophet (SAW) to disobey him even if they had to risk their lives. Whatever he commanded, was carried out without question. That obedience which the Holy Prophet (SAW) advised was demonstrated wholeheartedly and gladly accepted.

What is happening nowadays is that if there is an *imām* of a *masjid* and he tries to lead the people, they then question his integrity and accuse him of being useless but never question their own motives.[5] Why are we worried about someone else's duty? We will be asked by Allah about our own duty! However, these things are happening in our communities and that is why we are not making any progress. Trying to transfer one's

---

[4] The positive elements of *'ibādah* (worship) are fully and purposefully achieved. Ibid., 94-6.
[5] *Tazkiyah* and purification of the human personality.

obligations onto the shoulders of others is the great disease.
In any group of Muslims or organisation we will hear the conditions to do good. Akbar Ilāhabadi said: "If some Muslims come forward to do something for their community, they discourage each other and therefore nobody moves ahead. And then the quarrels start." All these are un-Islamic attitudes. The Holy Prophet (SAW) advised about the *imām* of the congregation:

> *Pray behind any Muslim, whether he is virtuous or a sinner.*

It is not that you are praying to the *imām*. It is only a form of bringing the community life together. If your attitude in prayer is good, you will get the benefit of prayer even if the *imām* is a sinful person. But if the *imām* is well known for his obscenity or crime, then, of course the community should not allow such a person to be the *imām*. But we are all sinful people as Jesus said, *Let him who is not a sinner, cast himself the first stone.* We are all sinners and imperfect beings, so we should have humility and try to seek Allah and not the shortcomings of fellow human beings. This is what we were taught and this is what was actually practised.

Recall the incident about Sayyidinā Khālid ibn Walīd, when, on the instruction of Sayyidinā 'Umar, he immediately handed the command of the army over to his subordinate and fought as an ordinary soldier. It is emphasised in the Qur'ān and hadith that *imān* means that a person must fulfil his promise regardless of the consequence. We have been told: *"fulfil the pledge."*[6]

We have become so low that we promise something and we do not carry it out and only make a lame apology. Islam regards this as the very negation of *imān*. The Holy Prophet (SAW)

---

[6] In other words, Islam encourages man to develop a positive attitude towards life, his environment and his quest for spiritual perfection. By contrast, negative attitudes breed pessimism and indifference to worldly life. *Islam An Introduction*, 8-9.

emphasised that in all our deeds of piety, the major factor is steadfastness. He said:

The best action is that in which you are constant.

If you are not constant with a good action of a high degree but you are constant with a good action of a lower degree, the latter will be considered more meritorious by Allah.

So a Muslim is a person who has to be steadfast and behave in a dignified way. He is not a cheap type of person who can be swayed any time. When he understands that something is from Allah, and that he ought to do it, he will do it. Nothing will cause him to deviate, and in this lies success. A person who pursues something constantly with discipline, even if there should be obstacles, he will succeed. Constancy is the key to success. Constant activity, even a little at a time, will some day prove fruitful.

A time comes when you suddenly feel that you want to remember Allah for eight hours during the night, but for the next week or two you are asleep, not remembering Allah for even half an hour, that will not help you. So, always start with the minimum quantity, then gradually increase it to suit your life.

What Allah demands from us is a healthy and sound spiritual heart. He does not want us to pile up hardships onto our lives, for He says:

I have not sent this dīn down as a hardship.

(22:78)

The points which I gave – don't think that they are few – you may find very difficult to practise, but do them with sincerity. I am sure you will feel the blessings which come through them. People have witnessed and seen that when *adhkār* is made, the saints and *malā'ikah* (angels) join them, and maybe Allah will enable some of you also to see this, *inshā-Allah!*[7]

---

[7] Cf. *Islam to the Modern Mind*, 302-10. Ansari refers to these forms of remembrance of Allah as Islamic Spiritual Quest. Unlike mysticism which in its

The members of the group are living in various areas and if it is too difficult to come together every week, then you may have two or three groups – each in a different area, but at least once a month, all should come together and perform the *adhkār*.[8] You will see that the *adhkār* I gave will take you about half an hour, so please take it up and be constant with it.

Remembrance of Allah (*dhikr*) as the fundamental exercise is directed to seeking the nearness of Allah, and cannot therefore be something formal. As such, firstly it should be undertaken in a state of 'withdrawal' - withdrawing attention from everything else and concentrating it solely on Allah. Secondly, it should be undertaken abundantly under all conditions and at all times. Thirdly, it should be joined to the contemplation of the Signs of Allah, which pervade the entire universe. Fourthly, it should be combined with a study of divine guidance as contained in the Holy Qur'ān and with a serious exercise in moulding one's life in accordance with it to the fullest extent possible. Fifthly, this entire exercise should proceed more conscientiously as well as most intelligently in order that the practical results and the tangible fruits of all this labour of love may be grasped at every step for enabling the pilgrim of eternity to undertake his spiritual flights and moral development at higher and higher levels with the attainment of ever-increasing refinement of the soul, on the one hand and purity of will for moral action, on the other.

---

very nature is escapist, Islam is activist in all dimensions of life.

[8] Ibid., 251-2.

PART 7

REFLECTIONS

It maybe emphasised that the members of Islamic brotherhood of Islam cannot be regarded as true to themselves and true to Allah and His Messenger if their attitude is not inspired by sentiments of sympathy and service. A true Muslim, therefore, who lays down his life in the way of Allah or who takes pains and undergoes hardships for preaching the message of Islam to non- Muslims does so as one who is inspired with love for humanity. In fact, a Muslim is he who loves all mankind and is the embodiment of goodwill for all.

18

Three Key Concepts

Brotherhood

Islam is the religion of the brotherhood of man *par excellence*, because it has not only preached that all human beings form one family, but it has also put this teaching into practice in a glorious manner. That this doctrine is a distinguishing feature of the Islamic religion is borne out by the fact that most religions and civilisations of the world have been averse to this ideal. For instance, Hinduism does not believe in the brotherhood of the Hindus themselves, not to speak of human brotherhood in general. Another type of religion in this connection is Christianity. Theoretically speaking, Christianity preaches the brotherhood of man. But in actual practice, the Christian church has been the greatest enemy of this ideal; for it is Christianity whose upholders are, even in the present age of democracy, instituting colour-bar (Apartheid) in South Africa, building separate churches for Whites, Blacks and Coloureds in Africa and Asia, and lynching the Black Christians in the most advanced Christian country of the world, the United States of America.

In Islam, the doctrine stands unadulterated both in theory and practice. The Holy Prophet (SAW) has given us the law once for all that all human beings are one family. This law in its turn is based on the verdict of Allah given in the Holy Qur'ān: "O human beings! Fear your Lord in your dealings among yourselves - the Lord who has created all of you from a single soul."

The practical instruments for the proper functioning of this idea have been laid down in the form of the principle that a Muslim is he who has goodwill towards all and ill- will towards none; and that a Muslim is he who hates evil but not the evil-doer and who loves good even though it is found in his enemy or in the enemy of his religion. Furthermore, the Holy Prophet (SAW) has laid down the maxim of Muslim life by saying: "None of you is a believer unless he loves for his brother what he loves for himself." It is obvious that every sane person loves for himself only that he considers to be good and he must in the very nature of the case always maintain goodwill towards himself. This means that so far as others are concerned, a Muslim should always desire nothing but goodwill towards them, irrespective of the fact whether they are friends or enemies.

Again, the Holy Prophet (SAW) says: "There is no superiority for the Arab over the non-Arab and for the Whites over the Blacks. All of you are the children of Adam and Adam was made out of dust." This means that all human beings should constantly keep in their minds the bond of unity and brotherhood that exists between them as a consequence of the common parentage of Adam and Eve, and that they should always practise humility and show love towards one another.

What generally cuts at the root of the idea of human brotherhood is not only colour-complex and other similar physical distinctions, but also the wrongs and injuries which the individuals and communities commit against one another. In all such cases most human beings lose their balance of mind, and their spirit of vengeance runs riot. But Islam has denounced such lack of balance and the consequent perpetuation of ill-will and injustice and has thus safeguarded the ideal of human brotherhood. The verdict of the Holy Qur'ān is explicit in this connection: "O believers! Let not the enmity of any people against you incite you to do injustice to them. (Indeed) be just towards all and under all circumstances." Finally, Islam has safeguarded the ideal of human brotherhood by propounding and guaranteeing for the first time in human history all the fundamental Human Rights to all human beings.

When we read Islamic history, we find that this concept of fraternity found its expression in the practical lives of Muslims in the most solemn manner. One of the most distinguishing features of the Islamic brotherhood is that people belonging to different races and different countries and possessing different habits and different modes of life were welded together in one brotherhood which forms the most harmonious international community. Islam came to a people who suffered deeply from race complex, regarding the entire non-Arab humanity as barbarians and unworthy of honour. Islam came to a country where the population was divided irrevocably into tribes and sub-tribes and who had been fighting against one another for centuries on the basis of the most flimsy notions. But it is one of the miracles of the Holy Prophet (SAW) that he transformed them into a solid rock into a group of brothers and sisters who were ready to sacrifice their all for one another.[1]

Dimensions of Tabligh

The word tabligh means 'to reach out the Message.' As a term it means 'propagation of the Message of Islam.' The Holy Qur'ān has given to it the status of an institution (3:104) and has ordained it as an important societal duty. The duty has been conceived to function at two levels, i.e. within the Islamic social order, and outside the Islamic social order where entire humanity comes under its purview.

The end it serves are:

- Preservation
- Development
- Perpetuation of the Islamic Community – and that in service to the cause of humanity (3:110)

The dimensions of this duty are:

- education of new generations of Muslims in Islam;

---

[1] Ansari, Table Talk, in *The Minaret*, September, 1996, 9-11.

- improvement in Islamic knowledge and inspiration for the grown-up Muslims;
- dissemination of the knowledge of Islam among non-Muslims.

Thus, tabligh stands out as a duty towards other individuals in respect of their spiritual and moral progress.

Also, it contributes simultaneously to the spiritual and moral development of the persons who undertake it, and thus it becomes a duty to Self. Its role, however, as a collectivistic or societal duty, remains supreme. Indeed, from that point of view, it stands out as the foremost duty without which the very existence of Islam becomes jeopardised.

As the Holy Qur'ān affirms, the Islamic community is meant to continue to exist for all time – upto the Last Day. This is in the very nature of the case, because the Holy Prophet (SAW) is the last and final Divine Messenger, and the Muslims are the last Divinely-raised religious group. As such, disappearance of the Islamic community at any time in human history is not conceivable. One of the most important instruments for keeping the Islamic community alive and functioning genuinely and truly is the repeated infusion of fresh blood into the body-politic of Islam. This has already happened in Islamic history, as, for instance, when towards the end of the 'Abbasid period, the Muslim world began to show signs of lassitude (lack of energy) and weakness, the conversion of Turko-Tartars revitalised the Islamic community to an extent that it could maintain its glory for several centuries more. The same seems to be the crying need today. But this need cannot be fulfilled without resort to an *enlightened, dynamic and multidimensional movement* in the field of tabligh, and not just a ritualistic or professional performance.[2]

---

[2] Ansari, *The Qur'ānic Foundations*, vol. ii, 33-5.

Status of Women in Islam

My dear sisters, beware of the ghost of modernism, of vulgarity, obscenity and shameless behaviour. That destroyer of the purity and dignity of womanhood is invading the homes of your country. The bacteria of this plague is here and spreading fast. If you wish to save your dignity and preserve the values of human life, you will have to take a definite stand against all this. I know that Muslim communities are tossing and turning between the evils of modernism and conservatism. I am sure most of you are educated and possess a sense of what is good and what is bad. I therefore appeal to all mothers, daughters and sisters to stand up and wage an all-out war against this devil of destruction which is in your midst and appears with an innocent face but with a dagger concealed.

The Holy Qur'ān and the Holy Prophet (SAW) exhorted us to approach marriage with dignity and decorum and not with vulgarity and eroticism. The pleasure of Allah is foremost and the sensuous bodily pleasures are secondary. It is natural that sensuous pleasure dies out the moment it is obtained.

How sacred is a trust from God? My wife and I felt for one another in this manner and therefore our life has been extremely happy. The husband and wife grow old together and the beauty of such a life is that they love one another more and more. This is possible only in the Islamic attitude towards marriage.

Allow me to give you another example, particularly for the youth to note: My mother's uncle was a landlord with estates and a farm. He had a palatial house: one section for the ladies and one section for the men. We used to go there every year for a holiday. He became very fond of me as he had no children. He was in his early thirties and a very handsome man. As a young boy I was shocked when I saw his wife for the first time. She was blind, deaf, dumb, and a part of her face as well as her body was paralysed. But her husband served her like a humble servant. After coming from *fajr* prayers, I saw the first thing he would do is to go to her room and wash her face, hands and feet himself in spite of there being twelve servants in the house. He would put oil on her hair and comb it. After that he would bring her breakfast and feed her with his hands. I could not understand what was happening and thought something was wrong with my mother's uncle. This thought lingered in my mind for a long time until curiosity compelled me to ask my grandfather why my grandmother was so ugly and he so beautiful. He answered, "When I married your grandma, she was very beautiful and we loved one another very dearly. This village is very far from the city and her first child was still born. There was no nurse and no doctor and only her life could be saved, not her health. Son, when I married her, I used to express my love to her, now that she is in this state, should I abandon her? As a Muslim, I should bestow more love on her so that her feelings may not be hurt. Therefore, I cannot marry another woman nor entrust a maid to care for her."[3]

---

[3] Ansari, *Islam to the Modern Mind*, 221-5.

www.ingramcontent.com/pod-product-compliance
Lightning Source LLC
Chambersburg PA
CBHW031238290426
44109CB00012B/346